The Virgin Vote

The Virgin Vote

How Young Americans
Made Democracy Social,
Politics Personal, and
Voting Popular in the
Nineteenth Century

JON GRINSPAN

The University of North Carolina
Press CHAPEL HILL

Designed and set in Merlo and Aachen types by Rebecca Evans
Manufactured in the United States of America

The paper in this book meets the guidelines for permanence and durability
of the Committee on Production Guidelines for Book Longevity of the
Council on Library Resources. The University of North Carolina Press has
been a member of the Green Press Initiative since 2003.

Cover image: Joseph Klir, *The Lost Bet* (1893), courtesy of the Library of
Congress, LC-DIG-ppmsca-19299. When an unlucky Czech tailor supporting Republican Benjamin Harrison lost his election wager to a friend who
backed Democrat Grover Cleveland in the 1892 race, he was forced to pull
a cart down Chicago's bustling 12th Street.

Frontispiece: Thrilled spectators watch an estimated 30,000 Tammany
Hall supporters marching through Union Square during the close, dirty
1884 presidential campaign. Most of those marching club members, and
many of the spectators, were in their teens and twenties. ("The Grand
Demonstration of the Tammany Hall Democracy," *Frank Leslie's Illustrated
Newspaper*, November 1, 1884; courtesy Library of Congress)

Library of Congress Cataloging-in-Publication Data
Names: Grinspan, Jon, author.
Title: The virgin vote : how young Americans made democracy
    social, politics personal, and voting popular in the nineteenth
    century / Jon Grinspan.
Description: Chapel Hill : The University of North Carolina Press, [2016] |
    Includes bibliographical references and index.
Identifiers: LCCN 2015038633 | ISBN 9781469627342 (cloth : alk. paper) |
    ISBN 9781469627359 (ebook)
Subjects: LCSH: Youth—Political activity—United States—19th century. |
    Politics, Practical—United States—History—19th century. | United
    States—Politics and government—19th century—Social aspects.
Classification: LCC JK1717 .G75 2016 | DDC 324.70973/09034—dc23 LC record
    available at http://lccn.loc.gov/2015038633

MIX
Paper from
responsible sources
FSC
www.fsc.org   FSC® C013483

Contents

The Virgin Vote

Introduction

Democracy Out of Doors

The night before he turned twenty, Oscar gave his first big speech.

His friends called him up before the rural Ohio meetinghouse. Oscar climbed the stairs, pocket watch ticking in his vest, Adam's apple strained against his collar. He stared out at the packed pews, crowded with slack-jawed boys, respectable ladies, and old farmers. He felt embarrassed by the attention.

Someone smiled. A stranger cheered. Friends hooted nicknames. Warmed by the support, Oscar launched into his talk on the coming election. He stomped the low stage, endorsing Abe Lincoln and mocking the Democratic Party. His handsome face—with its falcon nose, inquiring eyes, and frame of floppy brown hair—lit as he gathered momentum. When the skinny nineteen-year-old schoolteacher was finally through, the applause felt deafening.[1]

Before his speech, Oscar was pretty ordinary. He stood 5′8″ and weighed 135 pounds, typical for a man of his generation.[2] He lived in south-central Ohio, at the dead center of the U.S. population, according to the Census Bureau.[3] And he was nineteen years old, going on twenty, exactly average for an American in 1860.[4]

Oscar meandered into political life. He left home in his teens, packing a carpetbag with a diary, a Bible, and a bowie knife and setting off on an aimless "wander year."[5] He tramped across Pennsylvania, Virginia, and Ohio, lodging with strangers, drinking and dancing, and making note of which towns had the prettiest young ladies.[6]

Oscar finally settled in Hocking County, Ohio, where he found work teaching school. Someone invited him to join a debating society in town. Soon he was there almost every night, considering the "Women's Rights Question" or arguing about whether George Washington went to hell for owning slaves. Oscar loved these debates, joining in with a sometimes entertaining, sometimes irritating faith in his own unbending logic. He

Daguerreotype of Oscar Lawrence Jackson, the "boy orator" who stumped for Abraham Lincoln in the 1860 presidential race in Ohio, speechifying before roughly 10,000 people at age nineteen. (Oscar Lawrence Jackson, *The Colonel's Diary: Journals Kept before and during the Civil War*, ed. David P. Jackson [Sharon, Pa.: Privately published, 1922]; courtesy Library of Congress)

alternated between stiff pride and gawky modesty, a talented nineteen-year-old enthralled and embarrassed by his new powers. Local Republicans liked his swagger and promoted him as a "boy orator" in the heated 1860 race. After Oscar proved himself with his first big speech, politicians started calling him up before torchlit town squares.[7]

Speechifying made him notorious. To Republicans he was a partisan prodigy; to Democrats he was "impudent, foppish, immature."[8] Soon a crew of rowdies were heckling his late-night speeches, drinking whiskey, hurling apples, and running their horses through the crowd. Oscar refused to back down, teasing the toughs from the stage, seeing how far he could push them. Around him stood a posse of unsmiling "Wide Awakes"— young Republican men clad in shimmering black cloaks and soldiers' caps, revolvers and knives hidden under their capes. They eyed the troublemakers and would "have shot and sliced them like dogs if any one of us had been struck."[9]

Young women offered him protection as well. When he wasn't politicking, Oscar spent much of his time courting. Local girls returned the attention, sending the handsome orator anonymous Valentine's cards, inviting him to play a "kissing game," or asking him to escort them home after dances.[10] Some of the high school girls offered to stand around Oscar in a protective wreath, linked by their handkerchiefs as he lectured. No rough would be so ungentlemanly as to try to push past these bodyguards.[11]

But the schoolgirls could not protect Oscar. At night he heard his name cursed in the street. When lecturing indoors, he saw the furious faces of Democrats fogging the windows at the back of meetinghouses. Each rally or debate, each foray into what Oscar called "the democracy out of doors," made him more of a target. Oscar began to keep one hand on his bowie knife when he lectured, a challenge to "the maddest set of humans" threatening him at every speech.[12]

One October day Republicans organized the largest gathering that Oscar's region had ever seen. Thousands poured into the town of Logan, Ohio, from the villages that dotted the foothills of the ebbing Appalachians. Farmers and miners swept hay or coal from their wagons, wrapped them in handsome bunting, and rolled down the main streets in a massive procession. Squads of young ladies wearing pleated blue blouses and red and white striped skirts rode in on horseback. They mingled with companies of young men, some in Wide Awake capes, some in high collars and muddy boots. All sat down at long tables set out in an old oak grove to feast on four roasted bulls, their garnet meat smoky from a long night over wood coals, accompanied by hundreds of chickens, loaves of dense white bread, pickles, relishes, jams, and 2,000 pies.[13]

As night fell, the crowd lit bonfires and the speeches began. The main attraction was David Kellogg Cartter, a forty-eight-year-old former congressman believed to have cast the deciding vote that made Abraham Lincoln the Republican Party's nominee.[14] Cartter spat out his lecture with "extraordinary force and pungency," riling the massive crowd for the coming election.[15]

Then it was Oscar's turn. Again he found himself nervously climbing a stage, but this was no lecture before a few worn church pews. Turning his back to the fat columns of Logan's courthouse, he looked out at the biggest crowd he had ever addressed. Thousands of partisans were fired up, less than sober, and eager to hear what the earnest young man had to say.[16] How was it that Oscar Lawrence Jackson, too young to vote and new in town, with little money, few connections, and a spotty education, now shared the stage with Representative Cartter, the fierce kingmaker? Why was it that none of the multitude assembled seemed to think the presence of this boy orator at all unusual?[17]

Torchlight flickered across rapt young faces, illuminating the answer. Many in the crowd were Oscar's age. Several other speakers were in their twenties. Those ladies in blue blouses were even younger; most were between fifteen and twenty-one, in an age when young women took enthusiastic interest in politics before slamming into the wall of disenfranchisement. The Wide Awakes standing to attention were younger still, many members in their teens and their national leader just twenty-three.[18] When Oscar stood up to give his talk, a sea of youths stared back.

So many aspects of Oscar's life were average, but was his political engagement just as ordinary?

Rulers of the Land

This is a book about growing up and going out. Out into the public square, into wild schoolyards, flirtatious saloons, and tense polling places. About a forgotten time when young Americans found maturity in politics. About

Political parties hosted many barbecues to rally voters or celebrate victories. Usually several oxen, pigs, or sheep were roasted all night over oak coals and basted with their own drippings. Several hundred partisans made short work of such massive feasts, often accompanied by tankards of ale. ("A Democratic Barbecue," *Frank Leslie's Illustrated Newspaper*, October 18, 1884; author's collection)

how, during the loudest, most excited, least understood phase in our nation's democracy, young people played their greatest role.

From 1840 to 1900, young people fueled American politics. They developed a reciprocal relationship with political campaigners, trading their energy, and eventually their votes, for identity and importance. Party elites lobbied newsboys and farm girls, while ordinary young people seemed fixated on each rally or convention. In the words of William Alcott, the foremost author of advice books for young people, the "blustering politician of twelve or fifteen" usually knew more about a campaign than most adults. They were, in Alcott's view, "the rulers of the land."[19]

Some young people cared about shaping policy, others turned out for "fun and frolic," but nearly all used their political system to achieve personal goals.[20] In a tumultuous era, underage activists and first-time voters saw that public politics could help their private lives. They could find friends and mentors, identity and entertainment, advancement and even romance at rallies. Young Americans fueled their political system, not out of youthful idealism, but because all of their individual hopes accumulated to make them a public force. For many young people, the political was personal.

This is a crowded story. There were over 100 million votes cast in presidential elections between 1840 and 1900, and youth was the one condition that all Americans knew intimately.[21] We will meet some of the children, youths, and young adults who stepped further into democracy as they aged. There is the southern girl deciphering her parents' anxious politics on the eve of the Civil War, the enslaved boy spreading political rumors across slumbering plantations, the young cowboy galloping off to cast his first ballot, the gangsters in Baltimore, the lovers in Indiana, the sleazy Manhattan bosses recruiting young voters with cash or beer. Together their stories show how youths bundled their private struggles with public affairs.

It had not always been this way. Historians have grown so used to enumerating all of those left out of nineteenth-century American democracy that they often lose sight of how many were, for the first time, welcomed inside. For all its flaws, American citizens played a greater role in their government than in any other state in history.[22]

And they streamed in suddenly. The word "democracy" did not appear in the Constitution. John Adams warned that removing property qualifications for voting would cause "lads from twelve to twenty-one" to demand the ballot. Noah Webster planned to raise the voting age to forty-five.[23]

Here and there, elections grew heated and young men rallied or rioted, but early American politics were usually halting and unsystematic, dominated by a slowly widening republic of older property owners.[24]

Something broke open in the early nineteenth century, bringing forth a tide of democratic politics and culture, dragging young men and women with it. The big change came on the ground, as new states threw out property requirements for voting. The process was jerky and uneven, but while three in four states had required voters to own property in 1790, barely one-quarter did so by 1840.[25] States replaced these qualifications with a jumble of rules on race, residency, and mental competency but shared a rare consensus about age. For all states, twenty-one marked the dividing line between youth and political manhood.[26]

These seemingly dry reforms revolutionized America. Elections transformed from usually quiet affairs to mesmerizing spectacles. In the 1820s only a quarter of eligible voters cast a ballot; by 1840 four in five went to the polls. After the thrilling 1840 campaign—the first in which two populist parties squared off, providing free drinks and crazed parades—intense popular involvement became the norm. Over the next six decades, voter turnout reached unprecedented peaks, climbing to 70, 80, 90 percent of eligible voters in some states. Even the quietest presidential election during this era drew a far higher turnout than the most popular campaign in recent memory, in 2008.[27]

These turnout statistics chart, like elevation points, the age of popular politics, an era that stretches over the usual periods that divide the nineteenth century. The Jacksonian and antebellum eras, the Civil War, Reconstruction, and the Gilded Age are like mountains joining this massive range. Each dramatically altered American life but shared basic political patterns.[28] In the words of one Iowa electioneer who saw the plateau, not just the peaks, "we work through one campaign, take a bath, and start in on the next."[29]

Campaigns became the centerpiece of the new American culture. Citizens who lacked a shared ancestry, religion, or entertainment began to unite in barely contained competitive fun.[30] There were some regional differences, but the most politically excited parts of the country—the Mid-Atlantic, the Midwest, and the Upper South—were also the most populous.[31] The presidential elections that drove Americans wild came every four years, but nineteenth-century election cycles meant that there was always some local battle to be fought.

The result was a seemingly endless succession of "fun election times."[32]

Turnout

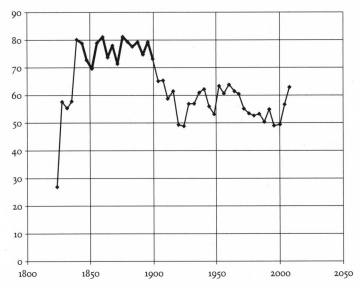

Historians have long known about the incredibly high voter turnout rates in nineteenth-century elections—hovering between 70 and 80 percent of eligible voters from 1840 to 1900 and crumbling in the twentieth century—but few realized the role that young first-time voters played in fueling this intense involvement. (See Appendix, "Eligible Voter Turnout in Presidential Elections, 1824–2012")

The average American already consumed several gallons of pure alcohol each year, and campaigners invited them to congregate around barrels of whiskey or cider or lager or gin.[33] One bored and sober immigrant wrote home that he could hardly wait for the next campaign, when "the Americans will be happy again."[34]

This wild democracy did a strange double duty, simultaneously electing leaders and providing the most popular form of entertainment. Politics bound entertainment and governance together in a three-legged race awkwardly stumbling across the century. The result was a captivating contradiction: an idealistic experiment in popular government tied to a brassy, sleazy, fleeting form of show business.

The age of popular politics coincided with the wild years of American youth. European visitors agreed that the nation swarmed with pugnacious boys and brash little girls, full of opinions on grown-up affairs. British tourists labeled them "precocious"—a polite English way of calling them wild and disrespectful. Many were equally struck by American adults' willingness to listen to their children, encouraging them to expound on politics or national affairs. Just as democracy revolutionized politics, it remade American child rearing, jettisoning many of the age hierarchies of the Old World. For much of the nineteenth century, these "democratic sucklings" focused their irrepressible energies on politics.[35]

For most young men, the new voting laws turned age twenty-one into a sharp boundary between youth and adulthood. Before, the right to vote had depended on an external factor—how much property one possessed—but after 1840, voting said something about one's internal identity, regardless of wealth or status.[36] Lacking many other rites of passage, boys looked forward to voting as the moment they would become men.[37] In an age when voters brought their own tickets to the ballot box and polling places often turned into wild partisan confrontations, casting that first vote was a thrilling initiation. This book explores the long-forgotten rituals by which growing a scraggly mustache, clutching a crumpled paper ballot, and running a gauntlet of hollering vote-challengers came together to announce admission into citizenship and manhood.

When a young man finally placed his ballot in the box, he would brag that he had cast his "virgin vote"—or even his "maiden vote." Americans meant the comparison. Voting, like losing one's virginity, marked a beginning and an end, a commencement and a commitment. If handled properly it could launch a vigorous manhood; if abused it began a long, tragic decline. After a prolonged campaign courtship, a young man needed to give his first ballot to a truly worthy party. And he must always remain true; that first time should "determine the voter's politics for life."[38] In typical Victorian fashion, partisans expected monogamy.

Though they could not vote, young women found their own place in this raucous democracy. Voting laws denied women adulthood, as well as citizenship, by excluding them from the same rite of passage as their brothers, but many refused to wait on the sidelines of the thrilling political culture.[39] Because American democracy was so intensely social, women could influence the men in their lives without ever casting a vote. Young ladies could help shape the politics of their brothers or beaux, at a time when their convictions were still fluid. They could wield moral influence to drive apathetic young men to the polls or don costumes and march in roaring processions. Many even used their sex lives for partisan ends; clever young ladies' flirtations often expressed suppressed beliefs.

Young women struggled, however, to discern the limits of their involvement. While men saw a series of clear stepping stones toward adulthood, women waded through the murky task of deducing, at each stage of youth, how far into public democracy they could venture, which lines they could step over, and which were never to be crossed.

Things were even more confusing for young African Americans. If white women found the boundaries of politics murky, black men found them jagged. For most of the period from 1840 to 1900, the majority of African American men could not vote and stood little chance of directly influencing the ballots of white men. But when they could vote, black voters streamed into the political culture suddenly, joining thrilling campaigns almost overnight. Many went from slavery to casting their virgin votes in a few short years. Others grew up planning to vote but saw that right taken away before they reached twenty-one. This unpredictable political culture meant that underage African Americans did not usually enjoy the same long political apprenticeship as white children.[40] But because their rights were so frequently contested, African American children, youths, and young adults could not ignore politics. In freedmen's schools and churches, at covert Union League meetings and bloody Reconstruction-era polling places, young African Americans found identity and adulthood in popular politics.

While American democracy halted at gender and racial boundaries, it leapt over class divisions. The political culture incorporated America's white laboring majority as no other system, anywhere in the world, managed to do.[41] Party headquarters located in saloons and butcher shops invited in struggling young people, offering them mentors, networks, and jobs. Poorer Americans often cared more about politics than wealthier citizens. While farmhands and hod carriers turned out in droves, lawyers and bankers—disgusted with political parties seemingly dominated by mobs of common men—often retreated to private clubs, grumbling the mantra "A gentleman never votes."[42]

Youth politics loomed the largest in the vast middling classes in American life, running from the stable poor to the comfortable middle. There are some mansions and shanties in this story but mostly log cabins, clapboard farmsteads, and brick boardinghouses. Regardless of class, politically active young people often shared a striving, struggling, bumptious ambition, a faith that their young lives could be improved with the help of a political party.

But what was in it for them? Why invest the energy? Why take the risks? In his modest diary, Oscar Lawrence Jackson explained the real motivations attracting him to politics in 1860. Though he filled his lectures with ideological arguments, in a section "not intended for public view" he gushed about the attention his speaking won from adult Republicans (and "very good-looking young ladies"). Party platforms aside, Oscar admitted that he was driven by the "ambition of anyone my age."[43]

Young Americans' private aspirations pushed them into public politics. Voting, speechifying, and electioneering allowed Oscar and many like him to feel like they were contributing to the governance of their nation. They usually expressed little interest in improving young people's collective status in America. Instead, most focused on what politics could do for them.[44]

Growing up in an era of tumultuous change, young people needed this boost from politics. Contemporary Americans may imagine the nineteenth century as a golden age of carefree, small-town childhood, but young people's lives were never more rootless, disparate, and confusing. During those years America's population ballooned from 5 million to 75 million people, as sprawling cities blossomed along riverbanks and massive slaughterhouses sprouted up where deer had grazed.[45] For the children of that era, each death of a parent from cholera, each relocation to a distant state, each new job in a clanking, stinking factory shook the rickety bridge to adulthood. The nineteenth century was not a single moment of revolution but a hundred years of change upon change upon change, and each new shift made it harder for youths to find their footing.

Party politics offered scaffolding to their unstable lives, promising structure regardless of boom or bust. American society lacked many age distinctions in those years; at workplaces, churches, saloons, and especially rallies, "the young folks and the old folks mingled."[46] Nineteen-year-olds like Oscar could impress adults in debating societies and political clubs, looking up the ranks to pick out spots they hoped to occupy. In a shaken society with little permanence, The Party was often the most accessible institution.

The world's largest democracy did not run on the hopes and dreams of nineteen-year-olds alone. While the young used politics in their personal lives, parties used the young in political life. For all the thrilled youths finding adulthood at public rallies, there were party bosses and electioneers scheming to draw new infusions of "warm fresh blood."[47]

These partisans structured every aspect of American democracy. They wrote the newspapers, printed the ballots, selected the election locations, and even chose the poll judges.[48] Membership in a party was instilled from birth and bound up with ethnic and religious background. Most voters would never go against the party of their family; more than 90 percent endorsed the same organization in election after election.[49] Men who switched parties were mocked as "old ladies" or "parasol-holders."[50]

These parties behaved in very similar ways. Campaigners focused little effort on winning over the undecided; instead, "nonsense carried the day" at rallies, firing up the faithful with vicious slogans, false accusations, and plenty of booze.[51] With each campaign shouting so loudly, voices all ran together. Conflicting beliefs distinguished parties and factions but rarely shaped *how* Americans participated. For one thing, elections were simply too competitive, and campaigners quickly adapted their opponents' techniques. Ideological rivals often looked the same on the ground. Even within a movement, well-versed partisans mingled with those who did not know the name of the candidate. Orators like Oscar tried to present the issues in rational, well-researched speeches but were often drowned out by roaring crowds and deafening fireworks. Spectators admitted they "never heard a political speech to the end."[52]

Politicians knew how difficult it was to change the mind of a regular party man, so instead they focused on harvesting the "large crop of new voters" turning twenty-one every year.[53] By 1840 campaigners realized that "new voters" almost always meant "young voters"—though usually committed to their family's party, men in their early twenties were the most politically flexible.[54] The older a man got, the more ballots he cast for his party, the harder it became to pry him lose.[55] But first-time voters "pay especial heed" to the campaign before their initial national election.[56] Win their virgin vote, and they would support your party for decades.

Politicos would have scoffed at William Alcott's claim that young people were the "rulers of the land." Most manipulated youths, accepting their votes and assigning them tedious campaign tasks. Kids ran errands, emptied spittoons, and filled out crowds. Rowdy "b'hoys" served as foot soldiers in the violent campaigning of the era, ready to "awl" a rival with a shoemaker's spike. Abraham Lincoln made use of them in his early career, advising a friend to "gather up all the shrewd, wild boys about town, whether just of age or a little under age," into a boisterous political club.[57] Lincoln went further, recruiting a young man he had defended in a murder trial (the youth admitted to the stabbing in a drugstore brawl but swore it was in self-defense) as an aggressive political operative for the Republican Party.[58]

Campaigners who relied on young Americans still treated them with condescension, rarely addressing youths' concerns or working to improve their collective status in society. Though doing away with many hierarchies, American politicians still looked down at young men and women. They were happy to accept supporters but mocked young rivals as "babies."[59] Like the youths who participated in politics without any thought of generational uplift, few adult campaigners wanted to alter age relations when they riled up the "shrewd, wild boys."

It was convenient that young people needed politics as much as politics needed them. The second half of the nineteenth century was a time of extreme instability for young Americans and intense recruitment by politicians. While ambitious novices sought social power in their personal lives, campaigners saw political power in those waves of hopeful first-timers. This dual use of politics, for the personal and the structural, for the young and the old, for entertainment and governance, explains why popular politics could climb so high and last so long.

Historians have long debated the "fit" of politics into public life, arguing over whether nineteenth-century democracy was popular and well-informed or artificial and superficial.[60] But the meaning and practice of politics shifted with each stage of youth and adulthood. Participation looked different at sixteen and sixty. Young people show that American democracy could simultaneously be grassroots and top-down, intimate and public, deeply felt but shallowly reasoned.

The overlapping uses of the same system pose the question: is this the story of ordinary young people's surprising agency, or of elite politicians' self-interested cunning?

The Waking, Thinking, Purposeful Age

Oscar wrapped up his speech sometime before midnight. He considered it "a rather poor affair," but the newspaper that reported on the barbecue seemed impressed. Organizers fired off the last volleys of rockets as the happy throngs began to depart, and Oscar headed home, into the dark October night.[61]

He kept speechifying for the next month. By Lincoln's November 6 victory, Oscar was a local celebrity, known for delivering eighteen speeches in four counties to roughly 10,000 people. The "drunken crew" who hassled him melted away; he never had to use that bowie knife of his. Oscar gave up orating once the war began. He volunteered in William Tecumseh Sherman's army, leading charges, surviving a gunshot to the face, and finding manhood in violence, not voting.[62]

Even as Oscar walked off the stage, new young people were taking his place. There were plenty of ambitious nineteen-year-olds craving the attention, the adulthood, and the fun of popular politics. Oscar had been born in September 1840, in the midst of that first youth-driven whirlwind campaign, and young men and women would keep pouring into politics for the next half century. Across the decades, a twenty-year-old in 1840 had much in common with a twenty-year-old in 1860 or 1880. This steady supply of new partisans spanned generations, the usual unit used to explain youth culture. But the age of popular politics defies such tidy groupings. Forget generations. It is far better to see a fluid reservoir, with youths bubbling up to replace washed-out adults.[63]

Politicians understood the trajectory of political excitement. After one hard defeat, a Republican paper printed an open letter to young men entering their "waking, thinking, purposeful age" who might cast their virgin votes in the next election. They asked these young Americans to consider "how many thousands of you there are; and think how, behind you, their heads reaching to your shoulders now, are pressing the boys from thirteen to seventeen. . . . This army of younger brothers behind you will be sure to follow your lead."[64] Campaigners saw that democratic participation had a predictable direction, a constant flow of new blood, an endless succession from youth to maturity.

Issues, parties, and even a civil war came and went over the age of popular politics, but campaigning, on the ground, remained remarkably stable. Stepping back from the thrilling specifics of each race, popular participation in 1860 looked a lot like many of the other elections between 1840 and 1900.[65] The symbols and the slogans evolved over time but within patterns that were deeply familiar. In an era of dramatic change in nearly every other aspect of American life, this repetition offered an appealing stability.[66] Instead of targeting new demographics or tackling neglected issues, politicians often focused on passing this existing culture down to young people.

Rather than follow the drumbeat of recurring political campaigns, this book asks how young Americans stepped further into public life as they aged. How did children learn about democracy? How did youths use politics to manage social, economic, and romantic crises? What was it like for a virgin voter to cast his first ballot, and what did it mean for his sister to have to sit at home that day? From the other perspective, what did adult campaigners offer young supporters in exchange for their labor and their votes? Historians tend to focus on change, revolution, and disruption, but this is a story about a culture reproducing itself over time, about a formative, forgotten era when Americans worked to make their democracy sustainable.

A wise and witty narrator helps explain the stages that defined aging and politics. Before William Dean Howells came to dominate American literature, before his buddy Mark Twain joked that his cynical motto was "Fry me an optimist for breakfast," Will was a hungry Ohio boy, quieter than Oscar but just as ambitious.[67] Popular politics helped him escape his hardscrabble childhood and realize his literary ambitions. As he moved through life, Will Howells returned compulsively to his youth. In memoir after memoir he recast himself as a wild but watchful child, a striving youth, and an "over-proud" virgin voter.[68] Born into politics, Will Howells spent adulthood studying youth, chuckling, "These days I'm all autobiography."[69] He will be our guide.

The world Will Howells and Oscar Lawrence Jackson knew did not last forever. At the end of the century, the plateau of popular politics suddenly began to crumble. After 1900, voter turnout plummeted, bottoming out in 1924 at less than half of eligible voters, the worst turnout in a hundred years. Here too, the young led the way. Older partisans kept showing up, as they had been trained to do, but new voters did not.[70] A new youth culture—those famous teenagers of the twentieth century—seemed to need politics less. Campaigners, for their part, grew worse at appealing to youths, falling out of touch with what young people might want from politics. Something happened to the accidental alliance of young people and campaigners that had sustained popular democracy over the nineteenth century. Youth participation fell, and "democracy out of doors" went inside. Politics—though cleaner and fairer—has never recovered.

But for the half century before 1890, young Americans used democracy to mark maturity. They linked each stage of youth to another step into the public world. For all their differences, these barmaids, belles, newsboys, and sharecroppers moved in the same direction. As in one of their massive political processions, each carried their own torch, unique and thrilling, but together they bathed a long era in a shared light, marching out from individual interiors to a common adult destination.

This strange history has been lost, locked up in sixteen-year-olds' diaries and ward bosses' memos. Their quiet writings and booming campaigns help tell the fascinating story of how democracy developed from Jackson to Roosevelt, and how Americans matured from birth to adulthood.

1 » Violent Little Partisans

It began at home. For Susan Bradford, home was a green-roofed, white-washed country mansion at the center of the Pine Hill Plantation. There she lived with her father, mother, extended family, and 142 enslaved "servants." Beyond the mansion and slave cabins stood 3,000 acres of the finest red land in Florida, planted with flower gardens, fields of cotton, and dense stands of pine.[1]

Susan first discovered the mystery as an eight-year-old in January 1855. Though the weather was unusually cold for Leon County, her father and several local leaders gathered outside for a hushed conference in a frosted rose garden.[2] Always a curious little detective, brown-eyed, square-jawed Susan watched through a low window. She did not know that the men were all prominent southern Democrats, sharing conspiracy theories about abolitionist agitators. She knew only that "there is something wrong somewhere" and wished, more than anything, that an adult would explain "what they were talking about."[3]

A few months later "something funny happened." Susan watched as a visiting northerner gave her father a copy of *Uncle Tom's Cabin*. She noted the way his face flushed when he recognized the cover. Over the next day he read it repeatedly. Father and daughter sat together in Pine Hill's ornate library, Susan on the couch, scribbling in her diary, her father stiff in a chair, his sad brown eyes scanning Harriet Beecher Stowe's abolitionist epic. When the guest approached and asked what he thought of the gift, the dignified Dr. Bradford, the master of Pine Hill, with his proud, mournful face and slicked gray hair, carefully placed the book in the snapping fireplace. Bradford looked his guest in the eye as the pages blackened and declared the coals "the best place for it."[4]

Susan was puzzled. "I wanted to read that book myself," she wrote in her diary that night, "but it must have been a bad book for Father, who loves books, to have treated it that way."[5]

Even the woods seemed to contain adult secrets. Her nanny, an enslaved woman named Fannie, began to whisper terrifying rumors about an "Abolition crew" lurking nearby.[6] Susan did not know what "abolition" meant but worried that someone planned to hurt her father. Another slave, an older man known as "Uncle Kinchen," told her a confusing story about accompanying her grandpa on a trip north, where they observed a gathering of abolitionists. Whatever Fannie and Kinchen intended when they told Susan these rumors, they had the effect of terrifying the girl. She had nightmares that abolitionists—monstrous "devils" with horns and cloven feet—"were after me," chasing Susan through the Florida pines.[7]

Soon she began to push her parents to explain the ominous references to "abolitionists" and "Republicans." One evening she awoke from a nap on the parlor sofa to hear her mother and uncle anxiously discussing the North's plans "to make trouble for us." Susan listened for a while, pretending to sleep, but could not contain her nagging curiosity. She bolted up and blurted, "Oh, uncle Daniel, please tell me all about it!" Her mother sent her straight to bed.[8] All she knew was that "there is trouble in the air but I cannot find out just what it is."[9]

Susan filled her precocious diary with questions that intrigued most American children. Sons and daughters observed adult political passions long before they understood what they meant. From an early age they learned that their family supported a party, or sensed a rivalry with another movement, yet grasped the ideological differences between these organizations only when they had grown much older. Adults taught children to ape their politics, sing campaign songs, and jeer the rival party. It took years of such instruction before teens began to read the partisan press, and even longer before young men could legally vote. The American political nation did not emerge, fully formed, at age twenty-one. By the time they cast their first ballots, many virgin voters were veterans of at least a decade of popular democracy.

Politics seeped into children's consciousness in a sloppy manner. Most experienced an education as haphazard as Susan Bradford's. They overheard a debate at the dinner table or nodded through a confusing lecture from a towering adult, which piqued their interest but left little knowledge.[10] Elders who warned curious children to stay out of worldly affairs only heightened the mystery, especially for determined kids like Susan. This untidy education taught many American children to view politics as an alluring hallmark of adulthood.

Adults knew a secret. Americans could never agree on how to formally introduce partisanship to their children, so they framed their politics as a slowly unfolding mystery.[11] Children learned new clues at each stage of their passage into the public world. At home, kids eavesdropped on political debates and took note of their parents' heroes and villains. In the semi-public realm of the classroom, children puzzled over the slogans chanted by older students and the biases of their teachers. By ten or twelve, boys and girls were allowed to join in rallies, parades, bonfires, and barbecues. Eventually some found their way into smoke-filled party headquarters, running errands for bosses. Along the way, boys and girls pieced together evidence about what politics actually meant.

I Know a Little Bit Now

"My earliest recollections are of endless political discussions," Sally McCarty reminisced about her childhood in Leesburg, Virginia, in the 1840s. Like Susan Bradford, Sally grew up with political talk, but her folks let her in on the secret. The stridently Whig McCarty family indulged Sally, an only child with few playmates, letting her "sit up with my elders when I should have been in bed."[12]

From that perch Sally absorbed the exploding political culture of the early 1840s. She claimed to be "tolerably conversant with the great questions of the day" by age seven, when she led a squad of little girls in a torchlight procession for William Henry Harrison. She learned to sew by watching ladies stitch Harrison banners, a new form of political expression for women in Virginia.[13] And she felt, viscerally if superficially, the ups and downs of partisan commitment. Sally remembered refusing to dance "the hop" with a boy at a party one late summer evening in 1841, claiming she was upset because "Tyler had vetoed the Bank Bill," whatever that was.[14]

Children like Sally did not know the difference between the organizations their parents loved and hated. They did not know that the Democrats were the oldest party in the country, formed in the 1820s as an alliance of aggrieved common men in the North, planters in the South, and frontiersmen in the West. They did not comprehend the party's fundamental belief that class conflict shaped American politics or its fear that a big government would privilege wealthy merchants or meddle with slavery.[15]

Nor did they understand the motivations of the Whigs, organized to battle Democrats in the 1830s. Whigs rejected the Democrats' belief in social conflict; they wanted an active federal government to help build infrastructure, stabilize the economy, and encourage harmony across class and region.[16] These children did not understand the dynamics that led the northern Whig Party to give way to the Republicans in the 1850s, joined by marginalized Democrats and the antislavery fringe. This new movement wanted to assert the northern majority's control over the country, halt the spread of slavery, and expand the federal government. Children born to parents who backed third parties—Antimasons, Free Soilers, Know Nothings, or Populists—had an even weaker grasp of their parents' beliefs. No wonder so many Americans, young and old, were deeply confused about the platforms of their preferred party.[17]

Sally McCarty's erratic education was typical. For most children, partisanship was overheard before it was taught and performed before it was understood. Sometimes kids decoded the information themselves, as in Susan Bradford's case, while others had it thrust upon them. Elders led the way, though with so many early deaths and dislocations, this might be a stepfather, an aunt, or a talkative neighbor.[18] Historians have long acknowledged the link between family background and party allegiance, but few have looked inside the home, at the political socialization of seven- or eleven-year-olds, to uncover the fitful yet abiding mechanisms that taught boys and girls to be Republicans or Democrats.[19]

Adults imbued children's lives with partisanship from the very start. Infants were "born a Whig" or "drank in Democracy with their mother's milk."[20] Some parents proclaimed their zeal by naming their sons for favored leaders. There were plenty of little George Washington ——s in the Early Republic, but this tradition peaked with the high tide of political enthusiasm and fell off suddenly around 1900. Starting in the 1830s, Andrew Jackson Smiths and Henry Clay Joneses proliferated in the census rolls. The popularity of such names often said more about a parent's views than it did about the success of the namesake. There were, for instance, twenty-five times more little boys named Rutherford in 1880 than there had been in 1870.[21] Children with such names carried the marker of partisanship from birth.

More children began their political education, like Sally and Susan, by eavesdropping. In a society with little separation by age, many boys and girls happened to be present when their elders talked politics. As "the main subject of conversation," adults often discussed upcoming elections, especially when traveling with strangers, and few noticed their children listening in on the deck of a steamboat or while lodging at an inn.[22]

Once they observed adults' intense interest, many kids wanted in on the fun. The writer and activist Lydia Maria Child recalled a bright little five-year-old girl who made it her mission to "to keep me booked up" on events in the 1856 election. Whenever the girl overheard political news she would dash over to Child's house, holler something like "Miss Child! Pennylvany's all right!" under her window, and then skip away again.[23]

Children of politically divided households often found themselves drawn into adults' disagreements. One Georgia girl, sick of her family's bickering, wished there was no such thing as politics, "for they are a never-ending source of warfare in the house."[24] Overheard debates filled children with misconceptions. Growing up in the late 1830s, Andrew Dickson White watched his Whig father quarrel fiercely with his maternal grandfather, an old-school Jeffersonian Democrat. The two stubborn men sent each other competing pamphlets, arguing ceaselessly over Martin Van Buren's plan for an "Independent Sub-Treasury."[25] Like Sally McCarty, the eight-year-old White sided with his dad. He parroted his father, declaring that the Van Buren plan was "the most wicked outrage ever committed by a remorseless tyrant," but later admitted that he had "not the remotest idea" what a Sub-Treasury was.[26]

This confused political education, all outrage and no instruction, led to a moment of genuine terror for poor Andrew. Early one April morning in 1841, his mother shook him awake. She told him, breathlessly, that President William Henry Harrison had suddenly died. The eight-year-old White panicked. His parents' hero was dead, and he anxiously wondered, "What would become of us?" No one, it turned out, had told White that there was a vice president.[27]

Many children were left to puzzle out their parents' politics, which could introduce real adult crises, as the elderly Alabama sharecropper Ned Cobb explained to interviewers in the mid-twentieth century. Ned's dad, Hayes Cobb, had been born a slave but was emancipated at age fifteen. Ned recalled watching his father head off to vote with other black men throughout Reconstruction. So what if he sometimes sold his vote for a hunk of side meat or a sack of flour? "My daddy was a man that voted," bragged his still-proud son nearly a century later.[28] Then one day Hayes Cobb stopped voting. Instead, he spent Election Day hunting in the nearby swamp or hanging around their cabin. Ned "never did hear my daddy say nothing 'bout losin' the vote. But I believe with all my heart he knowed what it meant."[29]

No one told young Ned that black voters were being systematically disenfranchised across the South. No one needed to. Ned Cobb explained: "I *seed* that . . . I was old enough to look at folks and hear the talk." Many young Americans learned political lessons this way, overhearing "the talk" as Election Day neared. Ned's testimony captured the muffled frustration—with the men who stole his father's vote, with his father for accepting its loss—of a child observing his parent's helplessness. This dull resentment lasted throughout Ned Cobb's long life. At age eighty-four he told interviewers that he had never voted and never would. "They tell me now I can vote and I believe I could. But I been disencouraged so bad."[30]

Adults sometimes deliberately trained children to support their party. Fathers usually took the lead. The majority of men had strong political affiliations and hoped to pass a partisan inheritance on to their children. But fathers were often distant from their preteen offspring. Girls and infant boys lived in a mostly maternal world, and young boys were not much help to their working fathers before age ten or so. Over the second half of the nineteenth century, children spent more time in school and fathers worked farther from home. This combination of patriarchal authority, partisan zeal, and paternal aloofness meant that fathers' instructions were often muffled and unclear, coming down like the decrees of a distant king. Boys and girls attentively followed this guidance, which did more to excite than inform.

Fathers tended to lead by example, bringing their children to political rallies but providing little explanation. At such events, adults chatted and drank while their sons and daughters ran alongside processions or assembled bonfires. Older siblings provided some useful interpretation. Nineteenth-century families tended to space out births over many years, so ten-year-olds frequently looked to siblings in their mid-twenties to explain what their fathers were trying to communicate.[31]

Many children came to see their fathers as individual embodiments of politics, especially because dads often relayed important political news to the rest of the family. Election Day entries in children's diaries frequently report waiting for "Father" to return from the political scrum or local saloon, bearing an update about the margin from a key state.[32] This link led many children to connect voting with masculinity and adulthood.

For as long as he could remember, young William Dean Howells associated his eccentric, "sunshiny" father with politics.[33] Among his hazy first memories, he recalled seeing his dad dressed in a fringed frontiersman shirt for the Whig campaign in 1840. Three-year-old Will understood that election only through the prism of his grinning father's strange costume. In another flash of early memory, Will sat with his family at an abolitionist meeting when a rock crashed through the window, hurled by some unseen opponent outside. Over the 1840s, observant little Will watched as anti-slavery politics became his father's "main worldly interest."[34]

Will followed his father to the printing office of his struggling Whig newspaper, battling for readers in Democratic southern Ohio. In his memories, Will's father was a lively figure forever writing editorials, tinkering with machinery, and chatting with politicians who stopped by, all the while pouring out "a great many theories and a great many jokes."[35] Will Howells's sense of himself emerged in that printing house. He was the oddly serious boy in the corner, nicknamed the "Old Man" by the journeymen printers, his sharp eyes peering out between high cheekbones and shaggy brown hair.[36] Slowly, Will began to see glimpses of his own hazy future, as a Whig and as a writer.

Outside of the printing house, Will followed his father's lead, running with a pack of wild Whig boys. Though they held "distorted and mistaken views of most things," they turned out at each election, marching and singing and hassling the sons of Democrats. The boys brought along Will's sweet but ugly gray mutt, named "Tip" (short for "Tippecanoe"), "a Whig dog" who would happily pull wagons full of screaming children in political processions.[37]

Then, in 1848, everything changed. Will's father suddenly left the Whig Party, refusing to support its nominee for president, the Mexico-invading, slave-owning Zachary Taylor. After years of growing agitation, Howells had enough. He denounced the war with Mexico, the expansion of slavery, and the Whig Party as a whole. His small paper had never been popular in the Democratic region, but refusing to stand with the Whig nominee made Howells a minority of a minority. He sold his paper, the sole source of income feeding his wife and seven children, and joined the Free Soil movement.[38]

For the rest of his life, William Dean Howells revisited this traumatic moment. At first his father's bolt from the Whig Party was "a terrible wrench."[39] Opposing the war with Mexico was humiliating enough for a patriotic eleven-year-old; to Will his father seemed "little better than a Mexican."[40] But his dad had even abandoned the family party and was hanging around with former Democrats in the Free Soil movement. Raised to view Democrats as "enemies of the human race," Howells was scandalized to see his father talking politics with such monsters.[41]

Then, before he realized what he was doing, Will Howells followed his father, snubbing his Whig friends and "roaring out songs against Taylor."[42] He joined a Free Soil club, even though its rallies were dull affairs. Will chose father over friends or fun. Looking back from 1916, Howells reasoned that, at first, a young child knows only "things it has been told of itself." But slowly "a wavering outline of its nature is shadowed against the background of family."[43] For Will Howells, his father's bolt from the Whig Party provided that moment, clarifying his politics and his personality for life.

Other fathers directed political lessons to their daughters. There are more accounts of father-daughter political talks than of those between fathers and sons, and daughters seemed more attentive to these partisan instructions. Sally McCarty lived in awe of her father's political wisdom, particularly his knack for thinking up campaign songs and nasty rhymes.[44] Other young women admitted that they had "quietly adopted father's views" or simply proclaimed, "I am a Democrat because my father is one."[45] Fathers may have made more of an effort to instruct their daughters because they trusted their sons to form their own alliances, whereas a woman might adopt those of her future husband. If a Democratic father wanted Democratic grandchildren, he had to make sure his daughter would pass on the lineage. Ironically, this patriarchal view meant that some daughters received better political instruction than their brothers.

While fathers talked politics with their daughters, mothers used their sons to express their political voice. Building on the culture of Republican Motherhood, which taught that mothers must mold their sons into virtuous citizens and future voters, many women saw it as their duty to be sure that boys were conversant in politics.[46] In the 1884 election, the *Salt Lake Tribune* highlighted the belief that sons enacted their mothers' politics when they turned twenty-one, announcing, "The mothers of 1863 are going, through their sons, to vote."[47] Some mothers saw no tension between political instruction and more domestic roles. Almira Heard's letters to her traveling son mixed furious criticism of the Know Nothings with maternal notes hoping that he "got a nice breakfast this morning."[48]

Down in Florida, Susan Bradford's mother had not been nearly as helpful. Rather than explain who planned "to make trouble" for the masters of Pine Hill, she had ordered her daughter off to bed. Only through years of eavesdropping would Susan come to "know a little bit" about the secret. By her early teens she figured out that the Bradfords were Democrats and began to refer to the party's candidates as "ours." She learned what abolitionism meant and deduced that a new Republican Party was working toward "the freeing of the Negroes and the downfall of the South," though she admitted, "I am only a child but reading the papers, that is the way it seems to be."[49]

Susan now understood politics enough to find fun in them. Her contrarian Whig brother-in-law had an adorable little daughter named Mattie. After witnessing a "hot fight" between her otherwise Democratic family and the black sheep, Susan and the other children teased nine-year-old Mattie until the girl felt she had to defend her father. "Mattie is so cute," Susan wrote of her cousin; "she shakes her golden curls and turns up her pretty little nose" when the family sang Democratic songs, which "to Mattie is like shaking a red rag at a bull."[50]

Yet there was much about party politics that remained mysterious. One spring day in 1860, Dr. Edward Bradford happened upon his fourteen-year-old daughter in their library, inscribing her confusion in her diary. In the very room in which he had incinerated *Uncle Tom's Cabin*, Susan's father asked, "What is my baby writing? It has brought a real grown-up frown to her face."[51]

Susan let her father—"the very best man in all the world"—read her diary. After a long silence, Dr. Bradford said, "You are getting to be quite a politician. I didn't know you felt such an interest." He explained to his daughter the coming presidential campaign, the division of the Democratic Party, and calls for secession. He also advised her to read partisan newspapers and the speeches of John Calhoun. Bradford ended the conversation by telling Susan that men and women were obligated to stay informed about political affairs and that she should come to him with questions.[52]

For five long years, Susan had viewed politics as a secret preserve of adulthood, and she wanted in on the mystery. That her parents proved incapable of shielding her from politics, or of even keeping quiet about it when she was in the room, speaks to the frequency with which Americans discussed their democracy. On top of this, Susan had learned that her family was Democratic, and that Republicans and abolitionists were their enemies, half a decade before her father finally explained the meaning of this difference. Most American families similarly teased children with the allure of politics while failing to deliver clear explanations about what it all meant.

Democrats Eat Dead Rats

Children first saw democracy reach beyond their homes in the classroom. Nineteenth-century schools acted as a petri dish for popular politics. Local districts drew together children of all ages, mixing uninformed toddlers with virgin voters.[53] Schools combined the sons and daughters of Democrats, Whigs, Republicans, and other parties in one big room, repeating songs and slogans picked up from parents or siblings. Teachers were often young men, at the peak of their political excitement and vocal about their beliefs. On top of this, few instructors followed official curriculums or educational theory.[54] Schools were disorganized, teachers were untrained, and students learned more from the social environment than from their textbooks.[55] American schools were better at encouraging the kind of social mixing on which popular politics thrived than they were at keeping out partisanship. This casual political education expanded upon the haphazard but zealous instruction that had already begun at home.

During campaigns students refused to leave their new partisan knowledge at home. Many dragged their family's politics into class, teasing rival children with aggressive campaign slogans. "Democrats eat dead rats" was a favorite, hollered by Whig boys in the South and Midwest.[56] Young Will Howells relished the chant, before his father abandoned the Whigs. The budding poet loved the rhyme, which left his Democratic classmates with no obvious retort. "Whigs eat dead pigs" hurt few feelings in a nation raised on salt pork. The slogan—catchy, competitive, and meaningless—nicely summed up children's engagement with politics.[57]

Classrooms hummed with political gossip on Election Day. Many teachers teased their students with the sense that something tremendously important was transpiring just outside those sod, log, or brick walls. In Martha Van Orsdol's Kansas classroom, there was very little studying during the 1884 vote. "Politics, more than lessons, were discussed," and her teacher snuck out to check the returns "real often for us."[58] In another Kansas classroom, William Allen White's eight-year-old Republican classmates used his "Tilden and Hendricks scarf"—sold to Democrats during the 1876 presidential campaign—to choke him until he passed out. With a half century's bemused nostalgia, he wrote, "No valiant defender of Democracy lay there on the brown prairie grass, but a little pop-eyed, redheaded, freckled-faced, gasping, ashy-blue Democrat."[59] The *Newark Evening News* was not exaggerating when it mused that a visitor to an American schoolhouse will find "the great majority of children violent little partisans."[60]

"You look loike wan of thim dirty Republicans — an' if yer don't shout for me fader and HANCOCK, I'll black the eye of ye."

For many nineteenth-century children, democratic involvement did not begin with voting, reading the newspaper, or studying the issues but with brawling, bullying, or getting bullied by young opponents of one's inherited political party. (*Harper's Weekly*, October 16, 1880; courtesy UNC-Chapel Hill Libraries)

Frances Willard, the future women's rights activist and president of the Woman's Christian Temperance Union, was delighted to see partisanship in her classroom. "Frank" taught in a large school in Illinois, along with a male teacher. She idealized the political process, even though "under the present system I was not allowed to vote," and supported the other instructor's decision to read the election returns aloud after the 1860 presidential election. In her diary, Willard depicted the scene as the tall teacher announced state-by-state returns to a throng of children. "All of my little girls," she wrote, "crowded around and listened attentively." One young student "dances up and down exclaiming, 'Are n't you glad, Miss Willard, that Lincoln is elected?'" Willard was glad. To her the moment captured "the genius of a Republican government, an organization in which every member, male and female, large or small, feels a keen, personal interest."[61]

"Republican government" often found its loudest expression in the schools the Freedmen's Bureau organized to educate former slaves after the Civil War. During night sessions in a makeshift classroom—often unplastered log buildings with no stove and a few stools—elderly freedmen poured over family Bibles while boisterous boys and girls studied as if the right to an education had not been denied them just a few years earlier. Such schools often served as the educational and political nexus of southern black communities, organized by black women and taught by northern Republicans. Teachers explained the meaning of democracy during class, and after hours semisecret political clubs held meetings for the Republican Party. Unlike white political organizations, which could claim public squares without fear of violence, African Americans turned schools into the "political hub" of the Republican Party in the South. In many black communities there were no politics without schools and no schools without politics.[62]

In most American schools, teachers were hardly professionals. For much of the nineteenth century, teaching was "considered a youthful and temporary employment" for aimless men in particular.[63] Few had formal training or any intention to make education a career.[64] Some tried teaching because, in the words of one sarcastic newspaperman, "it was easier than working in a saw-mill."[65] The diaries of new teachers demonstrate how unprepared they were. One young man switched to teaching after working in his brothers' failing wagon shop, mostly because the school offered cash while his old job paid him in unsold wagon parts.[66] Another examined his new workplace and sighed, "Who can get an education in such a place?"[67] It should be no wonder that these accidental educators ignored pedagogy, preferring to talk politics.

American schools were often wild places, packed with children who deliberately made education difficult. Mischievous girls tortured bashful young teachers, laughing, "Oh! What a time we girls will have. . . . We will make life miserable for him."[68] Bullies in Baltimore threw their inkstands at their teacher and wondered why anyone would take a job that "entailed so many wounds, cuts and bruises."[69] A would-be educator in Ohio asked himself that same question, noting that on his first day teaching he had "24 *very bad* scholars." He quit within a week.[70] In such a wild context, teachers were lucky if they could distract their students with politics.

To be fair, nineteenth-century American schools offered education to an unprecedented swath of society. The fruits of this success were borne out in the stellar literacy rates and impressed descriptions by European visitors.[71] These schools fostered exactly the kind of motley social space in which popular politics thrived. By gathering so many impressionable children of different ages into one classroom, often guided by a passionately partisan young teacher, American schools broadened the political socialization begun within the family. The buzzing political chatter, overheard at home, grew louder in the schoolhouse.

That Barbarous Republic of Boys

Will Howells was one of those students who made his teachers miserable. He particularly tortured a high-minded schoolteacher who refused to beat his students, interpreting his idealism as weakness.[72] But for Howells, and for millions of boys and girls growing up in the nineteenth century, school was just a momentary break from their real existence: a parallel universe in which gangs of barefoot scamps swam, fought, set fires, chewed tobacco, and threw rocks. Outside of school and his father's printing house, Will Howells was just another wild kid. He spent much of his childhood traipsing the woods and wetlands of southern Ohio, Tip the Whig dog by his side.

Looking back from 1890, Howells recalled the independence of midcentury childhood. Starting around age five, kids entered a separate culture threaded "all in and through the world of men and women."[73] Many felt this sense of being "apart-together," mixing among adults but in a separate kingdom with its own rules.[74] For male children in particular—encouraged to get some rowdiness out of their system before meeting the expectations of self-restrained manhood—this "boy culture" offered a temporary reprieve.[75] Every fistfight, every bonfire, every raccoon bite confirmed the independence of what Will Howells called "that barbarous republic of boys."[76]

This world was ephemeral, evaporating earlier for some and later for others. Some children were thrown into a hard life of labor at age eight; others ran wild until fifteen, their fate determined by class, race, region, and even physical size rather than by chronological age. But this "boy culture" taught lifelong skills. Many of its highest values—boldness, aggression, the ability to organize groups and battle rivals—reappeared in political campaigns designed to appeal to excitable young men.

Boy culture emerged because of changes in parenting, work, and environment. Most boys lived in a maternal sphere for the first few years of life, and fathers took responsibility for their sons' instruction in their early teens. But in the half decade in between, many male children found some freedom to get into trouble. The growing predominance of wage labor meant there were fewer apprenticeships to occupy boys' time, and more parents worked away from home, employed in nonagricultural jobs that their young sons could not assist them in.[77] On top of this, Americans' style of child rearing astonished European visitors as radically democratic and undisciplined, resulting in "painfully precocious" boys, more like "small stuck-up caricatures of men and women."[78] Finally, burgeoning urban spaces gathered together larger groups of boys, enabling complex gangs and rivalries.

Few girls enjoyed such independence. Most young women were expected to take on more of their mothers' domestic responsibilities as they grew. The fact that men were increasingly exchanging their labor for wages heightened this inequality. Few employers wanted to hire seven-year-old boys, but mothers could assign their daughters exhausting housework for free. Both girls and boys worked throughout their childhoods, but boys were allowed more free time outside the home.[79] As a result, girls usually developed along a more linear path to adulthood, without a similar period of wilding.[80]

The rites and practices of boy culture varied over time and place. In the earlier parts of the century, and in rural regions, boys focused far more on outdoor pursuits. In cities, groups of boys were often larger and spent more time hanging around adult male hotspots like party headquarters or firehouses.[81] By the 1900s, as education expanded from a periodic distraction to a genuine school system, boy culture lost much of its independence.[82] But throughout the middle of the nineteenth century, American boys, in roiling cities and frontier villages, fixated on violence, fire, and crowds. Each allowed them to exorcise their wilder instincts, and each reappeared in political spectacles.

Nineteenth-century boys were killing machines. Squirrels, frogs, rabbits, quail, and deer died by the thousands, pursued by groups of boys roaming the countryside. Many rural diarists hunted every day, killing much more than they could eat. The introduction of repeating rifles made them even more bloodthirsty, as post–Civil War boys seemed to wield their Henry rifles and Spencer carbines with particular relish.[83] Urban boys satisfied their penchant for violence on each other. Will Howells explained that the real importance of the constant fights was not who won but the unspoken refusal to let adults resolve a conflict. The boy who called for his mother burst the bubble of their independence. When not fighting, boys were "always stoning something."[84] Unfortunately, such boys frequently harassed racial and ethnic minorities, targeting Irish Catholics in 1840s Philadelphia, African Americans during the New York draft riots, and Chinese immigrants in Gilded Age California.[85]

If petty violence was boys' daily bread, fires were longed-for treats. Anyone living in a nineteenth-century city, built of wood and packed with blistering stoves and belching furnaces, knew the chaos the fire bell signaled. But the alarm always seemed to draw more boys than firemen.[86] George Templeton Strong, remembered for his urbane diary of the Civil War, spent his boyhood chasing the blazes that threatened his lower Manhattan home, evaluating each "as he would a stage performance."[87] Children loved the hypnotic power of fire and often started blazes of their own. Future marshal of the Baltimore police force Jacob Frey recalled watching his buddies set fire to garbage in alleys and amuse themselves by hurling stones at the fire companies who arrived to extinguish their fun.[88]

Fires and violence offered fleeting entertainment, but crowds left long memories and introduced boys to public politics. As a "live boy in a live city," Jacob Frey "followed the crowd whenever there was any commotion." Years later he could still vividly recall the public hanging, cheered on by a massive crowd, that he happened upon at age nine. The sight of that dangling corpse taught him more than "my teachers in the public school could."[89] Benjamin Brown Foster, an otherwise conscientious boy in Maine, also seemed incapable of resisting the urge to join whatever throng he happened upon.[90] Such boys populate crowd scenes in every Victorian novel, present in Dickens's Britain but ubiquitous in younger, wilder America.

The rowdy boy culture fit perfectly into the age of popular politics. Partisan rallies offered the crowds, fires, and potential violence that thrilled boys. Girls, denied such excitement most of the time, also indulged in these spectacles with the sanction given to political events. Of course, children were drawn to any crowd, whether partisan rallies or public executions, and were hypnotized by both accidental trash fires and jollification bonfires. But public politics distinguished itself by begging young people to participate in a way that hangings and burning buildings never did. Campaigners wanted children's attention and calculated their events "to catch the eye of a boy of nine years of age."[91]

Children made up a large portion of the spectators at political events.

Adult onlookers encourage a parade by partisan, torch-wielding, uniformed children. Some child-sized uniforms are still in existence, preserved at the National Museum of American History in Washington, D.C. After a parade, children were likely to begin collecting scrap wood for mammoth election-night bonfires. ("A Phase of Campaign Enthusiasm," *Frank Leslie's Illustrated Newspaper*, November 13, 1880; courtesy Library of Congress)

They gamboled along with marchers, got lost in the throng, or shouted themselves hoarse perched on balconies and lampposts. Kids seemed to inhabit a parallel dimension at rallies, running among the adults but focused on their own little dramas. Will Howells spent "my whole youth" immersed in raucous political gatherings—first for the Whigs, then for Free Soilers after his father's bolt from the party—but mostly cared about the battles that broke out between rival groups of children.[92]

In the hours before a big rally, while adult campaigners amassed barrels of liquor and crates of torches, brigades of children went to work as well. The more industrious prepared "fire-balls." First they gathered spare rags and deployed their meager sewing skills to stitch them into cloth balls. Overnight, they soaked these balls in oil or turpentine. Come the parade the next evening, daring children would light these incendiaries and deftly hurl them out over the crowds to make a "splendid streaming blaze." Ideally, these fireballs burnt up before coming down on onlookers' hats.[93]

Many kids built Election Day bonfires, a tradition that lasted well into the twentieth century. In his autobiography, Adolph "Harpo" Marx gleefully looked back on his turn-of-the-century New York childhood, spent building giant bonfires from scavenged lumber "in the middle of the street and the cops wouldn't stop you."[94] Marx reminisced about watching an election night blaze with his grandpa as flames leaped almost as high as their tenement, shimmering in the windows across the street and turning the sky into a great red curtain. His grandfather, a German Jewish immigrant, puffed on a free Tammany cigar and sighed, "Ah, we are lucky to be in America. This is true Democracy!" Young Adolph nodded, though, like many bonfire-building children, "I had no idea what Grandpa was talking about."[95]

Children found public politics so thrilling that they even turned out for the opposing party's events. In gold rush San Francisco, Frank Leach and his young friends were "indifferent to the party with which they paraded so long as they secured a torch."[96] Another Californian claimed that "kids played no favorites" and could never ignore a procession. He added, however, that a boy caught marching with the wrong party risked a severe beating by his dad.[97]

Some kids were just mature enough to see that political fun had consequences. Bettie Ann Graham, a Virginian at boarding school in Philadelphia, realized this as the 1860 election unfolded. The fifteen-year-old was increasingly aware of a political distinction between her southern family and her Spruce Street schoolmates. The eye-catching Republican campaign of that year forced her to choose sides. Like Will Howells, she sided with family over friends, but it was no easy choice. One October night, companies of uniformed Wide Awake marchers streamed directly under her row-house window, accompanied by blaring brass bands and cheering children. Graham "would have enjoyed very much" the thrilling procession "had it not been in honor of Lincoln." She shut the windows and tried to ignore the torchlight dancing on her ceiling.[98]

Public political events were more than inadvertently popular with children; if anything, they seemed to be specifically designed for them. This sense appears again and again in diaries and memoirs from the era. Sally McCarty, the seven-year-old who would refuse to dance because Tyler vetoed the Bank Bill, felt that there never was a "device so impressive to a childish mind" as the rolling log cabins debuted by Whig campaigners in 1840.[99] Others agreed, exaggerating that rallies were aimed at "a child of five years old."[100] Howells claimed that the politics of his town were designed for "the diversion of the boys" and that, on election night, "it is best to be young."[101]

This juvenile audience helps explain some of the stranger devices campaigners employed. Parades featured a menagerie of creatures and symbols that have baffled historians ever since. Floats wheeled out caged (and very angry) raccoons, foxes, and bears, not to mention tethered gamecocks and occasionally eagles. They rolled giant leather balls from town to town and dragged fully rigged ships on wheels, emblazoned with names like *Constitution* or *Tariff*. By the 1860s and 1870s, marchers favored ornate military uniforms and armed themselves with a variety of torches, some of which shot flaming bursts of explosive lycopodium powder. Clubs brought brooms—to sweep away their rivals—or else labeled themselves "the chloroformers," to knock out the opposition.[102]

Each of these devices carried a symbolic meaning for audiences during the age of popular politics, and historians have mined them in their study of political culture. But campaigners unveiled all of these raccoons, leather balls, and pyrotechnics for an audience that was often strikingly young. Parties seemed to be contending for the attention of twelve-year-olds, and this might explain some of their goofier contrivances.

Boys and girls alike felt that rallies, barbecues, and even brawls were "as entirely for their entertainment as the circuses."[103] To be a child in nineteenth-century America entailed certain prerogatives; chief among them, ten-year-olds "had a right to throw fire-balls or roll tar-barrels" at political events.[104] At the same time, such activities reinforced the political education children received at home and school. Once again, the impassioned, competitive aspects of the democracy drowned out issues of governance or rational choice. But unlike the socialization parents passed down at home and teachers let slip in the classroom, rallies begged boys and girls to join in the fun. Campaign spectacle helped the wavering outline of a child's nature form into a personal, political identity.[105]

The Ward 8 Dynasty

Some older children graduated from spectators to organizers, working as errand boys for political machines. They carried messages, fetched pails of lager, and dragged tipsy voters to the polls. Boys usually considered these chores a privilege. In the words of George Washington Plunkitt, the bombastic Tammany Hall district boss who got his start at age twelve, "You can't begin too early in politics. . . . Show me a boy that hustles for the organization on Election Day, and I'll show you a comin' statesman."[106]

These "comin' statesmen" found work and identity on the lowest rungs of partisan organizations. James Michael Curley, an impoverished teen who eventually won nearly every office in Boston, chose politics "because industrial conditions were deplorable."[107] Working for the Democratic Party meant better pay, cleaner lungs, and more adult guidance than his previous job in a sweltering piano factory. As urban labor conditions deteriorated and the system of apprenticeship crumbled, boys with few connections could still find healthy employment and devoted mentors within party machines.

James Curley's introduction to Boston politics offers a perfect example of how children became political actors, passing along traditions from generation to generation. Nineteenth-century Boston's party headquarters, tucked away behind butcher shops and funeral homes, often hosted bosses at the tables and boys leaning against the walls. Those smoky back rooms launched a dynasty of plucky, striving young ward leaders. Each got his start around age twelve. But no one is born a boss, and their successive initiations tell a story of how elders finally explained the inner workings of politics to select children.

The shambling immigrant neighborhoods of Boston's West End, particularly the notorious Eighth Ward, cried out for better leadership during the Gilded Age. Open sewage canals marked the lines between neighborhoods. Some blocks were dense with brick buildings; others wound randomly, made up of oddly spaced wooden shacks. Dirt roads divided most, like arteries bleeding out into the marshy mud flats of the Charles River. The locals, a confused mix about one-third Irish, one-third Jewish, and less than a quarter "native American," felt ignored by the Brahmin elite and looked to the Democratic machinery for salvation.[108]

They settled, for a time, on an unlikely choice. Martin Lomasney got his start as an orphan bootblack, the child of Irish famine immigrants. Locals remembered the taciturn young Lomasney for his penetrating blue-gray stare and the way he used his silence to command a room. During the 1870s the youth ran a street gang. His hustling caught the eye of a Democratic boss who recruited him with odd jobs and extra cash. That boss found Lomasney easy city work as a lamplighter and helped him open a political club. As the boy matured into a boss, he coined the political dictum "Never write if you can speak; never speak if you can nod; never nod if you can wink." Lomasney even had a drink named for his precinct (the highest honor any Boston politician could hope for). The "Ward 8" was essentially a whiskey, made bloody with grenadine.[109]

The whole ward knew Lomasney as "the Mahatma," the very stereotype of a "jut-jawed, heavy-set political boss."[110] As he built his empire, won office, and survived an assassination attempt, taking a bullet in the leg, Lomasney began to recruit the next generation of young Democrats. One of his favorites was Nathan Sodekson, a fatherless Jewish immigrant.[111] Sodekson—a nervy ball of energy—lived in a tenement across the street from Martin Lomasney. He hung around Lomasney's headquarters until "the Mahatma" began assigning him chores in the club and errands around town. Lomasney eventually entrusted Sodekson with the party checklist on Election Day. Together they made a distinctive team: the hulking, mute Mahatma, wearing his trademark yellow straw hat, his moustache twitching, peering sternly out through gold-rimmed glasses, standing beside the skinny, restless twelve-year-old, monitoring the polls and dispatching runners to round up malingerers.[112]

Eventually Nate Sodekson moved on, unionizing Boston's newsboys, but he passed down "the Lomasney tricks" to another generation of aspiring wire-pullers before he went.[113] One of Sodekson's students, James Michael Curley, carried on the Mahatma's legacy. While Lomasney relied on his commanding personality and Sodekson used his deep knowledge of the local voters, young Curley traded on his ability to persuade. He hung around the ward's cheap groceries, buttonholing voters by the corned beef and the pickle barrels. He could switch into Gaelic if he wanted to endear himself to an old timer or say something "the natives" should not hear. From there, Curley put his education to good use through a term as Massachusetts's governor, two terms as a U.S. congressman, and four terms as Boston's mayor. Not to mention two stints in prison.[114]

Boston's Democratic machine recruited Lomasney, Sodekson, and Curley by using the same tactics as professional guilds and organized crime. Apprenticeships began sometime between the ages of twelve and fifteen and started with the "honor" of performing menial tasks. Each generation was expected, in time, to pass along its secrets to the next. And young partisans came to view their actions in much the same way as a master craftsman or a lifelong criminal. Theirs was a trade or task, usually free of moral or ideological considerations. Several generations found this the easiest way to bring in new blood.

The Eighth Ward crew all shared something else: each was fatherless. Lomasney had lost both parents as a boy, Sodekson's dad disappeared somewhere back in the old country, and Curley's father died trying to lift a heavy load of bricks at a Boston construction site. Of course, many millions of Americans never knew their fathers, but partisan mentors often played a paternal role, fitting neatly into the usual pattern of children's political socialization. Those without fathers to drag them to rallies or argue politics at the dinner table still found their way into the party and may have responded to the presence of caring role models, especially given so few other options.

My First Job

When Susan Bradford peered out of Pine Hill's dark windows at night, scanning the woods for abolitionist "devils," and when Dr. Bradford gathered local planters to scare each other with rumors of Republican infiltrators, they were worried about young men like George Washington Albright. Though he was the same age as Susan Bradford, Albright stepped further out of childhood as he crept from plantation to plantation, spreading political news as slavery crumbed in Civil War–torn Mississippi.[115]

George Washington Albright was always feisty, combative, and funny; years later he would brag that the Ku Klux Klan had labeled him "a dangerous nigger."[116] He grew up enslaved on a northern Mississippi plantation, raised by his mother after his father was sold away. Though teaching a slave to read was forbidden, his mother picked up bits of the white children's lessons as she cooked for them and taught George what she could each night. Piece by piece George slowly learned about the growing struggle against slavery. While news of John Brown's raid shook Susan Bradford's thirteen-year-old world, George Washington Albright quietly delighted at how it "threw a scare into the slave owners."[117]

Albright stepped beyond simply receiving adult rumors as the Civil War enveloped the hilly counties of northern Mississippi. He learned, through the "grapevine telegraph," of the Emancipation Proclamation. George, his mother, and most of the slaves in the Confederacy were free, as far as the Lincoln administration was concerned, but local slave owners worked to suppress the news. So at fifteen George joined the "4Ls"—Lincolns' Legal Loyal League—a secret political organization designed to spread the news of freedom.[118]

Late at night Albright would sneak away from his cabin, ducking through tangles of scuppernong vines, padding up and down the red clay hills and hollows on his way to other plantations. The sleepy lanes were perilous—every time he turned the corner on some dark path he might happen upon Confederate raiders, vicious slave patrollers, or unpredictable Union troops. But Albright grew up with a slave's version of boy culture, in which young men frequently snuck out at night to play in the woods. Like the runners who pounded the pavements of Boston's Eighth Ward, a crafty young person could often achieve what a full-grown man could not. So he made his quiet way to the waiting cabins, knocked four times, and was welcomed quietly inside.[119]

The 4Ls used passwords, hand signals, and secret grips throughout the

South. We do not know which signal Albright preferred, but other Mississippi runners would hold their left hand to make an L, with their fingers vertical and their thumb perpendicular. Then they tapped each finger to their thumb, symbolizing the four Ls of Lincoln's Legal Loyal League.[120]

After the formalities, Albright told small gatherings the joyous news. In dim cabins the men and women must have struggled to quietly digest the revelation: they were free. Runners had to keep moving, though; Albright would return to his plantation while youths headed out to spread the news to other hushed assemblies.

Even when Albright was safely back at his slumbering plantation, there was more to do. Lighting a makeshift candle—usually just a cup of meat drippings with a wad of cotton as the wick—he would produce another thrilling secret: a copy of *Uncle Tom's Cabin*. Under the guttering flame, Albright would settle down on his cornhusk cot and pour himself into Stowe's novel. The world she described ten years before was crumbling, thanks in part to his young efforts. While Susan Bradford longed to read that "bad book" and Dr. Bradford considered his roaring hearth "the best place for it," George Washington Albright devoured it in the flickering glow of his rough cabin.[121]

At fifteen, Albright was no longer a child piecing together bits of overheard gossip. The young man, a future Mississippi state senator, threw himself into "my first job in the fight for the rights of my people."[122] Albright's efforts were unique, but by their midteens most Americans took a more active, personal interest in politics. While adults sometimes scoffed that children's participation was "little more than a game"—entertaining and external but not linked to their interior selves—partisanship took on a new meaning between fifteen and twenty-one.[123] Though their elders had indelibly shaped their politics, as they aged youths stopped simply following adults' leads. They made the democratic system their own, important in their lives as well as to the nation. When George Washington Albright dozed off reading *Uncle Tom's Cabin*, in his own cabin, he fit the national political conflict into his young life.

From Florida belles to Boston thugs to Mississippi slaves, young Americans saw that politics required personal assertions, and offered individual rewards, by the time they reached fifteen or so. The further they stepped into political life, the more mature they felt. At the same time, the rising crises of youth buffeted many with waves of social, economic, and romantic uncertainty. Young Americans saw politics as a life raft.

2 » The Generous Ambitions of Youth

Though he was four years, two months, and twelve days too young to vote, Ben was up early on Election Day, 1848. He looked unkempt, even for a sixteen-year-old boy on a foggy Maine morning. Ben was short and solid, with a serious brow and a heavy jaw fringed with hopeful muttonchops. He donned a tattered black coat, torn at both elbows, and strode intently toward Orono, Maine's waking polling place. He could not yet vote, but he hoped he might "advance a boy's opinion" with those who could.[1]

Why should Ben care about this election? How, he asked his candid and neurotic diary, had he become so caught up with a subject "not intimately concerning myself"?[2] What Ben did not realize was that, like many nineteenth-century youths, he dove into politics precisely because it did not intimately concern him. As Ben struggled in his economic, romantic, and social life, he sought out politics as a source of external identity and achievement. Like millions of Americans his age, Ben saw democracy as a tool to cope with the looming uncertainties of adolescence in an adolescent nation.

Beyond politics, Ben was constantly frustrated by those pursuits that did intimately concern him. A sneaky employer cheated him out of his pay, apprenticeship after apprenticeship fell through, and he jealously tracked the lives of wealthy young people in his town.[3] He felt teased by his desire for progress, a "shuddering discontent that crawls over me."[4] The sixteen-year-old berated himself, on his birthday, for being "ignorant, poor, fickle, wavering, without brilliancy, talents, wealth or influential friends." Ben's anxiety—"my eternal pest"—haunted his romantic life as well. He consistently failed to impress local girls. One popular young woman mocked him as "the dirtiest looking object she ever saw." Another girl seemed interested, but on a romantic sleigh ride together Ben lost his nerve and they "indulged no indecent familiarities."[5]

Frustrated in work and love, Ben first turned to self-improvement, putting his faith in the pseudoscience of phrenology. Based on a reading of the shape of his skull, he swore off butter and fatty meats. He slept with the windows open, in Maine, in winter. He suppressed his natural goofiness in a bid to seem sober and serious. None of this helped him find a job or a wife.[6]

Phrenology could not sate Ben's stifled ambitions, but politics could. Inspired by a dinner with fugitive slave lecturer Thomas James and provoked by partisan newspapers, Ben threw himself into antislavery activism. He read constantly, devouring not only Poe, Dickens, and the Brontës but also the *New York Tribune*, the *Liberator*, and the *National Era*. He shared those publications' hatred for slavery but chafed against their frustrating faith in moral persuasion alone. He believed that political parties were "America's salvation . . . the cement of the Union" and, at fifteen, penned an article calling for an antislavery political party.[7] When the *Bangor Gazette* published his anonymous battle cry, Ben felt a first blush of success in his otherwise stifled life.

So on the state election day in September 1848, he woke early, washed his neck, pulled on his muddy brown boots and his torn black coat, and headed out to the polls. There he watched as Orono slowly awoke. Dazed and sleepy voters, many of them caked with sawdust from the lumber town's humming mills, began to cast ballots. Some voted with deep "regard for principle," while others seemed "reckless, careless." Poll hustlers would catch men "by the buttons and drag them as the spider doth a fly" to vote Whig, Democrat, or—as Ben hoped—Free Soil.[8]

Ben went to work too, not pressing ballots on the undecided but simply talking to whoever would listen. He indulged his irrepressible "love of talking," his massive head bobbing in animated discussion with those who shared his distaste for the "Slave Power." Others "coolly reminded me that I was a boy." At the end of the day, Ben walked home through the dimming autumn light, sure that he had convinced some men to change their votes. Back at his parents' house, Ben recounted the thrilling election in his diary. He had never "felt so much interest and excitement."[9]

This politicking would not satisfy "the wealth-phantom," teach him how to flirt, or reshape his skull for better phrenological results. It did not directly solve any of the sweaty anxieties Ben poured into his journal. It did, however, offer the self-critical sixteen-year-old a hint of adulthood and influence. The election showed Ben a clearer path to manhood than he had seen before. Usually, he fretted about turning twenty-one, when he

A young African American orator takes part in the "speech-making mania" popular among freed slaves in the years after the Civil War. In this scene, the youthful speaker engages a mixed-age, mixed-gender crowd in Virginia, including the young boy in the back balancing a bucket on his head. Youths like the speaker often worked to win the attention of adults, part of an effort to affirm their adulthood during an uncertain phase of life. ("Electioneering at the South," *Harper's Weekly*, July 25, 1868; courtesy UNC-Chapel Hill Libraries)

would have "no home to fall back upon." But at the polling place, Benjamin Brown Foster felt just the opposite, wishing "that I was for one year, and on this one topic, a man, a voter."[10]

From Basements to Steeples

When Benjamin Brown Foster sighed, "My life is already probably a quarter or a fifth gone and with what result?," he joined countless worried youths.[11] From the Pennsylvanian who fretted that his big plans would probably "vanish for the lack of money," to the Tennessean who felt that she did "nothing but eat and wear and be in the way," a diverse swath of young Americans expressed the same mixture of self-improving ambition and self-pitying pessimism. Most believed that they alone were failing to progress toward adulthood.[12]

These worries were not limited to young Americans of a particularly morose type. Confident, arrogant, even smug youths expressed the same sense of obstructed progress. A Great Plains buffalo hunter who survived a stabbing at Deadwood, boxed for Calamity Jane's amusement, and kept track in his diary of all the animals he had shot frequently groaned about his future.[13] An evangelical street preacher who could work massive Philadelphia crowds into frothing anti-Catholic agitation filled his diary with lamentations that he was "qualified for nothing" and found it "humiliating indeed" that he still lived with his parents at age nineteen.[14] Something ineffable held back even the most self-assured youths.

What seemed like the individual failures of millions of youths was, in reality, the result of massive structural changes unleashed in the nineteenth century. American life transformed more radically during the nineteenth century than it ever had before. Between the 1830s and 1900, America's population quintupled, splitting cities' seams and peopling the vast frontier. At least 18 million immigrants arrived from Europe, more people than had lived in all of America in 1840. And the economy exploded, creating an industrial juggernaut that surpassed all other nations.[15]

These unprecedented changes filled the lives of fifteen- or twenty-year-olds with gnawing uncertainty. Many struggled to discern where "childhood ends and youth begins and where youth ends and manhood begins."[16] Pushed by a faith in progress and pulled by the disorderly modern world, young men and women hoped for success but saw no clear way forward.

Such upheavals disturbed the usual order of life. Before these revolutions, most youths simply hoped to replicate their parents' livelihood.[17] But beginning in the early decades of the nineteenth century, a growing market economy and desire for progress eclipsed that hope. By the Jacksonian era, few could plan to live as their ancestors had.[18] Slowly, over the rest of the century, moral reformers, social activists, and industrial capitalists built up a new structure, so that by around 1900 large institutions managed young people's education, employment, and entertainment. But for six decades in between, "every aspect of American life witnessed a desire to throw off precedent."[19] This unruly society shook the way young people lived, loved, worked, and voted.

Massive social change altered young Americans' most intimate experiences. Romantic relationships grew more complex as highly mobile men and women bounced around new cities and territories. Americans courted more partners and married years later than their ancestors.[20] Finding work became newly complicated; few young people had ever needed a job outside of their families' domestic economy and social network. As America refocused on unskilled industry, the tradition of apprenticeship that introduced so many young men to the middling classes crumbled. The market added formerly unimagined jobs, but most options were unstable and short-lived. Work that had once been collective, like farming, was replaced by individual labor in factories or warehouses.[21] The old institutions of a settled, rural economy fell apart, but the structures that shaped life after 1900, like schools, corporations, and unions, could not yet help most young Americans mature.

Just as their futures grew hazy, young people faced increasing social pressure to achieve. Each generation seemed more self-improving than the last, driven by a striving ambition that Americans often called the "go-ahead principle."[22] Though committed to the idea of progress and individual achievement, most young people experienced a phase of "semidependence" in their late teens. Many left home for six months of school or two years of work but returned to rely on their family while planning their next move.[23] Though the nineteenth century is often remembered as a time of decisive journeys—from farm to city, from agriculture to industry, from Europe to America—many experienced it as an era of false starts, finding themselves on a wagon returning to the family farm or on a steamer pointing back toward Europe. One young man in Ohio considered his teen years an alternating series of "baffling discouragements and buoyant hopes."[24]

Few nineteenth-century Americans called these young people "adolescents." That word's frequent use began around 1900, by psychologists describing a phase in which young people were particularly vulnerable, in need of protection while they matured. Between the 1840s and 1890s, men and women in this age range were called "youths," and they were treated far less gently, occupying, most believed, a transitional phase on the spectrum between children and adults. Their next step into maturity was not granted by age alone; they had to earn it. For men this meant achieving economic success or physical strength or manly virtues; for women it could mean marriage, motherhood, or the competent management of a household.[25] The wrong course, taken at this crucial turning point, could lead a youth toward a life of crime, violence, alcoholism, prostitution, or a host of other sins.[26] While the later idea of adolescence offered a temporary reprieve to grow, nineteenth-century "youth" demanded action.

Politics promised that feeling of progress. By joining parties, reading newspapers, attending rallies, speaking at debates, marching in processions, handing out ballots, or simply hurling bricks at the opposition, frustrated youths achieved a reliable sense of direction in life.

In an otherwise shaken society, popular democracy's regularity was one of its great appeals. Presidential campaigns could be counted upon every four years, congressional votes every two, and local battles raged year-round.[27] When all else seemed stalled, uncertain young men and women could jump upon this campaign merry-go-round, finding a sense of progress even if social forces blocked their path to adulthood.

Campaigners were happy to welcome unpaid young promoters. Though career ambitions might be thwarted and romantic crushes unrequited, parties always needed more boots on the cobblestones. Many politicians saw themselves as providing a service to uncertain teens. George Washington Plunkitt, who got his start at twelve, boasted that Tammany Hall assisted struggling young people who were "longin' to make names and fortunes for themselves at the same game."[28]

Walt Whitman, the "poet of democracy," understood how youths could use politics in their most intimate struggles. When a British traveler complained that young Americans were unruly, Whitman responded, "We are laying here in America the basements and foundation rooms of a new era. And we are doing it, on the whole, pretty well and substantially. By-and-by, when that job is through, *we will look after the steeples and pinnacles*."[29] As American society constructed a revolutionary new edifice, its young people puzzled over how to climb toward those promised but illusory steeples. Some of their most important ambitions—finding a spouse, a home, work, and an adult identity—proved particularly shaky. Millions used politics as a scaffolding to reach these goals. Walt Whitman, who began his writing career as a nasty partisan journalist, certainly did.[30]

Quite the Thing Here for Ladies to Do

Anna Ridgely hated politics. The eighteen-year-old Presbyterian was so devout that she refused to dance or play billiards, and she resented the drunken shouts, interminable oompah music, and celebratory cannon fire that drowned out her humble prayer meetings.[31] But the Springfield, Illinois, native changed her mind during the 1860 presidential campaign. The fact that her father played cards with Abraham Lincoln had some influence, but mostly she was interested in the young men who populated those profane processions.

When Anna began to "go with gentlemen," her admirers invited her to exciting campaign demonstrations. Some escorted her to rallies for Democratic leader Stephen A. Douglas, while others talked her into attending massive celebrations of Lincoln's nomination. Anna came from a line of staunch Democrats, and her parents warily eyed her Republican suitors. In spite of her former distaste for the wicked world of politics, she embraced the overheated campaign, sinking into what another midwestern girl her age described as "a solid mass of people, blowing every manner and kind of horns and whistles, ringing bells, beating pans and doing every thing to make a loud noise."[32] Temporarily intoxicated, with either the cheering crowds or her suitors' attentions, Anna exclaimed "Hurrah for Lincoln!" in her diary.[33]

Romantic entanglements could drag even the most apolitical young men and women into politics. At a time when Americans dramatically shifted their expectations for marriage, courtship elicited restless uncertainties. As the concept of romantic love prospered, Victorian mores tightened, and the number of potential partners skyrocketed, nervous teens sought an external tool in their awkward search for a mate.[34] Millions, like Anna Ridgely, stumbled into politics.

Large political gatherings offered a perfect venue for meeting the opposite sex. Youths saw these events as a democratically sanctioned excuse for public flirtation, and adults often smiled on the "young couples making love" at party picnics ("making love" had a vaguer romantic meaning than it does today).[35] Some young women used their courtships to express otherwise suppressed beliefs. The result was a messy jumble of national campaigns and personal romances.

The great shake-ups of the nineteenth century made courtship difficult for most young Americans. Single men and women increasingly lived in different places. Chasing booming industries, young men congregated in cities, the frontier, and bachelor communities like mining towns, lumber camps, railroad crews, and ocean-going vessels.[36] Nevada, California, Oregon, and Texas had far more young men than women. Women predominated in older communities along the East Coast and the Gulf, particularly in states like Maryland, Connecticut, and Louisiana.[37] Anna Ridgely, visiting her elderly aunt in a sleepy rural section of Missouri, missed the crowds of young gentlemen she had grown used to in booming Springfield.[38] Immigration furthered this mismatch. The majority of migrants pouring into the country were male, so that men outnumbered women in America by several million.[39]

This increased mobility inadvertently brought about a more restrained style of courting. Unwed pregnancy was common in the eighteenth century, but usually with the assumption that the expectant couple would marry. As the social unravelings of the nineteenth century made flight an easy option for young men, Victorians constructed a more restrained romantic culture.[40] Women were urged to act with modesty, lest they find themselves pregnant with the father disappearing along some turnpike or rail line. Meanwhile, male sexuality was denounced as predatory and in need of constant suppression.[41] All of this pushed the average marriage age well into the twenties, reaching an unprecedented peak by 1890 (in the twentieth century that average age fell dramatically, not to return to nineteenth-century levels until the 1980s and 1990s).[42]

While courting was complicated for young men emerging from their all-male boy culture, it had a far weightier impact on women. In addition to the threat of pregnancy, young women made their reputations through their courtships. Anna Ridgely worried about her active social life, reminding herself that spending too much time with gentlemen was "not profitable," for it made her seem scandalously available.[43] On the other hand, young women had to be active and assertive, devoting their energies to courting many different young men in their hunt for a lifelong partner. Women's reliance on their future husbands also meant that finding a spouse was likely to be the biggest choice they ever made, even as it was increasingly unclear how they should go about it. Though the older culture of picking a partner from a limited village selection had deteriorated, the structured world of "dating" had yet to emerge.[44] With high mobility and an inchoate system for meeting partners, young people floundered.[45]

In a dispersed and shaken society, public political events offered a much-needed solution. A big October rally—usually the largest gathering in most communities—could introduce couples that would otherwise not have met. Crafty campaigners manipulated these democratic flirtations, promising "wife-less young voters" that "all the handsome and intelligent young ladies" supported their party.[46] Young Americans openly acknowledged their use of public events for private liaisons. Charlotte Conant, a wealthy young Republican in Massachusetts, attended a Democratic rally, not because she supported that party but because two suitors had invited her and "it is quite the thing here for ladies to do."[47]

Nineteen-year-old Lester Ward certainly made good use of public events during the same 1860 campaign that won over Anna Ridgely. In his diary, the young Pennsylvanian wrote excitedly about courting "the girl" (diarists often avoided mentioning their romantic interests by name, to protect their privacy). Lester and "the girl" flirted in church and in letters, and when he happened upon her in town she seemed excited to see him "and spoke very fast." They even snuck off for late-night trysts, which "aroused my affection to a high degree," until her father would chase him off around 4:30 A.M. But Ward hoped to see more of her. So when he learned of a Republican rally that "everyone is planning to go to," he saw it as a good opportunity to rendezvous with "the girl" again.[48] Lester was lukewarm on politics but serious about his courtships.

Some young women used romance to express their political views. Denied more direct routes to activism, many relied upon flirtation as a source of influence. Newspapers joked that candidates with charming young daughters always seemed to win a large following among virgin voters.[49] Black women reportedly scorned men who cast their first vote for the hated Democrats during Reconstruction.[50] Occasionally, women turned down marriage proposals specifically because of a young man's political affiliations.[51] In the words of a twenty-year-old Indiana abolitionist, complaining about the poor prospects in her town during the Civil War, "there is no young men here except Copperheads and they are beneath our notice."[52]

Many young people bluntly admitted that they used popular politics to woo the opposite sex. The diary of Annie Youmans—full of charming exclamations like "ahem!" and "umph!"—shows how an assertive young woman employed political flirtation to reach out to romantic prospects. The twenty-year-old Republican learned to debate politics with young men, particularly those she found attractive. In September 1868 she had an animated, flirtatious debate with a suitor who argued that Horatio Seymour, the Democratic candidate, would win the coming presidential election. Annie teased that she hoped he enjoyed his delusions. In one entry she noted, "By the by this young man is very handsome." That same campaign, Annie placed a bet on Ulysses S. Grant's victory—for a pair of fine leather gloves—with a more serious suitor, who she described as having "splendad dark eyes." Though she certainly cared about politics, Annie admitted that her political bet with this dark-eyed suitor was a "pretense."[53]

Annie was outdone by Clay Anderson, a nineteen-year-old bank teller in Ohio. In the mid-1850s, Anderson penned letters to a friend bragging about meeting "fair and fascinating" ladies at Know Nothing rallies. At one event, attended by over five hundred "young folks," Anderson rode his mustang past a pretty young woman, also on horseback, who requested that he escort her along the parade route. Anderson gallantly, eagerly, agreed. That charming Miss Sarah Darlington ("a darling as well as a Darlington") shared Anderson's attraction, but she lived seventy-five miles away; they probably would not have met if not drawn together by politics. Anderson confidently concluded his letter, "I will have more to say of this young lady in my next." Unfortunately for the couple, he died of typhoid soon after the rally.[54]

Such courting did not make youths' focus on politics any less sincere. Instead, the political flirtations of Americans like Clay and Annie nurtured the idea that politics could be a gendered exchange. Young men used popular politics to perform their masculinity, waving torches, hollering slogans, and strutting ostentatiously. Women like Annie Youmans brought up campaigns, often in flirtatious mock debates, to engage men they found interesting. Where else but at a public political rally could a young woman seek out a male stranger in such a forward manner?[55] Again and again, young women's letters show their habit of talking politics when writing to men even as they neglected the subject in their communications with other women.[56] Party politics served as an ideal pastime, a popular event, and an external identity for youths to exchange in their clumsy flirtations.

Even so, politics and romance were not inherently connected. Most young people never linked these pursuits. Youths also flirted at spelling bees and camp revivals. Partisan campaigns simply made it easier for uncertain youths to announce something about themselves, so necessary in the confused romantic world of nineteenth-century America. Young Americans, struggling to find a spouse in the face of titanic demographic upheavals and moral reforms, used partisanship as a tool for courtship, bringing public politics to the aid of personal romance.

Off on a Wander Year

The uncertainties of nineteenth-century life often began with a young person's first steps away from home. Millions of Americans—most of them men—relocated in their late teens, lighting out for the territories, the city, or simply the next state over.[57] The mature self-assertion that came with leaving one's parents' house, the fleeting life of tramping across the country and living on farmers' charity—in the form of bread, milk, and prayer—and the socialization in boardinghouses and work camps all seemed to guide young travelers to party politics.

Such sojourns became a rite of passage. In 1850, William Alcott observed, "It is as rare now, to find a young man of thirty, who has not been beyond the limits of his native state, as it was thirty years ago, when I began to be a traveler, to find one who *had* been."[58] In one Wisconsin county, 89 percent of teenage males present in 1860 had left by 1870, and 90 percent of those present in 1870 were gone by 1880.[59] Travelers often set out with only the vaguest goals: a relative in a distant region, or a plan to rely on the religious good faith of fellow Methodists or Baptists along the way.[60] Impoverished young men were most likely to wander—heading out on what freed slaves called "frolics"—but students from Yale and the University of Virginia also set out for a spell after school.[61] Packing a carpetbag and hitting the road served as the capstone adventure for thrill-seeking graduates of nineteenth-century American boy culture.

In a fractured nation, the major political parties provided a national network for migrants to latch on to. Religious groups, youth associations, and entertainments varied greatly across the diverse country, but the parties offered a familiar presence from Connecticut to Louisiana to Oregon. A young wanderer could plug into this network in a new locale, finding instant allies and an active social life. When Oscar Lawrence Jackson—"the boy orator"—arrived in a strange corner of Ohio after wandering west from Pennsylvania, he hoped that his Republican speechifying would win him "introduction to the leading men . . . which is a great advantage to a stranger."[62]

Party hacks eagerly manipulated this unmoored population. Campaigners introduced one of the sleaziest tactics of the age of popular politics, a practice known as "colonizing," in which a group of partisans temporarily settled in a ward's cheap boardinghouses and voted to sway an election. "Young men out of employment" became the most likely colonizers, enticed with the promise of free lodgings and six drinks a day.[63] In Massachusetts's mill towns in the 1850s, ascendant Republicans worried that Democrats might manipulate the "very large number of young unmarried voters" to "carry any Ward they may choose."[64] Here, social uncertainty had concrete partisan implications.

The very act of leaving home, and the diverse characters met along the road, helped politicize young wanderers. Many experienced a powerful ideological emancipation upon moving away from their parents. Some found proof of their elders' wisdom, while others began to rethink the partisan education they had received as children. Bumming around

America by foot, hoof, and rail also introduced young men to adults who talked politics incessantly and to ideas and injustices that captured their imaginations.[65]

James Witham was one of the many young men who wandered away from home and into politics. Witham's early years in post–Civil War Ohio were marked by his family's poverty and his own irrepressible contrarianism. As he later described it, young Witham could never back down from an argument and went out of his way to be "the very worst boy in school." Pressed by the same species of nineteenth-century angst that worried Benjamin Brown Foster, James Witham struggled through a difficult youth. Often, when sent into the snowy woods to chop cordwood to support his family, James sat on a log and wept instead. Finally, in 1872, the sixteen-year-old left the Withams' ramshackle cabin and headed west.[66]

His political life began on a hot August day, crammed inside the caboose of a freight train with a few other passengers. As the train chugged out of Ohio, an obnoxious traveling salesman began to loudly mock the farmers' shacks dotting the countryside. Drawing from his intense reading of the progressive *New York Tribune* and unable to ever turn down a promising argument, Witham launched into a spirited debate. The ensuing quarrel— refereed by the train's crew—"commenced my defense of the men who toil on the farms." From this train ride, James Witham set out on a half-century crusade advocating farmers' rights and promoting radical midwestern politicians like William Jennings Bryan in newspapers and lectures.[67]

Though his memoir attacks the salesman as one of many silver-tongued hucksters who preyed on struggling farmers, the older man did James Witham a favor. The salesman's willingness to argue politics with an earnest young man offered Witham a sense of authority he had never before felt. The middle-aged traveler and the agitated sixteen-year-old shared a political culture, and though neither gave an inch on ideology, the debate left a lifelong mark on the youth.

The bustling world of nineteenth-century travel, of crowded passenger trains, bumpy stagecoaches, and interminable canal-boat voyages, helped politicize young Americans. Adults often proved willing to talk politics with young strangers in such environments. It became a trope in memoirs from the era: the intense political conversation between a prominent politician and a young man stuck together on a ship or train. Various writers proudly recalled their talks with Abraham Lincoln, Stephen Douglas, Daniel Webster, Sam Houston, Ben Wade, or James Weaver.[68]

"Wander years" could also bring regional conflicts into stark relief. In the antebellum era, a young northerner's voyage through the South, or vice versa, often posed crucial questions about slavery, race, and union, while cross-country trips during the Gilded Age often introduced eastern merchants and western farmers.[69] Even when wanderers arrived at a destination—particularly temporary camps focused on manual labor and populated with diverse itinerants—politics was always a frequent topic of conversation.[70]

Just as in the patchwork school system, age diversity and unabashed partisanship turned public spaces into political seminars. Adults did not shy away from debating with sixteen-year-olds; many felt a sympathetic desire to help young people learn to talk politics. A respectful debate with "a well-read man of some forty years" seemed to tickle the vanity of young travelers.[71] Coaxed along by the motley public world, the comfort with open political disagreement, and the intimacy found in shared travel, boardinghouses, and nights spent lodging with strangers, uncertain journeys began partisan careers.

The Poor Boy

Where to live and whom to marry had tangible answers, but the bulk of young Americans' concerns were not so concrete. Instead, many lumped together broad concerns about financial success, proving their maturity, and asserting their masculinity or femininity. This cluster of anxieties especially bedeviled eighteen- to twenty-one-year-olds trapped in the limbo of semidependence. It is no coincidence that this hazy phase separating youth and adulthood—considered "the most interesting and important, yet dangerous period of human existence" by preachers, educators, and parents—was also the moment when most Americans formed their own political identities.[72]

Young peoples' concerns about wealth, maturity, and gender played on each other. Adulthood and masculinity, for instance, were mutually reinforcing for young men. Americans considered manhood "a matter of age *and* gender" and used "manly" to distinguish men from boys as often as they used the term to separate the sexes.[73] At the same time, a culture of self-made capitalism increasingly dominated American aspirations, leading many to see financial success as proof of adulthood and masculinity. For young ladies, usually cut off from capitalist strivings, a feeling of uselessness undermined their sense of womanhood. Women frequently criticized themselves as foolish, frivolous, wasteful, and childish.[74] For young men and women, a victory in the realm of wealth, maturity, or gender strength-ened all-around self-image, but a setback increased their uncertainties across the board.

Politics appealed to many young Americans because their anxieties were so interwoven. This explains Benjamin Brown Foster's wonder at his zeal for a topic "not intimately concerning myself." Without earning a dol-lar, young political activists could win the regard of adults, making them feel mature and important. Without changing physically, campaign club members could achieve a sense of fraternity, strengthening their faith in their masculinity. Because their goals were so broad, external politics could often stand in for more personal achievements.

Michael Campbell knew these uncertainties more immediately than James Witham, Anna Ridgely, or even Benjamin Brown Foster. During the 1880 election, this immigrant factory worker learned how quickly demo-cratic activism could ease concerns about money, maturity, and mascu-linity. Popular politics helped Campbell, formerly "one of the poorest of street urchins" in New Haven, on his journey from factory packinghouse through Gilded Age boxing gymnasium and into the inner sanctum of one of the most powerful politicians in his state.[75]

Michael's parents had brought him to New Haven from Ireland as a tod-dler. His mother bore eight children, starting at age sixteen and ending at thirty-six, when Michael's father died of tuberculosis. As a young boy, Mi-chael ran wild in the alleys behind New Haven's bustling industrial water-front, but he went to work at age eleven.[76] In his late teens he lived with his family, worked in a packinghouse, and kept a poignant diary overflowing with personal frustration. In this dreamy, self-pitying chronicle, Michael sometimes referred to himself simply as "the poor boy."[77]

Some of that self-pity was warranted. The disadvantaged youth strug-gled during the "Long Depression" of the 1870s, marked by sixty-five continuous months of economic contraction, the longest in U.S. history.[78] Michael felt this worldwide downturn as a series of personal rejections. His application to apprentice in the wood pattern trade was denied. His boss at the factory shook his head to repeated requests for a raise. Michael tried night school, studying everything from bookkeeping to "scientifics" to child rearing, but could not raise the money for more courses. In one of his darker lamentations, he described his life as "strife day after day for it is a hard task for an Irishman without capital."[79]

His financial worries jelled with concerns about manhood. Michael Campbell was physically slight—5'7" and just 118 pounds—and kept obsessive track of his height and weight in his diary.[80] In an era increasingly captivated with muscular masculinity (when presidential campaigners bragged about the thickness of their candidate's neck), Michael fretted that he was "not a man in looks."[81] At work, he enviously watched his brawnier coworkers and complained in his diary that he was "laughed at by the stronger and better off."[82] The fact that young workers were often paid based on whether they were "big enough," rather than "old enough," meant that Michael's size had real monetary consequences.[83] In his late teens and early twenties, Michael Campbell's anxieties about his physical strength, his authority, and his job prospects mingled together. He comes across as one very insecure young man.

Perhaps the most striking thing about uncertain youths like Michael Campbell, or Benjamin Brown Foster or Oscar Lawrence Jackson, was just how ambitious they were. Most spitefully denounced "loafers" and launched multiple campaigns to better themselves. One of Michael Campbell's projects focused on gaining strength. At nineteen he began running in New Haven's parks; he joined a gymnasium soon after. Weight lifting was still considered new and eccentric in 1879, and Michael noted that his friends laughed at his "gymnastics." But he continued, exercising after his shift at the factory. Soon he started to practice fisticuffs, learning the art of bare-knuckle boxing in his search for size, strength, and, ultimately, authority.[84]

Michael's boxing was like Benjamin Brown Foster's phrenology. It gave him a temporary identity, but no one else really benefited from it. Political activism, on the other hand, aided Michael while making him useful to adults he wished to impress.

Less confrontational pastimes first pointed Michael Campbell toward politics. He joined the Young Men's Christian Doctrine and Library Association, an organization designed to reach out to young Catholics. This society helped introduce him to associational life, reminded him of his Irish roots, and drew attention to the reemerging conflicts over Catholicism in American politics in the 1870s. It is not surprising that a religious institution helped politicize Michael; no other sector of society focused more effort on recruiting young people. The roots of a distinctive "youth culture" emerged in Sunday schools and camp revivals before they appeared anywhere else. Though more important to evangelical Protestants, urban Catholics like Michael benefited from the same basic model. Such associations empowered young people as orators and organizers, playing an unmistakable role in preparing youths for politics.[85]

Zealous reading of cheap, sarcastic, combative newspapers introduced most young people to politics. The radical *New York Tribune* seems to have had the greatest influence, but thousands of other papers, including many that young people printed themselves, played a role in politicizing young Americans. (Charles G. Leland, *Pipps among the Wide Awakes* [New York: Wevill and Chapin, 1860]; from the Collections of the Division of Political History, National Museum of American History, Smithsonian Institution, Washington, D.C.)

He also became an avid reader. His older brother James, who took on a paternal role when their father succumbed to consumption, passed him Democratic newspapers. Michael made it his goal (writing in the third person) to "study and read all he can." He stocked the Christian Doctrine and Library Association's reading room with piles of party newspapers. In doing so, Michael Campbell joined practically every other politically active young person in the nation. Independent reading of the partisan press almost always heralded an interest in politics. Most young Americans even followed a similar pattern in their reading. Nationally prominent, ideologically aggressive papers like the *New York Tribune* or *New York Herald* framed partisan battles; the lurid, violent, immensely popular *National Police Gazette* heightened emotions; and the local press personalized national issues.[86]

This combination of reading and religion played a key role in Michael Campbell's political initiation. As he linked the shrill, entertaining partisan press with the camaraderie offered by membership in religious associations, he began to see politics as the antidote to his social worries—perhaps one even more rewarding than nights spent at the gymnasium.

Sixteen-year-old Michael observed the 1876 presidential campaign as an amused spectator. He attended flag raisings but, like a child, viewed such events as something external and distant. By the 1880 campaign, however, Michael Campbell needed politics. In the intervening four years he had faced rejection after rejection, attended his father's funeral, worried about

his masculinity, won friends in semipartisan clubs, and read up on the political battles of the day. By the time James Garfield's Republicans faced
off against Winfield Scott Hancock's Democrats, the "poor boy" Michael
Campbell was ready to take a side.

He became, predictably, a Democrat. He was an urban, laboring Catholic—a natural Jacksonian—and his Uncle Pat already worked in the New
Haven Democratic machinery. Michael made some halfhearted efforts to
explain his support for the party. Mostly, he harped on the Republicans'
defense of Chinese immigration.[87] Though there were, according to the
1880 census, fewer than two hundred Chinese people in all of Connecticut
and Michael Campbell was himself an immigrant, the anti-Chinese propaganda spoke to him most strongly. Driven into politics by economic uncertainties, many young Americans saw immigrants as rivals for entry-level
jobs and also complained that adult migrants could vote while native-born
youths had to wait.[88] Nativist mutterings run as a leitmotif through many
young Americans' writings during the age of popular politics, even, apparently, for the Irish-born Michael Campbell.[89] But, really, he had picked
his party based on family connections years before making these claims.

Michael bounded into party politics as the 1880 campaign took off.
After attending a Democratic rally and evidently liking what they saw,
Michael and his brother eagerly enlisted in the James E. English Phalanx,
a local political club named for Connecticut's wealthy former governor.
The night after they joined, the Campbell brothers stepped out in their
first procession, parading through the heart of "one the largest crowds
I've ever witnessed."[90] This immediate transition from onlooking nobody
to proud political demonstrator helps explain what young Americans got
from public democracy.

He rose higher still. The following Friday evening, Michael and his
brother James set out on the short, sweltering walk from their Franklin
Street house to Wooster Square, crossing an unmarked boundary between
their immigrant neighborhood and one of the wealthiest sections of New
Haven. The brothers climbed the steps of former governor James English's
cream-colored Italianate mansion. The established politician, one of the
most powerful in the state, welcomed the nervous young factory workers
into his home. Michael Campbell had a meeting with the governor.

Inside, the heat of the August city vanished. Beyond the three-story
spiral staircase, settled in one of the cool, soaring, marble-lined reception
rooms, Michael, James, and Governor English discussed possible designs
for the Phalanx uniform. Fireworks companies printed campaign hand-

A stern-looking member of an Iowa Wide Awake club, a militaristic Republican youth movement popular across the North in 1860. His uniform probably cost about two dollars and was designed to keep stinking torch oil from ruining his clothes. His torch staff could double as a club in fights with rival movements, although some Wide Awakes complained that such rods were made of soft pine and splintered after just a few blows to a Democrat's head. ("Iowa Wide Awake" from "'The Prairies A-Blaze': Iowa Wide-Awakes Carry Torches for Lincoln," *Iowa Heritage Illustrated* 77 [Spring 1996]: 43–46; courtesy Floyd & Marion Rinhart Collection, Ambrotype 382, The Ohio State University Libraries)

books, advertising vivid costumes and accessories, and from these Michael and the governor could chose uniforms like the "First Voters Legion," a loose white suit with red braids across the chest and a flat red and white cap, or for a bit more they might select the "Silver Knight," with its herald's tunic and spiked Prussian helmet. After that there were torches—so many torches—shaped like muskets or axes or eagles or top hats. Each minor detail mattered deeply to campaigners, who often spent more time on uniforms than ideology.[91]

Governor English promised Michael one hundred dollars—eight weeks' pay at his factory job —to buy outfits for sixty men. Michael Campbell, so nervous about his appearance, his authority, and his prospects, a young man who could not win an apprenticeship or get a raise or gain five pounds, felt elated by his sudden political importance. Floor-to-ceiling mirrors lined the reception rooms of English's mansion—did Michael see himself in one, the scrawny "poor boy" shaking the hand of the wealthiest, most powerful man he would ever meet?[92]

Governor English would not have seen an equal in those mirrors. The English Phalanx's mission stated that it was expected to "turn out on occasions when demanded by the Democratic committee."[93] From Governor

English's perspective, this was a top-down tool to win an important campaign. But to Michael Campbell, the political club offered a faster ascent than any of his other bids for self-improvement. Within a week of joining the Phalanx he had paraded in public and met privately with its namesake. Over the next three months, he attended six club meetings, conferred again with Governor English, and marched in ten processions. Compare this with Michael's more intimate affairs, such as his seventeen-month-long bid to win a small raise at the factory, and young Americans' use of politics suddenly makes a lot of sense.

Neither new uniforms nor meetings with governors could resolve the social and economic forces that blocked Michael's path to manhood. Eventually he found success, winning an important promotion and bragging, in his diary, about being assigned "quite a large charge for a young 'Irish' fellow."[94] Years later, the 1910 census found fifty-year-old Michael with many of the prizes he had yearned for as a younger man: a job as a mechanical engineer (he always loved to "talk scientifics"), a wife, and five children. Political activism at age twenty did not deliver any of these goals, but it did offer him a hint of importance, no matter how external or temporary, at the point when his worries seemed overwhelming.

Michael Campbell followed the same pattern as courting and wandering young people, bringing public politics to the aid of private identities. Like the courting teens Anna Ridgely and Annie Youmans, he used partisanship to facilitate a social exchange, repurposing exterior events as intimate tools. Like the wandering James Witham, his political involvement won him the attention of important adults. Grasping for maturity in the shaken nineteenth century, young men and women used the extroverted world of politics as a convenient handhold.

This use of politics inverted the equation established in childhood. For children, democratic participation grew outward from the private and familial to the public and national. Parents, teachers, and peers pushed children into party allegiance without explaining what it meant. By their late teens, young people began to "repay the debt," using democracy in exactly the opposite way, dragging partisan events into their intimate concerns.[95] Striving, uncertain, go-ahead eighteen-year-olds found some personal relevance in the immigration of Chinese workers to America, or in the place of slavery in the union, or in the relationship between businessmen and farmers. By age twenty-one, most Americans had received a thorough but contradictory education about the role of politics, making it impossible to distinguish where party life ended and private life began.

I Am 21 Years of Age To Day

The uncertainties of youth had a kind of miasmic weight that seemed inescapable in the nineteenth century but eludes historians today. One moment, however, crystallizes the shift from frustrated ambition to confident adulthood. Young people explained it best on their birthdays.

There was no "Happy Birthday" song in the nineteenth century.[96] Instead, many Americans between the ages of fifteen and twenty-one reflected on their failures and false starts over the past year. Some young people received gifts or had parties, but most felt that their birthdays were anything but happy. Usually, they marked the day with negative comments like "I am now eighteen and my feeling is regret—sincere regret," "Nineteen years of my unprofitable life are gone," and "My birthday—How much I feel to-day my own utter insignificance."[97] Such castigations did not resemble more modern concerns about growing old but rather show worries about failure to be further along the path to adulthood.

No one was more dramatic about his birthdays than William Dean Howells. As he grew from a rock-throwing boy into a brilliant youth, Will became bizarrely neurotic. He was convinced that he would drop dead the second he turned seventeen; only his father tinkering with the family clock dissuaded him. He also developed an overwhelming fear of rabies, worried that Tip the Whig dog had caught it.[98] Aside from these strange sensitivities, Will Howells sounded like a typically self-flagellating nineteenth-century youth. In one letter to his sister, Howells echoed Benjamin Brown Foster, moaning, "I am proud, vain, and poor," and concluding, "I pronounce myself *a mistake.*"[99]

Will's birthday worries grew from the fact that life was getting harder for the Howells family. His father's bold decision to leave the Whig Party and sell his newspaper had thrown them into poverty. They bounced around Ohio, chasing printing jobs, living in smaller and smaller houses. For a time they stayed in a decrepit log cabin, the cracks in its walls so big that snow drifted in and settled on young Will as he slept on the floor.[100] Though his father was as "sunshiny" as ever, life was tough. Will went to work as a "printer's devil" in his father's shop, laboring from 4:00 A.M. until 11:00 P.M. He "grew old enough very young."[101]

Finally the Howells family settled in northeastern Ohio, a region occupied by many radical Yankees who liked William Cooper Howells's Free Soil and Republican politics. Will, his father, and several hired printers

turned out a respectable partisan paper, working together amid the crank-
ing of the press and the hiss of a boiler forever threatening to explode. They
became the political hub of the community; the young assistants were "all
ardent politicians" in the midst of "the wander-years of a journeyman."[102]
Prominent leaders, including Ben Wade and Joshua Giddings, stopped in
to chat with Will's father.[103]

For all his worries about failure, death, and rabies, Will Howells was at
least getting good at courting. A photograph from 1855 shows eighteen-
year-old Howells as a handsome young man with sharp features, a piercing stare, and a carefully coiffed brown pompadour. He was funny, too,
describing himself as "a remarkably modest and unassuming young person."[104] Howells later looked back nostalgically on his years of late-night
"frolics" at Ohio girls' houses, especially the ritual of walking his favorite
girl home at midnight, relishing their "long lingering at the gate."[105] He
never lost track of politics, though, noting, when he escorted one young
woman home, that "hers was certainly a Republican house, as nearly all the
houses I frequented were."[106]

But courtship aside, Will Howells fit the mold of the era's ambitious,
worried youths. Typically go-ahead, he constantly reminded himself that
he was intended to become a famous writer. He had spent years watching his father pen editorials, and he began, over the course of his youth,
writing poems and stories and "reading, reading, reading."[107] He taught
himself Spanish and German so he could better enjoy his idols, Miguel de
Cervantes and Heinrich Heine. He fantasized about being published in the
Atlantic Monthly. When a Cincinnati paper printed a poem of his (secretly
submitted by his supportive father), Will crowed in his diary, "Just think
of that—they called me a 'poet'! I swear it beats all!!"[108]

But like Benjamin Brown Foster and Michael F. Campbell, he felt held
back by some unspoken force. Though he briefly took an impressive job
reporting on politics in Columbus, Will soon returned home. He was painfully aware of "the disappointment which my father delicately concealed"
when, like so many semidependent youths, he came home and took up
his old job.[109] In increasingly whiny letters, peaking around age twenty,
Will muttered, "The dull pool of my life stagnates again," and asked his
sister, "How am I to make a living? I want to make money, and be rich and
grand. . . . I am wretched. . . . I want to succeed, yet I am of too indolent a
nature."[110] Always self-deprecating, Howells thanked his sister for letting
him "write all this trash."[111]

In his late teens Will Howells felt stuck, each birthday affirming the "inaction of my life."[112] Looking back from sixty birthdays later, though, Howells found the perspective to interpret what he, and millions of young men and women, had faced. In one autobiography, Howells explained that nineteenth-century youth was an imperative condition, demanding action. Childhood had to be escaped; adulthood had to be earned. Young people had to *do something* to prove themselves. Youths must survive a phase of "blind struggle," Will wrote, often "ridiculous and sometimes contemptible," before they could enjoy "achievement and advancement."[113] Each disappointing birthday marked another year that this struggle went unwon.

With one exception. Though young Americans like Will Howells bemoaned their failings on their seventeenth or twentieth birthdays, they reveled in their twenty-first. Men in particular used proud, triumphant, nationalistic language to mark that anniversary. One street preacher proclaimed with dramatic flair, "All Hail, I am 21 Years of Age to day, Thanks be to God! The Laws of the Land declare me to be a man and a Citizen!"[114] Even the "poor boy" Michael Campbell, so prone to moping and carping, stuttered, "Today is an important day in my life no doubt for on to-day I am to commence my career as a man and not as a boy ... for on this beautiful day in may I have completed my twenty one years in this world."[115] On other birthdays the young looked back, considering mistakes they had made or paths they might have taken, but on their twenty-first men finally looked forward to adulthood and citizenship.

Turning twenty-one appealed to floundering young men in an era of foggy boundaries and few handholds, delighted by the idea that they had won adulthood through simple chronology. For once they did not have to do anything; the artificial and arbitrary boundary was like an unearned birthday present. Though young women excitedly marked their twenty-first birthdays as well, they felt the absence of the easy transition men enjoyed. But for a young man, his twenty-first birthday had some of the mystical power Will Howells had feared on his seventeenth. Overnight, no matter how indolent the rest of his life appeared, a young person glimpsed "some inspiration of a worthier future."[116]

The Union army veteran, Radical Republican, and civil rights activist Albion Winegar Tourgée best articulated the political weight of turning twenty-one. In his book *Letters to a King*, he linked democratic participation to the quest for manhood. Writing to a fictional young adult, Tourgée announced, "This is your 21st birthday. Yesterday you were an infant; today you are a man." Turning twenty-one initiated some kind of personal revolution, according to Tourgée: "Yesterday you were a subject; to-day you are a sovereign." The political system coronated young men; the nation, Tourgée wrote, "enjoins you to *be a king!*" [117]

With one enduring act, twenty-one-year-old men could put their frustrating pasts, their uncertain ambitions, and so many failed birthdays behind them. All they had to do was vote.

3 » My Virgin Vote

J. J. knew the river would be cold. By November, western Nebraska's North Platte hovered somewhere between a liquid and a solid, with broad wings of slush and floes drifting amid the sandbars. But the young cowboy had a mission that took precedence over warm breeches or dry boots. It was Election Day 1884, and John J. McCarthy had a ballot box to deliver. So he steered his old buckskin horse into the North Platte, its flailing hooves splintering the thin ice that lined the banks. Together they battled across the wide, shallow, freezing current, pushing toward the far shore, three-quarters of a mile away. Cold as it was, J. J. would not let his virgin vote go uncounted.[1]

A few hours earlier McCarthy had cast his first vote, along with thirteen other employees of the Ogallala Land and Cattle Company. The cowboys were all first-time voters, but a thorough upbringing in American political culture had taught them how to make ballots, in an age when voters brought their own to the polls. The problem was that they lived on the isolated Keystone ranch, on the far side of the North Platte from the frontier town of Ogallala. To the north stretched a choppy sea of mysterious sand dunes; J. J. and his partners were the first and only voters in their desolate precinct. Someone had to get their votes to the county clerk in Ogallala, and so McCarthy, a talkative Irish immigrant and an ardent young Democrat, threw the ballot box over his shoulder and set out for town.[2]

Hours later, a wet, cold, exhilarated McCarthy trotted into Ogallala. That "lively burg" of five hundred was as rough as J. J.'s ride had been. A key railhead on the Union Pacific, Ogallala drew pioneers and troublemakers from the East, many of them Union army veterans and strident Republicans. It was also the northern terminus of the Texas trail, and Democratic, former Confederate cowboys warily rubbed shoulders with hostile locals.[3] So when J. J. appeared on Election Day, bearing votes for Grover Cleveland, the Democratic candidate, the local Republican paper made a disdainful note of it. The *Ogallala Reflector* grudgingly praised the "wet and bedraggled messenger" for the risks he took in bringing in the vote but sniped that politics like J. J.'s "will bring ruin to all American industries."[4]

No Republican could dim McCarthy's glory. The twenty-four-year-old cowboy considered his ride through the North Platte a kind of baptism in the waters of politics. Despite an adventurous life, begun in County Cork and ended on the High Plains, his enthusiasm never "run higher than it did on that memorable day when I cast my first ballot."[5]

Though his ride was unique, McCarthy's experience connects him to millions of more ordinary first-time voters. He went out of his way (and through an icy river) to vote and believed that the ungainly ballot box strapped to his back contained a new, masculine, adult identity. Linking his virgin vote to an earlier rite of passage, J. J. wrote, "That first election was like my first pair of trousers, I shall always remember."[6]

Americans agreed that a first vote promised passage. Most considered it a boy's introduction into civic manhood. Other achievements, like marriage and fatherhood, were private, individual milestones, but none were as public, as collective, or as age-specific as voting for the first time. Younger men looked forward to their first vote as a moment of ascent; older men looked back at theirs as the roots of their stability. A young man's first ballot granted passage between two levels; it was the ceiling of youth and the floorboards of manhood. The day he cast that vote unfolded in the awkward crawlspace between those floors.

Whether splashing through the North Platte, staggering to the polls with half-drunk friends, or facing down partisan challengers at the voting window, male minors became active citizens somewhere in the course of that day. Stuck at home, women of the same age were forced to reckon with their second-class status in a way many had managed to avoid before. But a man's first vote, Americans believed, had deep consequences in his own life, in the life of the parties, and in the future of democracy.

Getting Sleeked Up

It began with a mustache. Or the shadow of a goatee. Or muttonchops, side-lilacs, a dashing Van Dyke, or a stern Hulihee. As November began and young men prepared to lose their political virginity, many asserted their manhood through these nervous trimmings. Evidence of the coming rite blossomed throughout American society with seasonable predictability, in boastful new mustaches sprouting under "twenty-onesters'" noses.[7] As their first election approached, most virgin voters tried to look the part they hoped to play.

A funny little book of cartoons offers our best guide to the strange rituals of the virgin voter. Its author, Charles Leland, was a folklorist who considered himself "a scholar and a wizard." He wrote *Pipps among the Wide Awakes* to recruit young men to the Republican Party's political clubs during the 1860 campaign.[8] His story of naive young Mr. Pipps's efforts to cast his first vote explored the thrills and doubts of the archetypal virgin voter. Armed with an arsenal of 1860s slang, from "Rip Sam!" to "Go it lemons!," Leland's sharp insights into Pipps's big day help dissect the rites and customs of casting that first vote.

Leland introduces young Mr. Pipps admiring himself in a mirror. Pipps announces that because "the horns are coming out under my nose," he could finally start voting.[9] Indeed, the age of popular politics coincided, almost exactly, with the high tide of American beardedness.[10] Preelection whiskers made a bold, self-conscious claim to masculinity and citizenship. Although this was part of an international trend, many young Americans linked beards and ballots. New voters hoped their facial hair would make them look old enough to participate—and, knowing that menacing party hustlers would "challenge" the votes of anyone who looked underage, they would need every follicle they could muster.

Older politicos commonly dismissed first-time voters as "beardless boys."[11] Partisan editors frequently used this epithet to write off novice rivals, mocking enthusiastic young men "with scarce a bit of down to shade their chin."[12] Connecting the dots between facial hair and political stability, Chicago's *Daily Inter Ocean* condemned an upstart Democratic faction as "men without hearthstones, or responsibility, beardless youths who wallow in the mire of dive politics."[13] The *Inter Ocean*, and many other publications, stressed a strict division between irresponsible, baby-faced youths and manly leaders with full beards and familial hearthstones. Virgin voters hoped a little "facial foliage" might help them join the men.[14]

American youths' aspirations went beyond preelection stubble. They often followed a predictable path of manly behaviors as they grew, from wearing boots and long pants, to smoking cigars, to spicy profanity, and finally to ostentatious voting.[15] First-time voters "sleeked up" before casting that ballot, which seemed to occur "at the precise age when young men pay particular attention to tooth brushes."[16] After the 1876 election, the *Milwaukee Daily Sentinel* chuckled at a stereotype of the average "maiden voter." A typical young man, the paper joked, awoke hours before dawn,

The caption accompanying this Republican cartoon, aimed at first-time voters in 1860, reads, ". . . having arrived at the age of 21 years," young Mr. Pipps "desires to cast his virgin vote at the coming Election." To prove they were men and voters, and no longer "beardless boys," young men like Pipps grew some "facial foliage," or at the very least a little mustache. (Charles G. Leland, *Pipps among the Wide Awakes* [New York: Wevill and Chapin, 1860]; from the Collections of the Division of Political History, National Museum of American History, Smithsonian Institution, Washington, D.C.)

fussed with his appearance, blustered at the breakfast table, argued politics with his father, dismissed his sister's views, and spent the day preening around the polls, his pockets stuffed with extra ballots.[17] Young voters put into their physical appearance exactly what they hoped to get out of voting, affecting the manhood they wished to achieve.

While young men fluffed their beards, donned new hats, and headed off to the polls, their sisters looked on with a combination of support, pride, and—sometimes—resentment.[18] Frances Willard, the future temperance and women's rights leader, certainly felt the latter emotion as a girl in 1856, watching her brother prepare to vote. Willard recalled "how proud he seemed as he dressed up in his best Sunday clothes and drove off in the big wagon with father and the hired men to vote."[19]

Unlike Willard, who wished that she too could cast a ballot for the new Republican Party, most American women accepted the ritual as a sacred preserve of men. Georgia belle Ella Gertrude Thomas encouraged her fiancé to vote, expressing palpable disappointment when he was too sick to drag himself to the polls on Election Day.[20] Even Sarah Ann Ross Pringle, a Ku Klux Klan supporter in Reconstruction-era Texas, sent her brothers off to vote, each menacingly "furnished with something to shoot with."[21] Lacking a vote of their own, most women saw their men voting as a victory for their family.

Young women watched as the men in their lives prepared to vote, but party activists refused to sit back and wait. Instead, they introduced a subspecies of political clubs, popular from the 1840s through the 1890s, to appeal to "those who give their first Presidential vote."[22] Big city machines particularly stressed these "First Vote Clubs," hoping to attract lonely new arrivals who "do not wish to go alone to the polls."[23] Party agents recruited for such clubs in the boardinghouses and pool halls where young men congregated. In Milwaukee in the 1880s, the Republican Party used such clubs aggressively, offering free bicycles to men who recruited enough new members. Milwaukee Republicans advertised one such club to gather new voters to their ornate headquarters and then employed their official Young Men's Republican Club—members clad in dashing white capes and bearing bright lanterns—to shepherd the bewildered novices to the polls.[24]

Joined by friends or club members, virgin voters converged on the town squares, warehouses, or saloons where voting would take place early on the much-awaited day. On their way they passed walls "papered three deep with humbug, banners, and inscriptions," preelection meetings reverberating from every grog house, and muddy fleets of farmers' buggies, drawn from the far edges of a precinct. A few secreted pocket revolvers or knives under their jackets, more clutched flasks or growlers, but most focused on their thin, unassuming paper ballots.[25]

How a young man stepped out to vote said much about his style and his values. In lower Manhattan, the elite, sarcastic George Templeton Strong headed out with cool disdain, wary of the "wretched, filthy, bestial-looking Italians and Irish . . . the very scum and dregs of human nature" swarming his polling place.[26] With his long black hair swept back, Strong, wearing a high cravat and a haughty expression, sneered at newspapers so ridiculously taken with the silly 1840 campaign that they would not have room to report it if "a live kraken were to sail into the harbor."[27] Beneath his contempt, however, Strong admitted that he was thrilled to exercise "for the first time the great and glorious right of suffrage."[28]

A generation later William Dean Howells rose early, still keeping the hours of a printer's devil, and sleeked himself up for a local spring election in 1858. He had always harbored "a secret longing to be a dandy," with a covetous love of calfskin boots, feathered Kossuth hats, and fine dark cloaks that usually turned into embarrassment once he actually wore them.[29] Upon turning twenty-one Will even grew out a "manly" mustache and a pointy little imperial and combed down his youthful brown pompadour.[30] In a photograph from this time he looks more substantial than the barefoot boy or the neurotic youth he used to be, prepared to enter adulthood by casting his virgin vote.[31]

And in "Mahatma" Lomasney's ward in Boston, the budding Gilded Age politico James Michael Curley strolled quietly to the polls for his first vote, more aloof than snarky George Templeton Strong or "over-proud" Will Howells. The canny young man was ready to graduate from listening to adults talk politics in the party headquarters behind "One-Arm" Pete's tobacco shop. Lean, sly, and conservatively dressed, Curley affected the nonchalant style of the boss he hoped to become. On his first trip to vote, he puffed a cigar, his eyes shielded beneath a derby. The fact that he "knew something about the art of self-defense" might also have come in handy at his rough polling place.[32]

As they left home, first-time voters often clumped into lively packs, said to blush all the way to the polls. Virgin voters were likely to vote in groups, often joined by brothers, fathers, and friends, and analysis of poll books shows that many excited new voters dragged along older acquaintances who had not participated before. Young immigrants, these same poll books suggest, rallied together before heading out to vote among the natives.[33]

As new voters neared the polling place, the sounds of a typical American election drowned out any hope of quiet reflection. Citizens often heard the drums first, their heavy beat resounding off distant buildings and exciting a martial, competitive spirit.[34] As voters got closer, they made out the clash and squeak of competing brass bands. Each party would field its own ensemble, causing musicians to favor volume over harmony. Some voters loved these street orchestras, while others complained that their tunes were "very trying to musical ears."[35]

Now within blocks of the polling place, young voters picked up the sound of many men, some of them deeply drunk, bellowing campaign songs. Parties put a great deal of money into printing political songbooks and usually favored easy-to-holler personal attacks.[36] The superficial messages of such songs changed little over the decades. In 1840, Whigs took aim at Martin Van Buren—the second shortest president in U.S. history—shouting, "Little Van's a used up man." Forty-eight years later, Republicans targeted the obese Grover Cleveland—nicknamed "Uncle Jumbo"—in much the same way, warbling, "Grover Cleveland's collar is an extraordinary size / So many men mistake it for a corset in disguise."[37]

The great clanking whir of the polling place, the loudest machine in nineteenth-century America, distinguished full citizens from everyone else. African Americans, for one, avoided the scene. Where black men could vote, they went out of their way to dodge the crowds of white men that coalesced over the course of the day. In the North, black men often made up the first few names in poll books in the morning, and during Reconstruction southern black voters frequently assembled off-site and arrived at the polls together.[38] Americans also considered elections "no place for women," even as observers, and so ladies spent the thrilling day at home, listening as concussive drums rattled their windowpanes.[39] Everyone within earshot knew a momentous rite was taking place, ringing loudest in the ears of those considered full citizens.

Young voters felt released, finally, from the seclusion experienced by all but adult men. Getting sleeked up and heading to the polls enunciated their membership in the American political nation. Virgin voters had long prepared for this moment—through childhoods of confusing, thrilling party instruction; through their awkward youth filled with the promise that voting brought stability; and most recently with hopeful goatees, stiff new collars, and long nights at wild rallies. Now, at twenty-one or twenty-three, young men finally turned a corner, ballot in hand, ready to join the throng of chanting, jostling partisans.

Like a Good Wife's Virtue

As first-time voters approached the polling place, a heavy consideration weighed on their minds. In the weeks before an election, young men absorbed many messages—some of them quite shrill—about the meaning of their first vote. Above the miscellaneous clatter of catchy slogans, nasty rhymes, and scurrilous implications, a single phrase lingered in their ears, calling them to cast their "virgin vote."

The term was still new when, during the 1856 campaign, the dissolute old poet N. P. Willis dramatically announced that after fifty years of ignoring politics, "I shall give my 'virgin vote' for Fremont."[40] Known more for his dandyish style than for his politics—he was fond of high beaver hats, flamboyant capes, embroidered vests, and literary gossip—Willis's public declaration did not receive the respect he had hoped for. Lydia Maria Child, the women's rights activist with a lightning wit, snapped, "It was pleasant to learn that he had anything 'virgin' left to swear by."[41]

Child's joke worked because Americans did not use "virgin" lightly. In a society that rarely spoke about sex—newlyweds' diary entries were masterworks of evasion—the term signaled a crucial rite of passage. How a young man handled losing his virginity said a great deal about him—it could signal the first step into healthy, vigorous manhood or begin a downward spiral ending in an early grave.[42] No wonder campaigners and voters chose this metaphor. Parties suggested that a miscast vote, rather than causing a bad case of syphilis, might trap a young voter with the wrong party. The concept of a "virgin vote" spoke to the combination of commencement and commitment, excitement and danger, youth and maturity, that casting a vote and sexual initiation had in common.

Most believed that the first vote cast, like one's first sexual experience, had long-term implications. On the one hand, an aspiring voter was supposed to anticipate his first vote "as the event of his life." On the other, older men were said to "refer to it in after years with pride and pleasure."[43] Recognizing this, campaigners and voters used language heavy with innuendo. During the 1876 presidential election, the Democrats aggressively warned young voters to be as careful with their virgin vote "as a good wife is of her virtue."[44] Virtue—sexual or political—could be established or forfeited by that first time.

Losing one's political virginity was risky, but it was also too important to avoid. Those who failed to cast their virgin vote, or to stick with their initial choice, were mocked as perpetual boys, indecisive "old ladies," sexless "neuters," or effeminate "Miss Nancies."[45] Changing parties indicated "you ain't no man," declared one former slave in Missouri; "you got to stand for your point."[46] While nonvoters were undernourished milquetoasts, voting made men "solid."[47] For nineteenth-century Americans, the central difference between boyhood and manhood was the self-restrained stability that adult men were supposed to embody. The best way for a twenty-one-year-old to distinguish himself from wild boys and uncertain youths was to declare, with his virgin vote, the virtuous constancy that marriage also symbolized. Voting wrong could mean "political defilement," but if handled with manly steadfastness, a young man's first time conferred manhood.[48]

What did Americans really mean when they talked about a young man's "virgin vote"? And when they employed the alternate term "maiden vote," what did *that* imply? What did these metaphors say about gender, sex, and politics? Why did Americans use this feminized language when discussing the moment that boys supposedly became men?

Maybe "virgin" was the best term Americans had for such a transition. Young men were usually referred to as political virgins just before they were about to vote; perhaps Americans chose the phrase to demonstrate the way a single act could move a person from youth to adulthood. Or was the metaphor more crass? Is this why first-time voters, supposedly so active, were put in the "maiden's" role? Were Americans suggesting that the parties were the aggressive partners, that virgin voters were being seduced?

Or did they simply lack the words to discuss male virginity? When referring to actual sex, many used language with female connotations even when talking about men. Pornographic books, for instance, sometimes referred to men as losing their "maidenhead."[49] Perhaps American culture was so fixated on women's virginity that it had few special terms to discuss what the transition meant to men.

None of these explanations is very satisfying. Few Americans really unpacked these terms during the age of popular politics. They were probably just thoughtlessly borrowed from other idioms like "virgin soil" or "maiden voyage." The best proof that "virgin vote" was a relatively shallow metaphor comes from the fact that Americans used it so boldly. "Virgin vote" and "maiden vote" appeared in newspapers, children's books, speeches, and broadsides. It seems unlikely that a culture that was usually so bashful about sex would use a suggestive term so frequently. This absence of awkwardness indicates that these expressions lacked much deeper meaning.[50]

Whatever its implication, the term "virgin vote" did not enter common speech until the age of popular politics established itself in the 1840s. Americans began to use it frequently only in the late 1840s; N. P. Willis still felt the phrase necessitated quotation marks in 1856. The fact that it took a few years for "virgin vote" to catch on hints at the metaphor's meaning to young voters.

In 1840, young people's political interest looked more like a momentary burst of enthusiasm than the beginning of a six-decade-long plateau. More first-time voters participated in 1840 than in any other election in U.S. history—nearly 40 percent of voters were new that year—but no one knew how they would behave four years later.[51] So in 1844, Democratic campaigners worked to assure young men who had chosen the Whigs that they could still rectify their mistake. Democrats played upon the camp revival model and organized "renunciation meetings," bringing forth former Whigs to testify that they had been "carried away by the whirlwind of blind enthusiasm" in 1840 but had been "born again" in the church of James K. Polk.[52] Though the Democrats won in 1844, they lost Ohio, North Carolina, and Tennessee, the three states where they held the most "renunciation meetings." Activists began to realize that a first vote was not a temporary fling but instead announced a sustained identity. Virgin voters were more monogamous than partisans had thought.

Campaigners met popular talk of "virgin votes" with their own phraseology, more decorous but more forthright. Lecturers, hustlers, and editors all began to warn young voters to "start right." The term, almost unused in publications between 1800 and 1840, flourished alongside "virgin vote" in American speech after the 1840s. Newspapers screamed some variation of "start right" particularly loudly in the days before a presidential election. On October 30, 1856, Massachusetts's *Pittsfield Sun* demanded of young men, "How are you going to cast your first vote? How begin your political life? There is no event of your life of more importance than this. Begin right. That is everything to you."[53] Five hundred miles west, campaigners in Cleveland bludgeoned young men at least as bluntly, ordering, "Cast your first presidential vote right! Old America expects Young America to do its duty."[54]

Leaders were picking up on virgin voters' view of their first ballot as more than a fling and began to stress the idea that one's political initiation determined decades of future behavior.[55] Young men advanced this rhetoric themselves. James Witham—the traveling farmers' rights radical who could not help but argue politics aboard midwestern trains during his wander year—agonized about his first vote, wondering if "as a young man with my life all before me, could I afford to take the wrong side?"[56]

Campaigners put aside the language of "renunciation"—as if the parties were false, momentarily enchanting gods—and took up the rhetoric of virginity instead. This change in the 1840s demonstrates crucial aspects of the era's political culture. Young voters introduced the rhetoric of the "virgin vote," and campaigners kept it going with their talk of "starting right." Virgin voters were not simply conned by clever campaigners, but neither were they deaf to their harangues. Instead, each side put reciprocal pressure upon the other, shoving each other out the door on election day. And the popularity of "virgin vote" and "start right" demonstrates the underlying logic of the age of popular politics, in which political virginity and partisan manhood, individual agency and structural power, all met at the polling window.

Tumble Up There

The polling place was its own nebula, densest at the center. On the edges, voters ducked into nearby buildings for a nip of whiskey or a glug of cider. Closer in, men hung around in loose constellations, some chatting, some arguing, some paying no attention whatsoever. Voters brought their lunch and spent the day hanging around the polls, munching sandwiches, greeting friends, and "kicking up old arguments."[57] Closer still, a broad belt of elbows seemed to sway between nervous young voters and the poll judge.

The ritual of challenging illegal voters at the polling place could frustrate many
first-timers, but it was also seen as a crucial, confrontational way to maintain the
purity of the ballot box. In this engraving in the Republican *Harper's Weekly*, an
honest-looking, fresh-faced young challenger denounces a supposed illegal voter,
depicted as a shady-looking Irish stereotype, complete with jutting jaw, bulky coat,
and ugly shirt, probably about to vote a Democratic ticket. ("Challenging a Voter,"
Harper's Weekly, October 26, 1872; courtesy UNC-Chapel Hill Libraries)

That official accepted ballots through the window of a saloon, warehouse,
or school selected as the district polling place. It was the sun around which
American democracy revolved.

Hustlers from both parties "challenged" the votes of men approaching the window as ineligible for reasons of age, race, or residency. They
hoped to deter anyone who seemed like he might vote for the opposing
party. Challengers learned to judge what a Democrat, Whig, or Republican
looked like, based on accent, clothing, or profession. The system turned
the ground before the window into a tense gauntlet. It also offered a
dramatic showdown for a first-time voter, the culmination of decades of
mounting political agency.

In a society with frequent migration, few government records, and a
tangled web of relations, virgin voters struggled to prove they were of
age. Many Americans knew their age only vaguely, and even those sure of
their specific date of birth could have trouble proving it. As a result, voters
often answered their challengers with convoluted calculations. One young

voter affirmed his age with the help of a witness who remembered seeing his mother, pregnant, at an execution twenty-one years earlier. Another was forced to chronicle the sex life of his mother, said to be a prostitute, to convince judges that he was old enough.[58] A third virgin voter calculated his age "from examination of a tombstone."[59] Casting one's virgin vote was often the only time in an American man's life that he was required to know exactly how old he was, further affirming the ritual as a crucial moment of adult self-assessment.[60]

First-time voters, who believed their ballot would help transform them into men, denounced challenges as "a most exasperating thing."[61] Those with strong roots in a community particularly resented being challenged in front of men they had known since birth. Some objections verged on the ridiculous. When one voter at an especially corrupt 1872 Philadelphia election identified himself as an employee of a local box factory, a feisty challenger pointed to his fancy clothes and remarked that he dressed "rather tasty for a boxmaker."[62] In *Pipps among the Wide Awakes*, Charles Leland joked that in casting his first ballot, young Mr. Pipps was "sworn in a little, and sworn at considerably."[63]

Popular accounts of confrontations with challengers often played on the fear that immigrants were perverting American democracy. A suspicious number of young writers report being challenged by an "immense Irishman," a "*Ferocious Irishman*," or "fifty Irishmen," whom cartoonists depicted as overgrown gorillas in bulky coats.[64] This fear of "gigantic" Irish poll hustlers makes little sense, particularly considering that most Irish immigrants had lived chronically malnourished lives and were smaller than the average native-born voter. Stories about having to battle Irish rowdies probably say more about young men's efforts to make their first votes sound heroic than they do about "Irish Democracy."

Challenges took their most atrocious form during Reconstruction, as white supremacists tried to intimidate black voters. Freedmen fought back through their Union League clubs. The leagues, descendants of the 4L club that dispatched George Washington Albright to spread news of emancipation, played a crucial role in helping many African Americans cast their virgin votes in the late 1860s.

The Union League took different forms in different places. In the North it served as a patriotic social organization for wealthy urban Republicans, gathering elites for sumptuous banquets in clubhouses in Philadelphia or Chicago. In the Appalachians the league helped organize impoverished white mountain communities to fight the lowland "big bugs" who controlled state houses. But it played the most dramatic role among freed slaves in the Deep South.[65]

For much of the year, Union League clubs met in secret, often in Freedmen's Bureau schoolhouses, discussing upcoming elections. Sometimes they trained as militias, marching, demonstrating, and occasionally arming themselves to fight off the KKK and other groups. On Election Day they poured forth from their hidden clubs, marching in formation to polling places threatened by white supremacists. Southern towns often saw a "solid phalanx" of black men striding in to vote together, singing songs, wearing flowing red sashes, preparing to cast their first ballots in the most hostile election environments in American history. These clubs offered protection and community and contributed the several hundred thousand ballots that won Ulysses S. Grant the presidency in 1868. Like the new voters clubs, the Union League showed that for many Americans, voting was a premeditated act, a social, collective, and public announcement. Marching to the polls and sporting red sashes and occasionally holstered pistols made a statement as significant as the actual ballot cast.[66]

Not all challenges were baseless, however. Throughout the nation, an ever-present minority refused to wait to turn twenty-one to vote. Such underage voting highlights young men's desire to join the adults, as well as Americans' undying love of plucky campaign trickery, but it mostly shows the powerful influence of the specific voting environment. Most illegal voting transpired in big cities and on the frontier, in unstable, scrambled environments where young men could get away with it. Casting an underage ballot was more difficult in long-settled rural communities, full of citizens who had known each other for decades. A family friend collecting ballots discouraged such behavior, but a stranger for a poll judge might encourage mature-looking nineteen-year-olds to try to pass.[67]

The two largest bursts of underage voting help explain how some got away with it. During the Civil War, many young Union soldiers voted prematurely. Leander Stillwell, an eighteen-year-old sergeant from Illinois, recounted his first vote in an army camp in 1862. Stillwell knew he was underage and had no plans to participate, but an older soldier took him by the arm and marched him to the camp's makeshift polling place: a few hardtack boxes set out under a tree. When the suspicious election officers questioned Stillwell as "a mighty young looking voter," his older friend blustered, "It's all right; he's a dam good soldier." Stillwell was allowed to vote for the Republican Party, heavily favored in the ranks. His capable

HARPER'S WEEKLY.

A JOURNAL OF CIVILIZATION.

Vol. XI.—No. 568.]   NEW YORK, SATURDAY, NOVEMBER 16, 1867.   [SINGLE COPIES TEN CENTS.
                                                                   [$4.00 PER YEAR IN ADVANCE.

Entered according to Act of Congress, in the Year 1867, by Harper & Brothers, in the Clerk's Office of the District Court for the Southern District of New York.

When large numbers of former slaves won the right to vote following the Civil War, they threw off the usual expectation that new voters would be young voters, aging into the system at twenty-one. This proud image depicts the breadth of the black community as the men cast their first ballots, running from the white-bearded elder to the young swell to the Union army veteran. It nonetheless honors the belief that a man's first vote bestowed a collective, masculine, nationalistic new identity. ("The First Vote," *Harper's Weekly*, November 16, 1867; courtesy UNC-Chapel Hill Libraries) fighting won him permission to vote, highlighting the linkage of voting and manly acts like soldiering.[68]

The other eruption of illegal voting took place along America's peripatetic frontier. In sodden, dripping tents perched on Sierra Nevada hillsides, in dusty Great Plains outposts with more cattle than voters, and in mossy north woods logging camps with more mosquitoes than voters, young men were often permitted to vote before turning twenty-one.[69]

Such voting was crucial in the unsettled western reaches of the nation, where so many young men gravitated. In 1850, white males between the ages of fifteen and twenty-nine made up the majority of the population of California.[70] Politicians pointed to "the emigration of young voters from the older States to the inviting fields of the Pacific slope" and believed a permissive voting environment might induce young men to put down permanent roots.[71] They also hoped to bolster their numbers at election time, to help along territorial bids for statehood. Local campaigners, especially in California, reached out to teenagers and to nonresidents. In the first election held in one Central Valley town, activists lined the San Joaquin River's banks, calling passing boatmen to cast their first vote, reasoning that they "were citizens of the world" and "might as well vote here as anywhere."[72]

Pioneers allowed underage voting using the same logic that gave Sergeant Stillwell a ballot at eighteen: a youth who had proven his manhood had earned political maturity. Tough young settlers—like "dam good soldiers"—deserved to vote. In gold rush California, one eighteen-year-old excitedly cast his first ballot, encouraged by a friendly poll judge who felt that "every one that had been able to make his way to the country" should get to vote.[73] In frontier Nebraska, a successful teenage speculator named Dick Darling was given special permission to vote underage because "he is considered one of the first pioneers."[74]

Frontier voting shows the power of America's political culture to replicate itself across generations and across a continent. Gold miners in California, feeling cut off from their birthplaces in Tennessee or Pennsylvania, looked forward to voting as "a refreshing reminiscence of home."[75] The Nebraska cowboys voting with J. J. McCarthy domesticated their wild district by holding an election on its soil. Those cowboys were all virgin voters but managed to cast ballots without any previous experience or official mechanisms, showing that democracy lived in their culture, not in a state apparatus.[76] Often election organizers selected a (legal) virgin voter for the honor "of casting the first vote that was ever cast" in a new district.[77] This

Coal miners in Pennsylvania vote early in the morning, in full gear, before descending into the mines. Three boys—possibly working in the mines as coal hurriers or breaker boys—look on, observing the special rituals of American democracy and American manhood. ("Pennsylvania Miners at the Polls," *Harper's Weekly*, October 26, 1872; UNC-Chapel Hill Libraries)

enthusiasm explains the sustained power of American politics, capable of reasserting itself for virgin voters on virgin soil.

Of age or under, on the frontier or back east, virgin voters put great meaning into this potentially banal scene of one man passing a slip of paper to another. The practice of challenging young voters enlivened this anticlimax, turning a civic rite into a tense confrontation. Though many complained about being challenged, the gauntlet of shouting poll hustlers created a dramatic crescendo out of the quiet act of voting. The rowdier the polling place, the bigger the challenger, the wilder the environment, the more tangible a vote's meaning.

When Will Howells "cast my first vote," wearing his manly new mustache and a little imperial, he felt this change.[78] Looking back at his sense of self-satisfaction, dawning at age twenty-one, Howells smiled: "I was prouder then than I can yet find any reason for having been."[79] He had finally *done something*. Voting transformed Will from an anxious boy, exaggerating his failures, into a self-satisfied man, exaggerating his achievements. Or, as an Indiana first-timer, far more excitable than pensive Will Howells, put it, "I was happy, and ranted and cheered, and made myself a burden."[80]

Perhaps Charles Leland's account of Mr. Pipps's first vote best captured a young man's struggle to express the weight of that little action. Once Pipps cast his ballot, Leland writes, "IT IS DONE. He hath voted! He hath. It's there in the box, as done as can be."[81] One can practically see Leland waving his top hat and cane, shouting, "GO IT LEMONS!"[82]

That simple moment was transformative, often recalled as "the proudest day of my life."[83] First-time voters echoed those campaigners who nudged young men to "start right." On this topic, if on little else, voters and leaders seemed to agree. The equation was balanced for once: what politicians put into voting, young men claimed to get out of it. As he strutted from the polling window, swigged ale, applauded friends, and hassled rivals, a young man reveled in his new identity.

Perpetual Minors and Vigorous Manhood

Voting altered gender as well as age. Placing their ballots "there in the box" not only turned boys into men but also elevated them above women. With that first vote, a scrawny twenty-one-year-old with a bad goatee stepped in front of all the schoolmarms, grandmothers, and senators' wives as a political actor. Each woman handled her disenfranchisement in her own way. Annie Youmans—that charming young lady who playfully flirted about politics with "very handsome" suitors with "splendad dark eyes"—dealt with her twenty-first birthday in perhaps the most typical manner.

For her twenty-first birthday, Annie did not speak out for suffrage or demand equality. Instead she had a picnic. She wore her white dress with a blue satin sash. She curled and crimped her hair. With ice cream, croquet, and dancing, Annie Youmans and her friends enjoyed themselves in late July 1869 along the banks of the Hudson in Westchester County, New York. She danced with multiple young men and enjoyed puzzling her friends about "who I really did like best." Annie had a great twenty-first birthday, the biggest celebration in her diary. The only hint of inequality was unintentional; afterward she wrote, "I shall always remember my freedom birthday with pleasure."[84]

What "freedom" did that birthday grant? Other young women used similar rhetoric when turning twenty-one. One living a few miles upstream from Annie's picnic wrote that since turning twenty-one, "I have tried to be dignified, as becomes my age." Another twenty-one-year-old wrote in her diary, "Am now of age, some say 'can do as you please.'"[85] Many women shared the sense that something changed at age twenty-one but could not point to the same concrete ritual as men. They celebrated their birthdays and rarely spoke about the rights they did not have, but their diary entries seem uncharacteristically numb.

Unlike those suitors she danced with, Annie's politics would not evolve with her "freedom birthday." She had long been a lively, honest partisan. At sixteen she had prayed for Lincoln's victory, acknowledging "the only reason I have for wishing Lincoln to be re-elected is because I do."[86] Annie enjoyed each presidential election as an entertaining fight, but she always expressed her politics through interactions with others. In 1864 she set her love of Abraham Lincoln against her friend Annie Schryver, who was "making a great time" for his rival George B. McClellan. At twenty, she argued for Ulysses Grant against a number of handsome suitors, winning a pair of gloves and a sense of maturity in the process. She learned about election results from her pa, who acted as a political informant because Annie could not visit the polls herself. The same was true of young men her age; before becoming voters they too had to use politics as an interpersonal tool.[87]

But while turning twenty-one allowed young men to physically enact their new, partisan identities, Annie could never take that next step. Like most women, she remained trapped in a youthful form of political involvement. Historian Corinne Field has written that disenfranchisement arrested young women's development, leaving them "perpetual minors" in the eyes of society. Casting a virgin vote implied that men walked a progressive path toward new rights and powers, while women waited at home.[88] And it froze their partisanship as a device to interact with others, rarely becoming an independent and internal identity. Women did not have to give up their interest in politics after age twenty-one, but they could only hope to be influencers, never actors.[89]

Most women accepted society's limitations on their involvement. But some spoke out, like Frances Willard, the future women's rights and temperance activist who watched her brother dress in his finest Sunday clothes and ride off to vote. At the time Frances felt almost sick with frustration, furious at the implication that she did not "love the country just as well as he." Her sister shushed Frances, warning her that if she kept up such talk she would "be called strong-minded." Decades later, Frances gave a gleefully strong-minded speech on the subject before the National Council of Women. Willard recalled how similar she and her brother had been until he cast his virgin vote. "There came a day when there was a separation," Willard shouted. "I saw that voting made it, and it seemed to me the line was artificial."[90]

This separation between men's and women's paths frustrated activists like Willard, but the majority of Americans supported such gender distinctions. Young ladies like Annie Youmans helped enshrine voting as a sacrament of manhood. Many celebrated the virgin votes of the men in their lives, bragging that an older suitor would soon "be 21 and able to vote."[91] So many Americans agreed that voting signaled "young and vigorous manhood" that it was difficult for a new voter not to see himself differently afterward. In *Pipps among the Wide Awakes*, Charles Leland makes a recurring joke, having Mr. Pipps assert some ambitious vision of himself, bolstered with the hopeful catchphrase ". . . or any other man!" as if tentatively affirming his membership in the club.[92]

The account of one first-time voter, Theodore Sutton Parvin, captures this sudden manhood. Theodore had been one of those wild boys playing in America's woods, until one day, at age seven, he jumped from a high dam and landed wrong. That fall "crippled me for life."[93] He could still walk, but with difficulty, and focused on books and education from then on. Fourteen years later, election day found twenty-one-year-old Parvin—now an earnest young lawyer with enormous brown eyes and a chin curtain beard—aboard a Mississippi steamboat docked at a small Iowa town. The boat's captain asked his passengers if they would like to go ashore and vote. Parvin shouted "Amen" and clambered up the muddy riverbank to cast his first ballot. Later he reflected, "It was a joyous privilege going forth from the steamer that afternoon a boy, and returning later to her decks a full-fledged man."[94]

It is tempting to think that first-time voters like Parvin were simply the type of romantic nineteenth-century youths who described every sneeze in florid, baroque prose, that virgin voters' claims of sudden manhood were mostly literary, of no more consequence than Annie Youmans's "freedom birthday." The difference was that most men went on to act differently as well, turning their rhetoric into reality. One action dramatically affirmed this new manhood: some virgin voters went so far as to switch parties.

Though most first-time voters supported the organizations they had been raised to revere, there was also a decisive bloc of young Americans who announced their adulthood, independence, and agency by rejecting the party of their forefathers. Some "smart alecks"—accused a miners' paper in Arizona—voted specifically "to show the 'old man' that they have a will of their own."[95] Though this was, theoretically, the proper way for a democracy to maintain itself, such rejection was rarely greeted with enthusiasm. Young voters grappled with the decision to join a new organization, and some only did so provided "mother and step-father didn't find out."[96]

"Bolts" by virgin voters followed a consistent pattern. New voters rejected the party of their birth, hoping to declare an independent path. By picking a new movement, such defectors distanced themselves from a long line of relatives—and from their own childhoods. This was usually deliberate. One gold prospector, voting deep in the Sierra Nevada, abandoned his family's party solely because he was "determined to go blind." He had already turned his back on his home and his kin and wanted to start fresh in California with new politicians, even though "I don't know a damned one of them."[97]

Lew Wallace, the future (mediocre) Civil War general and author of *Ben Hur*, rejected his "intensely Whig" family with his first vote in 1848. Like Will Howells's father, Wallace hated Zachary Taylor and began to give furious speeches against him. After one particularly harsh rant at the county courthouse, an elderly family friend approached Wallace and inquired, with genuine concern, "Your father is living, isn't he?" The old Whig could not conceive of a world in which a virgin voter would turn his back on the party of a surviving father.[98]

As they rejected their past, partisan apostates also looked forward, seeing their first vote as a long-term commitment. The wealthy Virginian John Herbert Claiborne had been raised, like Wallace, as a Whig but believed that he could not continue that tradition in the early 1850s. He felt that a new voter should "shape his course, true to himself," and he could not commit to the crumbling organization. Had he been an established voter, Claiborne would have held out in support of his family's party, but the rite of passage forced a moment of clear-eyed decision. Interpreting his first vote as a lifelong initiation, he became the first in a long line of Claibornes to vote for a Democrat.[99]

Though the majority of new voters stuck with their family's party, more Americans switched allegiances with their first vote than at any other moment.[100] Loss of political virginity provided a rare passageway between worlds; in the transition some young people changed parties, along with so much else about themselves. Some used the opportunity to ostentatiously assert their independent adulthood, while others saw it as a way to chart a path forward into manhood. Few women in their early twenties could make such a dramatic self-assertion. For over half a century, the world's largest democracy turned on the whims of such "smart alecks."

Haunted by Their First Time

A virgin vote did not end with a young man leaving the polling place. Instead it gained meaning in the days, months, and years that followed, as voters ornamented an emotional altar dedicated to their first election. Often, this legacy depended on how their first ballot fared. If a young man's first vote helped elect a ticket, he boasted of it for decades, and if his initial participation ended in defeat, it motivated an embattled, recommitted worldview. Many agreed with John Pope, the former slave still voting for the Republican Party in Arkansas in the 1930s. Although his state had not supported a Republican president for over sixty years, Pope promised, "I ain't going to change. That's my party till I dies."[101]

In 1844 William Saunders Brown learned about this legacy the hard way. The twenty-three-year-old clerk at a sleepy tidewater Virginia courthouse met his first election with vocal enthusiasm. Brown considered Henry Clay the absolute embodiment of an American statesman and wanted to do something to help. Over breakfast a few days before the vote, Brown and a friend hit upon the notion of raising a "Clay Pole" for their hero. For three late October days they wandered the tawny Virginia woods, felling trees, stripping their branches and bark, and splicing them together to form a seventy-foot pole. With the help of more friends, they hoisted the pole at a key crossroads and ran a thirty-five-foot-long Whig flag to its top. Proud of the beautiful construction, William then passed all of November 4 at the crowded election—the whole place "resounding with singing"—aggressively challenging hated "Locos."[102]

It was only after his thrilling first election that Brown saw that "times look rather squally" for his beloved Mr. Clay. The local Whigs rallied only about half of the voters they had hoped for. Worse yet, in the night some villains had torn down his beloved Clay Pole. Brown fumed in his diary, "No one but the most vile character would have committed such an outrageous deed."[103] He accused some young Democrats, who had erected their own "Polk Pole," of the sabotage, but they played dumb. From there on, Brown noticed more ominous clouds gathering. In the next few days, the older Whigs at the courthouse looked downcast, but Brown was young and exuberant and held out hope that his hero would win out "over such a man as Jas. K. Polk."[104]

Brown had some waiting to do; 1844 was the last presidential election held in different states on different days. Five days after Virginia voted, Brown happened upon an acquaintance while riding who informed him of the Democrats' victory in New York State, giving Polk the presidency. Brown took the loss hard. He raced home to write in his diary, worrying about how poor Mr. Clay would receive the news. Brown griped, "Shame upon the country that it chose its preferences in this way." That night Brown barely slept, turning over the defeat in his mind. The loss "haunted my sleeping hours." William Saunders Brown, not usually an emotive diarist, scrawled, "If crying would have done any good I could have shed a multitude of tears."[105]

As the most influential politician never to win the presidency (despite four attempts), Henry Clay invited special feelings. Four decades later, Alabama senator James L. Pugh and New Hampshire businessman Malachi F. Dodge reminisced, in the middle of a Senate hearing, about their first votes for Clay. The two agreed that they had feared "the country was ruined" when he lost, and—like Brown back in 1844—they "could not help shedding tears" at the news.[106] Their conversation reveals a long-petrified specimen of the same hurt that kept William Saunders Brown tossing and turning four decades earlier. Virgin voters, in New Hampshire, Alabama, or Virginia, in 1844 or 1885, felt much the same about their first loss.

Whether they backed a statesman like Clay or some more forgettable candidate, most voters clung to the legacy of their first ballot. Many young men felt that their first vote built a bond between them and their candidate, and they frequently remarked upon that connection. Virgin voters who had endorsed particularly iconic statesmen always took some credit. Well into the twentieth century memoirists still bragged, "I voted for Abraham Lincoln."[107] Alternately, those who gave their first ballot to a defeated candidate smugly believed that, had their man won, the whole course of American history might have been altered. Old men who had supported John Frémont in 1856 or Stephen Douglas in 1860 claimed that they could have averted the Civil War, and supporters of William Jennings Bryan felt that, had voters followed their lead in the 1890s, the nation would no longer bear a cross of gold.[108]

Even the minority of Americans who left their initial party could not live down the embarrassment of a miscast first vote. In his essay "How I Became a Socialist," radical organizer John C. Chase recounted his regrettable first time. Chase had labored in New England woolen mills and shoe factories since age eight. He came into his first election believing that the Democratic Party spoke for the workingman. Though he cast his first vote for a Democrat, Chase moved on to socialism and felt "stoop-shouldered in carrying about that load of shame" in the years since. He tried to forget that first ballot, but sometimes its memory "rises up to haunt me and I say to myself, what a fool I was!"[109] Like the Virginian Whig William Saunders Brown, with whom he shared little else, Chase chose the word "haunt" to describe his feelings on a regretted first vote.

There was something undying about a virgin vote. It had a meaning that lasted more than four years—as the Democratic organizers of "renunciation meetings" learned in 1844. An elderly Mississippi steamboat captain, writing to the Republican newspaper the *Outlook* in 1916, agreed. The eighty-three-year-old boatman shamefully admitted that he cast his virgin vote for James Buchanan but added, "If the good Lord will forgive me for that, I will take the risk on all the balance of my sins myself."[110] Good or bad, that first vote cast a long shadow.

Voter to Elector

J. J. McCarthy never let those around him forget how cold the North Platte had been. The Irish cowboy built a reputation around Ogallala as a talker, rambling on in his slurred County Cork accent. Usually, he spoke about horses, which he made a living riding and raising, or the romantic brilliance of Victor Hugo, whose works he would recount in after-dinner lectures to his less literate partners.[111] But often he would talk about his first vote. He bragged about it at the bar in Ogallala's Hotel Mellette, made loquacious by "the cup that cheers."[112] He lectured on the subject at Democratic rallies.[113] Settlers who moved to Ogallala well after the 1884 election knew the story but believed it had happened the year they arrived, as did his wife, Mary, whom he married a half decade after strapping the ballot box to his back.[114]

Even death couldn't shut J. J. up. When he passed away, in 1931, the *Keith County News* printed an admiring obituary, which described his famous ride. The details it included—J. J.'s "buckskin horse," the river of "snow, slush and ice"—made it clear that the obituary's author had heard McCarthy's story firsthand. The practice of mentioning a man's virgin vote in his obituary or eulogy was actually quite common, whether the story was as thrilling as J. J.'s or more mundane. For the generations of men raised during the age of popular politics and dying off in the early twentieth century, obituaries frequently noted a man's first vote as the detail that concluded his youth and commenced adulthood.[115]

Then, in 1938, a fifty-year-old woman named Bessie Jollensten paid J. J.'s aged widow a polite visit. Jollensten worked for the New Deal's Federal Writers' Project, assigned to round up life histories from her dusty region.

Seated in the sunny, modern addition of her rambling farmhouse, Mary McCarthy passed Jollensten an old document written by her husband. J. J. had penned "When I First Voted a Democratic Ticket" years earlier, to commemorate a central moment in his long and exciting life. Seven years after his death, fifty-four years after his ride through the North Platte, and a century after the beginning of the age of popular politics, J. J. went on telling the story of his first time. Bessie Jollensten included his account in the American Life Histories collection of the Federal Writers' Project. J. J.'s virgin vote had outlived him.[116]

From this perspective, J. J. McCarthy was the archetypal virgin voter. He saw his first vote as a personal initiation and dutifully kept his promise to "always remember." His wife, Mary—barred from voting for most of her life—curated the memory of his first ballot. But there is another angle. As he aged, J. J. matured from a young man galloping off to vote into a Democratic Party insider. By 1912 he even represented Nebraska in the electoral college, helping to make Woodrow Wilson the first Democratic president since McCarthy's old hero, Grover Cleveland.[117] At some point, he became the older man, pointing a new generation of youths toward the polling place.

No matter how long Americans lingered on the memory of their virgin vote, time pushed them into new categories. "Twenty-onesters" did not act alone; the largest, most powerful institutions in the country engineered their deeply meaningful first votes.[118] The tan ballots that virgin voters clutched while heading to the polls did not magically appear. Instead, armadas of ostentatiously jaded activists in their mid-twenties shoved them into the hands of new voters. Older men crafted the slogans and songs designed to get virgin voters to "start right," not to mention selecting the candidates and setting their platforms. A young American man's first vote signaled a transformation from boyhood to manhood, but his participation also heralded a transition from individual agent to cog in a massive machine.

Neither aspirational new goatees, nor flirtations at late-night rallies, nor bonfires set by eleven-year-olds can tell the entire story of the age of popular politics without balancing them against bullying poll hustlers, taciturn bosses, and condescending reformers. We have seen how young Americans pushed to vote, but how were they pulled?

4 » The Way for a Young Man to Rise

If you believe James Logan's defenders, the twenty-one-year-old did not begin Election Day by quietly loading a large revolver. He did not, they swore, hide that weapon beneath a bulky black coat. In fact, Logan's father-in-law later testified, the Baltimore gang member wore no such coat but donned a flashy plum jacket that morning. And the scrawny, sharp-faced, goateed Logan certainly did not slip a weighty cast-iron knuckle-duster into his pocket as he headed to Ward Fifteen's polling place.[1]

Others admitted that they came prepared on the morning of November 2, 1859. In a home far tonier than Logan's cramped quarters, twenty-nine-year-old George Kyle loaded a double-barreled pocket pistol and sheathed a long dirk. His brother Adam Kyle Jr. painstakingly prepped a revolver with powder, ball, and cap and then hefted a weighted cane with a metal head. Each grabbed a large bundle of ballots. With heavy pistols jammed against their hips and "Reform" tickets folded underarm, the scions of one of Baltimore's wealthiest families set out for the same polling place as Logan.[2]

The Kyle brothers had good reason to arm themselves. They represented Baltimore's Democratic establishment, with ties to proslavery, pro-southern, pro-immigration state and national organizations. They hoped to retake Baltimore by masquerading as a reform movement. But anti-immigrant gangs—with names like "the Tigers," "the Plug Uglies," and "the Blood Tubs"—had been targeting Reform candidates and election-eers. So, in addition to their own weapons, George Kyle had distributed eighteen revolvers to workers who would police other wards that day.[3]

As they marched into south Baltimore, the Kyle brothers knew they were entering "a hard neighborhood." The nativist Tiger club controlled much of the district. In addition to bullying immigrant and free black ship-builders, the Tigers spent their time intimidating Baltimore businesses for easy jobs, though they did notoriously shoddy work. They also hustled for the American Party, the official wing of the Know Nothing anti-immigrant movement. In return, the city council located Ward Fifteen's polls in the Tigers' favorite tavern.[4]

When they reached the Light Street polling place, teeming with voters and more than a few Tigers, the brothers went to work. Operating with the brazenness expected of nineteenth-century poll hustlers, George Kyle stationed himself just two feet from the voting window, practically leaning on it as he pressed ballots on voters. His brother Adam stood back, handing out more tickets amid the growing throng.[5] Few men showed any interest, either out of distaste for the Reform movement or from fear of what might happen if they took a ticket. Somewhere in the crowd, among the peaceable citizens and grumbling Tigers, James Logan seethed—allegedly.

The partisan tension was too much for Logan's boss. Joseph Edwards Jr., the middle-aged bartender who ran the Tigers, had seen enough of these gentlemen-hustlers and their Reform tickets. Looking to his club members, whom he had ordered to do far worse in the past, Edwards stepped up and hollered, "Snatch the tickets from them sons of bitches!"[6]

The crowd boiled over. Someone tore the ballots from Adam Kyle's arms. In the same instant, James Logan—if you believe those who testified against him—lunged forward and cracked Kyle in the side of the head with his iron knuckles, knocking him to the pavement.[7]

Had the young gentleman stayed down, it might have ended there. But Adam Kyle, still on the ground, began to thrash about with his weighted cane, driving the throng back. As the mob paused, Kyle drew his revolver and came up shooting. His thumb and finger frantically worked trigger and hammer, launching a swarm of unaimed bullets. One of his rounds wounded an attacker, a local rowdy who went by a nickname so improper that it was struck from newspapers after the shooting. Another bullet killed Basil Elmore, a boy who was either raising a flag or hurling bricks, depending on the account. With his attackers stunned, Kyle bounded into a nearby German candy shop and barred the door.[8]

The Tigers set after him. Five men smashed down the door and stormed up the stairs on Kyle's heels. They caught him on the third floor of the building and began to drag him back to the street. On the stairs, in full view of Regina Dochtermann, the German immigrant who ran the candy shop, someone who strongly resembled James Logan—same pinched and angry face, same dark goatee—drew a long revolver from under a heavy black coat, and executed Adam Kyle.[9]

Outside, the street rattled with the staccato of pistols. Other Tigers set upon George Kyle, who fought back, escalating from fists to blades to bullets. He stabbed a man with his dirk and fired both barrels of his pistol into the crowd. At least six men cocked their guns, but before they could shoot, a fast-fingered brick thrower pegged George square in the chest. He crumpled to the ground as most of the Tigers' fusillade sailed over his head. Bullets grazed George's temple, shoulder, and hip but would have done far more damage if not for that well-aimed brickbat. He stood up and scrambled quickly down the street, his empty pistol leveled at the surging crowd in an impotent threat. Always a gentleman, George Kyle paused to grab his hat and then limped home, leaving hundreds of bloody Reform ballots strewn across Light Street.[10]

Baltimore's 1859 election was on the bloody side. The battle on Light Street received the most attention, because it left a prominent young man dead, but partisans clashed at sixteen out of Baltimore's twenty wards. The *Baltimore Sun*'s tally of "outrages at the polls" reported at least eight shootings, four stabbings, and two dozen severe beatings. That count missed some attacks with shoemakers' awls, which did harm but were not always classified as stabbings, beatings not considered severe, and numerous "knock downs" of men waiting to vote "the wrong ticket."[11] Nativist gangs even kidnapped German migrants and forced them to repeatedly vote anti-immigration ballots at different polling places.[12] The American Party, collapsing almost everywhere else in the nation, took a lopsided 75 percent of the city's votes.[13]

After the fighting, but before James Logan's trial for the murder of Adam Kyle, gang members visited several key witnesses. Logan himself appeared at Dochtermann's candy shop, joined by two ladies who called for ice cream. The accused murderer reportedly warned Regina Dochtermann not to say anything about what she saw transpire on her stairway on Election Day, reminding the German immigrant that secrets had a way of leaking out in the neighborhood. After a trial in which many altered their initial testimonies, James Logan was acquitted.[14]

The havoc in Baltimore was an extreme example of what many considered simply "the ordinary incidents of a popular election."[15] Men in their twenties, far from children but still considered young, made up many of the canvassers, hustlers, and foot soldiers in each campaign. Away from the polls, they often took the lead as "lung workers," debating the issues over mugs of lager or games of billiards.[16] Young women, discouraged from overt politicking, joined in, trying to sway the men in their lives.

Acquainted with popular politics but still young and striving, Americans in their twenties served as the chief persuaders on the ground.

Parties relied on young adults to bridge the generations. Politicians preferred to delegate tasks to twenty-five-year-olds, who had seen a campaign or two but asked for less money and held fewer grudges than older activists. More-established men usually avoided the tedious requirements of on-the-ground campaigning, from explaining platforms to arguing with cranks to tracking down drunks.[17] Campaigners often considered young adults their best investment.[18]

Young adults could also reach out to virgin voters and youths in unique ways. They mixed with the next crop of juvenile partisans and knew, better than older activists, who might be most useful. While children and youths mostly focused on their own personal growth, young adults learned the arts of recruitment and delegation. They began to practice politics from a mature perspective, serving as a crucial liaison between the generations.

These young persuaders challenge the image, painted so lushly by some historians, of a political jungle divided between voracious campaigners and their unwitting prey. Most of the young adults who convinced friends, spouses, or strangers to vote went unpaid and unrewarded, acting as an unofficial auxiliary of older party activists.[19] They usually threw themselves into campaigns on a whim, climbing the low bar for entry into electioneering. Their participation shows how messy party organizations could be, more like an overgrown trellis, with weeds snaking up and down, than a trim and simple ladder.

This self-deputized posse began to reverse the path set out over the course of youth. Underage Americans had encountered partisanship first at home, then in school, and then in the streets. Their public activism usually peaked around the time of their virgin vote. At this age they were often America's most voracious political animals, supplementing their first votes by hustling voters, canvassing strangers, and threatening rivals.

But most turned a corner in their mid-twenties. Over the rest of their ebbing youths, Americans settled into increasingly private politics. As their commitments entrenched and their enthusiasms became routine, most men and women in their twenties slowly began to distance their political selves from open hoopla in the street. Though still intensely invested in politics, they learned to express their fascinations in less bombastic ways. Many young men turned to the quieter work of guiding younger friends and relatives into politics, while wives lobbied, often in private, to influence the votes of their new husbands. The arc of public political involvement, driven by juvenile insecurities, began to curve downward as youth came to an end.

The Love of Smart Dealings

Charles Dickens took away two big points from his disappointing tour of America in 1842. First, he concluded that the entire nation, particularly the Senate floor, was saturated with tobacco spittle. Second, Dickens came to feel that the dominating ethos of the country was a "love of 'smart dealings' which gilds over many a swindle and gross breach of trust."[20] Though America's democratic experiment made it unique in the eyes of the world, the nation was also notorious as the home of a striving, bumptious, sneaky brand of capitalism. This "love of 'smart dealings'" soaked into the political culture, and many young adults participated in campaigns to try to sell their party to strangers. The changing model of politics, more countinghouse than schoolhouse, moved democratic persuasions into new and more aggressive territory.

Canvassing and hustling created an odd political marketplace, in which young people were both the most active salesmen and the most sought-after customers. Many young adults tried their hands at partisan peddling in a campaign or two. Most found that it wasn't for them. Electioneering required an artful blend of volubility and discretion. Successful young canvassers, talking politics in the final days of a campaign, worked to ingratiate themselves with doubtful voters, but on Election Day, hustlers swaggered like carnival barkers, foisting ballots on strangers.[21]

But even as they increased their volume, these partisan showmen retreated into more secluded venues. Though they performed in the public theater of politics, young adults focused more and more on the machinations of their parties, which secretly determined so much about nineteenth-century elections. Young Americans spent their time button-holing neighbors, manufacturing ballots, and intimidating voters in hidden locations where smart dealings verged on dirty tricks.

In public, campaigners rarely alluded to their behind-the-scenes scheming. Instead, electioneers relied on false familiarity, hoping to turn fleeting friendships into pledges of support. Younger voters particularly hated this approach. The "poor boy" Michael Campbell, who considered himself an active partisan after his work for the English Phalanx, complained that at a fair, crowds of canvassers surrounded him, "all calling my name as familiarly as if they were old friends of mine but for my part I could not recognize one."[22]

Americans worried that young voters were particularly vulnerable to these phony tactics. The Louisiana comic writer Marianne Marbury Slaughter published a brilliant piece on this during the 1878 election. She joked that young men needed to shield themselves from this "shelling of 'principles' and 'platforms' and this thundering bombardment of eloquence." Older men, Slaughter wrote, had learned to accept canvassers' free drinks and cigars without ever promising support, but virgin voters were too easily won over. Slaughter hoped for a refuge "where young voters with tender consciences can skip to on the approach of this suicide-inducing fraternity."[23]

Canvassers especially haunted groceries and country stores, selling party politics among the cracker barrels. These small establishments—often with a makeshift bar in the back—provided the perfect environment for partisans to treat potential voters to a dram of brandy or a jigger of gin. They were, political satirists joked, the cradle that "rocked into manhood the coming American politician."[24] Party activists would use a first toast as an introduction and then keep the drinks coming while expounding on immigration or banks or slavery. Americans became familiar with the image of nattily dressed young party operatives loitering outside such stores, idly talking politics as they waited to ambush shoppers.

Electioneers always worried, however, that too much free bourbon would undo their hard work. Nineteenth-century American drinkers rarely believed in moderation, and partisans hated the idea of spending hours refilling the cup of a man who might never remember a word. A voter who was "just a little bit tight," activists learned, was more useful than one who was three sheets to the wind.[25]

From their perch "squatting," one writer put it, "like a venomous toad upon the corner of a block," these "liquor groceries" enabled unusual politicking.[26] Sometimes the woman who ran the counter used her position to lobby for her party in a manner that would have been unacceptable outside of the store. One such woman was the tough young Mrs. Con Donoho, who ran a grocery in New York's Five Points slum in the mid-1840s. Mrs. Donoho's husband was a "zealous, firm, hard-fisted Democrat." Con commanded the local street sweepers, offering them easy city work in exchange for occasionally turning out to smash the hat or break the nose of a party rival. While Con fought his political battles with squadrons of local thugs, Mrs. Donoho used her store to influence an army of partisan wives.[27]

Donoho's grocery was pretty typical. Up a few narrow stairs, past an open barrel of shimmering herring and another of matte black charcoal, stood an elaborate bar of home brews. Locals joked the couple manufactured both "ardent spirits" and "ardent voters."[28] Mrs. Donoho watched over the business, smiling at the immigrant women who came in to buy a fish for dinner or to refill their milk pitcher from the gin barrel. She would coyly quiz her customers on their husbands' preferred candidates in local races, usually for alderman. If a wife answered that her man backed the wrong politician, Mrs. Donoho would sell only the smallest fish or green, eye-specked potatoes from the depths of the barrel. She would add, with a wink, that if the wife could change her husband's mind, he might find work in Con's crew, ten shillings a day. This was the kind of quiet electioneering, meted out in spuds or gin, that built local political empires.[29]

The Donohos' gin, made bright red with a dash of lemony ratafia, was not enough to win over everyone.[30] Though alcohol played a central role in American politics, canvassing was never simply an exchange of votes for booze. There were too many teetotalers for that. Middle-class religious folk were particularly likely to denounce "the beverage of hell." And they were not all old church ladies: the youth-oriented Sons of Temperance was among the most popular organizations for young Americans.[31] Party activists had to be careful whom they treated. Though there were more temperance supporters among the Whigs and Republicans, some young Democrats were also passionately anti-liquor, so canvassers had to avoid pressing the bottle on the wrong voter.[32]

The safer approach was to simply talk their ears off. John Young had the perfect personality for this. Born a slave in South Carolina on the Fourth of July, 1855, Young nurtured a bombastic, unceasing love of conversation. He never seemed to hold to any one subject for very long but would explode "like a bunch of fire crackers about anything that pleases or annoys him." Young was prone to belly laughs, mustache-wiggling asides, and exclaiming "Pshaw!" when agitated. Though he focused his big personality on politics well before he turned eighteen, it was in his mid-twenties that Young perfected his electioneering.[33]

Young dove into politics during Reconstruction, bringing his bombastic oratory to the ferocious elections of 1870s South Carolina. He seemed to be constantly speechifying, reminding black voters about the virtues of the Republican Party. Young's strategy was to "nevah lets 'em forgit" about coming elections. He liked to begin a conversation by "guessing" that some stranger was planning to vote for his candidate, making it seem like the

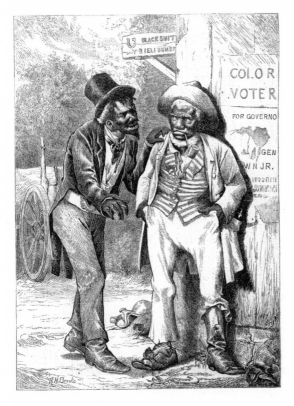

Capturing two common stereotypes in one image, this engraving depicts a grotesque stereotype of an African American electioneering in Virginia in 1872. This portrayal expresses the growing disgust with electioneers—increasingly mocked as "lung workers," "sidewalk committees," or "shoulder hitters"—who cajoled or coerced potential voters. The partisan, sleeked up in a fancy jacket, with shiny hair and boots, hustles an older, skeptical-looking voter. ("Canvassing for Votes," *Harper's Weekly*, November 2, 1872; courtesy UNC-Chapel Hill Libraries)

voter's idea. As they spoke, Young worked to keep the name of that Republican politician in the air. The only information a voter needed was the name of the candidate he should support and the name of the other guy, the one who wanted to take his vote away. By the end of a conversation, Young bragged, "I had dem people ready to promise anything before I lets up on 'em."[34] Young could talk for hours and had no problem pestering people: he was an ideal canvasser in a democracy that often ran on the social skills of talented talkers.

The drugstore arm-twisting, the free five-cent cigars, and all that phony good-fellowship ended the day before an election. At this point, campaigners traded the soft sell of canvassing for the frantic commerce of hustling. Young men, more than anyone else, were expected to do the legwork.[35] Considering the forty-eight hours of electioneering that stood between him and the closing of the polls in 1856, one twenty-year-old Brooklyn Republican anticipated the "tickets to be printed and distributed, votes to be looked after, repeaters to be guarded against, frauds to be discovered and defeated."[36]

The key to hustling, if not to the whole of nineteenth-century democracy, lay in the ballots. The parties printed and distributed their own ornate tickets, and an election could be decided before the polls even opened by particularly sneaky "smart dealings." Friendly newspaper presses printed most ballots the day before an election, and these clanking presses, hidden away in obscure newspaper offices and unheated warehouses, acted as home bases for parties fighting a behind-the-scenes war to control an election.

Parties worked to keep the design of their ballots secret. Otherwise their opponents would print bogus ballots, designed to look like one party's tickets but listing candidates from the other. Illiterate voters might be tricked into casting ballots for the wrong side. Or one party, the Republicans for instance, might print thousands of mock Democratic ballots with the politicians' names all spelled wrong so that they would be disqualified by election judges once the polls had closed.[37]

One California newspaperman described the secret battle, fought during an early 1870s election in Vallejo, to copy rivals' ticket designs and distribute counterfeits before the other party learned about the scheme. Both sides had quietly sent teams to San Francisco by rowboat to buy up all the colored paper available. Once the voting began, runners sprinted from the polls to the newspaper offices, breathlessly reporting on the opposition's ballot color. Then journeymen printers and political operatives rushed out new ballots in that same shade. "Again and again the change of color was made," and every twenty minutes hustlers appeared with new ballots to trick voters.[38]

Hustlers in their mid-twenties presided over these printing wars, watching as newspaper presses manufactured the instruments of democracy. Once the ballots were prepared, teams of young adults, supervised by older men, went to work in party headquarters. Like sweatshop laborers, they bent over wide desks, cutting and stacking the sheaves of ballots. Each organization had its own style. Tammany Hall preferred canvas sacks stuffed with ballots; various Republican organizations wanted them bundled like greenbacks. District leaders watched this manual labor closely. Without ballots, there were no votes: sabotage of these flimsy paper bundles would mean "no election could take place."[39]

The newspaperman who watched the Vallejo printing war came away with a trenchant insight: older partisans controlled the political process from nomination through the printing of the ballots, but once those votes were handed off to hustlers, elections were decided by young activists on the ground.[40] "The indefatigable industry of young enthusiasm," agreed a Republican organizer, "is worth a thousand speeches from great leaders on the night before the election." The "real, substantial warfare must be at the polls."[41] Put another way: once a twenty-five-year-old stuffed his pockets with blue or gold or green tickets early on Election Day, "the fight was on."[42]

In Brooklyn, twenty-year-old Lyman Abbott decided to help John C. Frémont's presidential bid in 1856. The future preacher of the Social Gospel was then a "quasi-bohemian" in his early twenties, a high-foreheaded young man with a slick mustache and piercing black eyes. An antislavery Republican, Abbott worried that "America will either remain in God's service, an exponent of individual freedom, or it will go over to Satan." So he organized his brothers, with whom he shared a rented room in Brooklyn Heights, and picked a polling place nearby. The Abbott boys stationed themselves around the polls, one out before the window and the others at the ends of the street, pushing Republican ballots on whoever walked by.[43]

The brothers were doing a passing job, working the polls in their "cold-blooded, reserved" way, when a rough-looking fellow in an old yellow coat appeared. Abbott worried that the thug was a Democrat there to run interference, but he grabbed a bundle of ballots and let loose with the kind of vigor that blurred the line between politics, salesmanship, and show business. His yellow coat flapping, the stranger stomped up and down the Brooklyn street, vociferating at the top of his lungs, "Here's your regular Republican tickets!—Free speech, Free soil, Free press, Free men, and Frémont!—Free speech, Free soil, Free press, Free men, Frémont!—Free speech, Free soil, Free press, Free men, Frémont!" Hollering the greatest slogan from the age of popular politics in a rolling tongue twister, the rough fellow pressed large handfuls of ballots on Brooklyn voters that day.[44]

The Abbott brothers were not wrong to worry about an approaching tough. Most parties made use of thugs to police the polls. In 1844, the *New York Herald* reported that both Whigs and Democrats were arming "the fighting men—the bullies—the 'sporting men'—the 'gentleman of fancy' as they are called in their own slang." Respectable citizens, the *Herald* accused, were employing "the dregs of a population, drawn from all parts of the world," collected in brothels, saloons, and the rougher theaters, to hustle and intimidate. The article asserted that in the run-up to the heated election, hardware stores were selling off whole boxes of new Colt revolvers.[45]

Much-feared "b'hoys"—an urban stereotype somewhat akin to "thug" today—seemed particularly involved in street-level politics. From the 1840s on, the respectable classes noted their presence at city elections, strutting around in their red shirts, leather vests, high boots, wobbly top hats, and slick, plastered forelocks. Some were the gambling "sporting men," others were career criminals putting their sleight of hand to partisan use, but most were simply "young bloods." These aimless troublemakers in their twenties were not active criminals, just bored and wild. They turned up at elections "as uncouthly sociable as a company of young bears."[46] One young Bowery tough, who made his living boxing in brothels as the "downstairs" entertainment, rented out his services to campaigners from New York to Maryland.[47] Another, a Philadelphian who kept a wager book detailing every dogfight, horse race, and "rat match" he attended, instead scrawled "busy canvassing" in his fight book during the heated 1868 campaign.[48]

One New York boardinghouse resident reported on the "fast young man" who shared the breakfast table each morning. The youth talked of nothing but an upcoming race, made out his housemates' election bets in the proper English book style, spent his evenings talking politics in pool halls, and "falls up-stairs every night, full of information."[49] Down in Baltimore, James Logan—revolver on his hip, knuckle-duster in the pocket of his bulky black coat—fell into this same category.

Urban b'hoys were not the only hustlers. Young men pressed ballots on voters from North Carolina to South Dakota. In rural regions, parties could not afford as many professional politicians, so Americans in their twenties formed "electioneering parties." Young men would grab some growlers of beer and wander from house to house, dragging voters to the polls from miles away.[50] These hustlers carried more weight than their urban equivalents. In a large city, a voter could usually procure a ticket for whatever party he preferred, but this took more work in highly partisan stretches of the countryside. It was nearly impossible to find a Republican ballot in South Carolina in 1860 or a Populist ticket in 1890s Vermont.

And their appeals worked. Though many associate nineteenth-century campaigning with cities, the rural but settled regions of the country had the highest turnouts. Campaigners in Indiana or upstate New York knew their neighbors most intimately and stood the best chance of dragging them to the polls.[51]

The fact that there were fewer rural hustlers meant more power for each one. In big cities a party could diversify—having amateurs hustle ballots

An election takes place in 1850s New York City amid brawling men and dogs. Note the young hustlers offering sheaves of ballots and the boy waving a sign. This image should be interpreted as a bit of propaganda, depicting the worst version of Election Day rowdyism. Really, beneath the hollering and the fighting, a complex, age-defined political culture structured what often looked like chaos. ("At the Polls," *Harper's Weekly*, November 7, 1857; courtesy UNC-Chapel Hill Libraries)

while focusing more experienced (or intimidating) operatives on challenging and threatening voters. By 1860, New York's parties became so specialized that Republicans organized a task force to monitor Democrats, and the Democrats responded with a squad to monitor their monitors.[52] But in rural areas, young hustlers doubled as enforcers. There were few strangers in these small towns. In an 1862 election in rural Missouri, for instance, an elderly man complained that a young family friend, who was handing out Republican ballots, had threatened him. The youth blocked his elder and ominously hissed, "Uncle Jake we do not want any democrats to vote."[53]

Buying off voters represented the ultimate expression of the love of smart dealings. An ever-present minority illegally sold their vote—usually for about two dollars—and many smiled at this sneakiness.[54] One Norwegian immigrant reported on a Minnesota state senator who paid the opposing hustlers to tear up their ballots and go home. His smart dealing "was considered clever and not concealed."[55] Yet young adults were seen as more honest, law-abiding, and naive, and many thought they were less likely to sell their tickets. Though there is very little evidence of anyone bragging about selling their ballots (for obvious reasons), there are particularly few examples of young people doing so. Young adults enjoyed many of the sneaky battles of nineteenth-century partisan warfare, but they were still learning the arts of political corruption and were thought to be less easily bought.[56]

Whether canvassers or hustlers, gin-drinkers or teetotalers, big city "sporting men" or country store electioneers, a large bloc of young adults participated in the doubly American mixture of salesmanship and democracy. While hustling ballots might seem more active than merely voting, in reality it represented a step away from the full emersion in public politics, anticipated by youths and enjoyed by virgin voters. Like a business, the front end of political persuasions seemed open and extroverted, but the back end fed into a more covert world. As young people aged and as they climbed party ladders, their politics moved away from noisy bandstands and roaring town squares to lamplit grocery store bars and cobwebbed printing rooms. There was a low bar for entry into the world of hustling and canvassing, but it marked the beginning of a climb away from the public politics of youth.

Looking Out for the Little Fellow

Most young adults advocated for their parties in a quieter fashion. Many retraced the steps that had led them into the world of rallies and elections, back toward the families that pointed them towards politics as children. While fifteen- or twenty-one-year-olds seemed particularly focused on the world outside their home, Americans in their twenties began to consider how they might influence the rising crop of younger brothers and sisters.

One blunt editorial explained how they could do so. Following a close, ugly defeat in the 1884 presidential election, the Republican *American Reformer* explained exactly how new voters were created. Looking to its youthful audience, the paper editorialized, "It's the 'big fellow' that holds the admiration and allegiance of the 'little fellow'" and does more to frame his politics than "teachers or parents or books."[57] If the party hoped for virgin voters next time (and about a thousand more Republicans in New York would have swung that election), it had better get the "big fellow" and the "little fellow" talking.[58]

The *American Reformer* hinted at a forgotten truth about popular politics. Dividing the electorate into generations was the wrong way to reach out to that "little fellow." Instead, the better increment to subdivide citizens, the fundamental unit of partisan demographics, was the quarter-generation. A twenty-two-year-old stood the best chance of getting a seventeen-year-old reading the papers, and a twenty-six-year-old made an ideal escort for a virgin voter. Rising young people often listened most attentively to the lobbying of men and women roughly five years their senior.

Everyone seemed to have an older sibling or friend who could make politics feel lively and accessible. Susan Bradford, still deciphering the meaning of partisanship in Florida in her late teens, shared her family's mansion with a strident brother-in-law who provoked partisan debates at the dinner table.[59] When William Saunders Brown wandered into the Virginia woods to fell the trees for his "Clay Pole," a friend nine years his senior carried the ax.[60] And James Witham, that contrarian farmers' rights supporter who argued politics on midwestern trains, hung out with a group of older friends in rural Iowa. They frequently debated the issues, though Witham's buddies were "pretty rough company" and could make him "decidedly uncomfortable" when they disagreed.[61] Which, knowing Witham, was frequently.

These persuaders were usually about five years older than the friends they influenced. They had seen one more presidential election and were a step further into work, marriage, and parenthood. They often had a particularly strong effect on Americans in their late teens who no longer received much instruction from their parents. Though these older peers never had the same formative influence as one's mother or father, they stood as encouraging markers along the path to politics, waving on youths and virgin voters.

Casual mixing of age groups enabled this kind of persuasion, and campaigners worked to create the right blend in political clubs. Marching companies rarely set age limits. Instead, their rosters show a healthy mix of youths and young adults.[62] Though they won attention with flashy public rallies, clubs also drew together different age groups for smoke-filled, whiskey-soaked late-night meetings in their rented headquarters.[63] Perhaps most important, the bonds between clubs members were as mixed as their ages. Some knew each other well, but others were only casual acquaintances.[64] These loose bonds helped persuade young Americans to imitate their immediate elders.

Children's fiction reflected the habit of older peers guiding the politics of young Americans. Writing for *Harper's Young People* in the early 1880s, Mary Densel published a story about a young girl disguised as a boy who accompanies her brother to a political rally. She is cheered by clubs of bois-terous young men for getting involved while so young; they holler that there is "nothing like getting boys on the right side."[65] In Charles Leland's *Pipps among the Wide Awakes*, Mr. Pipps is also guided to participate by older acquaintances. One gives him a speech on the importance of "the Elective Franchise being transmitted unimpaired to the rising generation," while Pipps's "Bruising Friend"—drawn as a massive, bearded fellow—lectures his younger buddy on fighting his way to the voting window.[66]

William Dean Howells became one of these literary persuaders in his mid-twenties. The budding writer had grown beyond his years whining about "the dull pool of my life," hiding from adulthood in his father's print-ing office.[67] After casting his virgin vote he shook himself free from his former gloom. By 1860 Will was an up-and-coming political journalist in Columbus, battling on behalf of the rising Republican Party.[68] To his ambi-tious mustache and imperial he added a narrow, bohemian chin scruff. He even published a poem in his beloved *Atlantic Monthly*. But to win greater fame as a writer, Will realized he should turn his literary talents to guiding the politics of young Americans.

Will's editor convinced him to write a quick campaign biography of Abraham Lincoln. Howells cared little for the candidate and even turned down an opportunity to meet him—though he later moaned that he "missed the greatest chance of my life."[69] The ambitious young man sim-ply wanted the attention (and the money) that came with an easy-to-sell biography. Will poured out the book in little over a week and filled the preface with assurances that he could write something "a great deal better" if he tried.[70] Instead of focusing on Lincoln's policies, Howells aimed his biography at younger readers, stressing the link between youthful aspira-tions and politics. *The Lives and Speeches of Abraham Lincoln and Hannibal Hamlin* stands as an artifact of hungry Will Howells's calculation that per-suading younger Americans to support Lincoln would win him important connections.

Howells's short biography used the words "young" or "youth" twenty-one times in a few dozen pages. Will clearly drew from his own youth, asking readers to empathize with Lincoln as a young man driven by "men-tal exuberance" and "restless ambition," struggling for "his path to man-hood."[71] In a dramatic crescendo, Howells stressed the model of succession that powered the age of popular politics. Will proclaimed that Lincoln's life should inspire students beginning their political lives, young immigrants wandering "toward some Illinois yet further west," and especially "the rustic boy, who is to be President in 1900."[72] In a campaign that courted and won the votes of young westerners, Will hit all the notes the Republican establishment would have wanted him to.

Will Howells's first book demonstrates a logic common to young adult persuaders: he would reach down to younger Americans in exchange for a step up the political ladder. Howells had mostly lost interest in the partisan entertainment his father had raised him to enjoy, but he still saw political involvement as his chance "for a shot" at fame.[73] After Lincoln's victory, Will felt that "I who had written his life ought to have" a political office of his own. In a system powered by patronage, Will Howells used his connections in the Ohio Republican Party and the campaign biography to win a consulate job.[74] He knew that sometimes, lobbying "the little fellow" was the best way for "the big fellow" to impress those even higher up.

Of course, most young adult persuasions were less literary and more personal, aimed at friends or younger siblings. This peer education differed from the long socialization passed down by parents. For the most part, children received their elders' guidance as a neatly wrapped gift, a cohesive tribal identity, and the majority accepted it wholesale. On the other hand, most young Americans were somewhat leery of their friends.[75] They tended to view acquaintances with an attitude of competition or distrust, or as cautionary examples who were taking the wrong paths in life. So while they listened to their political beliefs, young Americans were much more critical of their peers' views. Some, like young Blanche Butler, demanded more political information from her parents to balance out the unreliable news "the girls get round."[76]

If there was one point where young Americans weighed party ideology rationally, it was in partisan chats among young adults. Benjamin Brown Foster, for instance, held heated arguments with his older brother Charles. The two would lie in bed, in their frigid room early in the Maine morning, debating which party was more antislavery in the coming 1848 race.[77] Similarly, Oscar Lawrence Jackson would stage public debates with a clever young Democrat named William Rehren. Jackson and Rehren were good friends and enjoyed testing their new arguments on each other.[78]

Though meaningful, this kind of peer persuasion met striking limitations. Most of the evidence of such interactions comes from the younger person, recording what an older friend or relative imparted. Older persuaders passed down political information, but they did not seem to value such conversations enough to record them. Often they looked up the hierarchy, more fixated on established adults than on aspiring youths. Many enacted, on a lesser scale, Will Howells's exchange of a biography aimed at young people for a political job. Moreover, young adults' efforts could not replace the decades of political socialization most Americans received from their parents. Though more substantive and free-form, peer socialization was also weaker and less intentional, showing the diminishing returns of political persuasion as a voter aged.

Do Not Say You Are Not Comeing Home to Vote

When Mattie Thomas put aside her Bible and her baking to write to her long-distance beau Uriah, her letters ranged from teaching Sunday school to her intense desire to see him to her burning hatred for the Democratic Party. Politics played a central role in this Indiana couple's tumultuous relationship, as it struggled over distance, war, and class. So when twenty-three-year-old Mattie wrote Uriah, with the 1868 election looming and their engagement stretching on indefinitely, she mingled the two campaigns that seemed to define her life.

By the time they were in their mid-twenties, most Americans were married or pledged in serious courtships. But young couples still used politics to help explore the boundaries of these relationships. New husbands felt their vote now counted for two, and wives never had a better chance at influencing a voter. Americans commonly expressed this in jokes, like one comedian's jest that his fiercely partisan mother permitted his father to "go thro the manual labor uv castin the ballot."[79] No longer courting adolescents, showing off their ostentatious political passions, men and women in their twenties treated politics as a chip in the negotiations that measured committed relationships.

Young women walked a blurry line. They were expected to guide the morals of the men in their lives but also to know when to keep out of "worldly affairs." How could they tell where domestic morality ended and political ethics began? Unlike street-corner hustlers, young women's efforts to influence their husbands or beaux were muffled, usually offered in hushed bedroom talks or quiet correspondences, easily drowned out by the thunderous hullabaloo of nineteenth-century politics. But an intimate conversation between newlyweds could carry more weight than the pontifications of a stranger in a country store. Young women's domestic politicking played a crucial role in persuading many men to turn out on Election Day.[80]

Photographs of Uriah Oblinger and Mattie Thomas, the young Indiana couple who let the 1868 presidential election play a key role in their long-distance courtship. Though she herself could not vote, Mattie urged her beau to come home, vote against the hated Democrats, and finally marry her. (Mattie Thomas Oblinger and Uriah Oblinger, Uriah W. Oblinger Family Collection, American Memory, Library of Congress)

When Mattie Thomas met Uriah Oblinger, neither thought much about politics. They knew each other from Sunday school, near Young America, Indiana, in the late 1850s. Uriah was then a handsome, square-headed youth, with bright blue eyes and a bad reputation. Mattie was petite and pretty, with a worried dark gaze, high cheekbones, and big stubborn ears. She wore her glossy black hair up in a complicated Victorian do. Where Uriah had a hot temper that quickly cooled, Mattie simmered with a persistent intensity. The two shared an attraction, but the Civil War intervened.

Uriah enlisted in the Indiana Cavalry and did extraordinarily well in the war. He reveled in the "hard fighting and good running" of cavalry raids and often wished, postwar, that he was still in uniform.[81] But Uriah was not solely focused on the conflict. In May 1864, Mattie Thomas received a surprising letter from her former classmate. Earnestly promising that he was "entirely free from all lady correspondents," Uriah asked for a letter from Mattie, if her parents approved. He closed by swearing that he would write no other lady until she responded.[82]

Mattie wrote back and they began a romance, first by mail and then in person when he returned. The two seemed perfect for each other; Uriah even became a Methodist, joining Mattie in her spirited faith in a better world to come. They spent the year after his discharge in an intimate bubble. She would tease him and tug affectionately on his dangling whiskers; he would box her big ears and pull her onto his lap.[83]

The couple struggled to overcome the divisions between them. Mattie's family was middle class, while Uriah had neither money nor concrete promise. While her parents played a guiding role her life, Uriah's mother had died when he was a boy and his father had been deeply depressed ever since. On top of this, their letters allude to vague, disreputable behavior that Uriah had perpetrated as a youth, before he found Mattie and God and the cavalry.

Uriah could not yet marry Mattie. Though they were pledged to each other, Mattie's father forbade it. Uriah pushed for a date in the future and Mattie evaded. This was typical of mid-nineteenth-century couples, in which the man advocated for marriage while the woman and her family delayed (she had far more to lose, after all).[84] Instead, Uriah needed to earn money and status before they could wed. So he set off "to roam the broad prairies of the beautiful west" until Mattie and her father agreed to a marriage.[85]

Uriah spent three long years wandering the Midwest, working odd jobs. He cut corn, dug ditches, peddled goods, and made, it seems, no progress toward financial stability. He would return to Indiana for a few months each year, but mostly their relationship lived on in yearning, heartrending letters. Uriah would write from makeshift camps in frontier Minnesota, a rifle by his side and a good dog on watch, and Mattie would respond from the stifling comfort of her parents' kitchen. They exchanged photographs, reminisced about their time together, and promised kisses (and more) when they were next together. Mattie, or her father, continuously pushed back the date when they could wed, from 1866, to '67, to '68.

By the summer of 1868 the couple was trapped in an unspoken standoff. Mattie's father still would not permit her to marry, and she was not about to disobey him. Uriah grumbled that her father was "glad that I am absent" and vaguely threatened that he could not stand "this single wretchedness" much longer.[86] But he was no closer to the wealth and stability he needed to win her family's approval. The only leverage Uriah had was distance; he implied he would stay away from Indiana until she acquiesced to marry. Mattie desperately wanted to see Uriah but could not yet offer him the one thing he wanted. As the tension grew in their seemingly unending courtship, the 1868 presidential campaign played a convenient and surprising role.

Mattie and Uriah were both Republicans, or more accurately, they both hated Democrats, whom they usually referred to as "copperheads" or "rebels." The central issue for both was not slavery, race, or an active federal government but the punishment of the South and the prevention of another war. Uriah bragged to Mattie that when a Democratic "copper-johnson" tried to win his vote in a Minnesota settlement, he threatened to murder the hustler, hissing, "I could kill him and all others like him with better grace than I ever shot a Johnny."[87] Mattie agreed that the conflict had not been resolved in 1865 and spent the rest of the decade worrying that a big Democratic win would mean "war here again among us."[88] Both fit perfectly into the paranoid postwar climate: while Grant's campaign urged "Let us have peace," many felt that another war was more likely.[89]

So Mattie Thomas began a campaign of her own as summer ended in 1868. If she could not bring Uriah back to marry, she might retrieve him to vote. For Mattie, the coming campaign did a double duty. She genuinely hated the Democrats and prayed for Grant's victory, but she also hoped to see "Uriah coming with his bright blue eyes danceing."[90] She displayed this overlap between her political and romantic self by angrily promising her family that she would "leave this Copper County."[91] She hoped to get out of Democratic Cass County and also to live with Uriah in a cottage some-where in the West, bundling together her romantic and political goals.[92] Mattie also knew Uriah well, and though he resolved to stay away, he often reminded her, "You know how easily persuaded I am."[93]

At first Mattie tried to use political jealousy to bring Uriah home to vote. In one letter she mentioned a run-in with a mutual acquaintance, an underage Democrat who taunted Mattie, saying that if he were old enough he would vote just to cancel out Uriah's ballot (and, by extension, hers). Mattie told Uriah how she spat back that the boy should have to "fight the Rebels" before he voted Democratic.[94] A few weeks later she was more direct, nudging Uriah, "I fear you will have trouble in getting to Vote by staying away so long."[95]

Uriah stayed away, trying to peddle pumps in Illinois. Either he still hoped to force Mattie to consent to a fall marriage or he did not notice her attempts to persuade him to return. So in early September, as the weather cooled and the campaign warmed, Mattie made one strident bid to bring him home. In a flurry of frustrated and partisan letters, she warned that not coming home would be the same as voting "on the rebles side," adding that it would be easier for him to "cast your ballot than shoulder a musket." In the most forceful tone she had ever mustered, Mattie urged, "Uriah I would feel real vexed if you would not vote this fall. . . . Do not say you are not comeing home to vote." She concluded this letter, which had stomped well beyond the bounds of ladylike diffidence, "Do not get offended at what I have said for you know I am true blue . . . your true and devoted Mattie."[96] If her message had not been clear enough, she added, as a final postscript, "Come soon."

Mattie's firm words broke their standoff. Uriah came home and voted, and their tortured letters ceased. In addition to having financial concerns for the couple, Mattie's father had worried that Uriah would not treat his daughter well but would "keep me at home."[97] Perhaps Uriah's responsiveness to Mattie's pleas won him some credit and eventual permission to marry. When Uriah next took up his pen, a few months after Grant's victory, it was to contact the preacher who would officiate at their wedding.[98]

I Was Young Once

Nineteenth-century politicking got no quieter than the scratch of Mattie Thomas's pen, inking her romantic and partisan emotions in carefully ruled letters to Uriah. Such intimate politics are easy to overlook, buried deep in personal relationships. Historians are lucky that Mattie Thomas was not the type to whisper.

By contrast, politics rarely boomed louder than that shoot-out in Baltimore, with a barrage of gunfire shaking the Light Street polling place. The tumult that left Adam Kyle and Basil Elmore dead echoed through the newspaper network and into several high-profile trials. Such violence, though not frequent, raised the volume of even the most tranquil American elections.

What do the yearning letters of an Indiana Sunday school teacher have to do with the execution of a wealthy hustler in a Baltimore candy shop? Through shoot-outs or weddings, Americans in the final years of their youth persuaded others to participate in popular politics. While Adam Kyle worked as an overt arm of a political movement and Mattie Thomas lobbied with more tangled motives, both sought to determine the actions of the young people around them. In the last step before maturity, young adults often formed political habits that would last the rest of their lives, shaped by the lobbying of their friends, their loved ones, and absolute strangers.

How many women were willing, like Mattie, to put such pressure on the men in their lives? And how many men strolled to the polls with revolvers rattling in their coats? Probably not many. In their final sprint toward maturity, young Americans spread out across the track. Some burst ahead, diving into campaign organizations and personal lobbying; some turned to encourage other runners; and some stopped completely. Unlike the political socialization of children, which was usually mandatory, young adults chose their paths. In their final steps, many passed along their political excitement before stumbling off into adulthood. Those who continued to pursue partisanship, more than anyone else in society, helped sustain the age of popular politics by transmitting it to rising youths.

And then, sometime after their late twenties, young people stopped being young. This happened sooner for some and later for others. There was no clear age line in the culture, but most agreed that the transition took place somewhere between twenty-five and thirty. (Surprisingly, the point of change seems roughly the same as it is today, despite very different demographics.) Americans generally considered young people unsettled and vacillating, jumping from identity to identity and job to job. When they developed "fixed purposes and a settled vocation," they were no longer young.[99] Politics showed this transformation. Democracy stopped seeming so new and enticing, at least for native-born Americans. In club rosters and voting lists, virgin voters were almost all under thirty; older first-timers were mostly born overseas.[100]

One clear sign that an American was no longer young was that he or she began to recruit the next generation. Young people tended to look up the age hierarchy and lacked a collective identity or desire to uplift their generation. Looking down the party ladder to recruit young people usually meant that you were no longer one of them.

Abraham Lincoln acknowledged this switch when he counseled his friend William Herndon to recruit the "shrewd, wild boys" of Springfield in 1848. Nearing forty, then-congressman Lincoln wrote, "I suppose I am now one of the old men . . . but I was young once." Youth evaporated somewhere between twenty-nine-year-old Herndon and thirty-nine-year-old Lincoln. When he was young, Lincoln recalled, he had focused on his own rise, angling to promote himself in any way he could. But now, "merely by being older," Lincoln found nothing more satisfying than knowing that "my young friends at home are doing battle in the contest." The two men were on opposite sides of some great political prism, with Herndon looking up to the bosses and his Lincoln looking down to the b'hoys.[101]

Who else was welcoming young voters, and what did they want? For most of their lives, young Americans—be they Oscar Lawrence Jackson, Susan Bradford, Will Howells, or Mattie Thomas—headed out into the public world of politics. What would they find as they entered the private club of party machines? Were adult politicians, as Benjamin Brown Foster put it, "spiders" preying on young men's votes? Or were they representatives, looking out for this uncertain constituency? Which stereotype—the sneaky boss or the wise statesman—beckoned young Americans into politics?

5 » Every One Is Fifty

Stepping back from public did not mean abandoning politics. Samuel Tilden, an odd little frog of a man, directed campaigns, tallied margins, and mobilized voters, all from the ornate seclusion of his Manhattan mansion. More than any other leader, Tilden participated in the span of popular politics from the 1830s through the 1880s. And though hidden away in the cloistered elegance of Gramercy Park, Tilden knew how to draw young Americans out into politics.[1]

The "Sage of Gramercy" would never bring a revolver to a polling place, or ride his horse through an icy river, or even flirt with Democratic ladies at torchlit processions. Since his youth Tilden had been weird and retiring: a chronic hypochondriac who complained of Victorian afflictions like "corrugated tongue," a brilliant student who dropped out of Yale because he disliked the food, a passionate Democrat for whom the party served as "wife, children, and church."[2] But he showed an unrivaled grasp of youth politics. While young people expressed their aspirations by heading out to join the noisy rallies, men like Tilden stepped back from the raucous public, binding their individual enthusiasms into something larger.

Tilden was once one of those American boys for whom politics was an engrossing sport. His family ran a country store in the Hudson valley in the 1820s, frequented by many of the founders of the Democratic Party. His father would sit young Samuel on the counter and have him explain the finer points of party ideology to Martin Van Buren or William Cullen Bryant. Tilden spent his teens giving speeches against the Bank of the United States, moneyed privilege, and "centralism," his lifelong foe.[3] He grew into a political mastermind. As an adult he loved organization, wooing editors, uniting feuding factions, and calculating likely turnouts. When he ran for governor of New York, Tilden not only won but estimated his margin of victory almost to the voter.[4]

In private letters and whispered deals, Tilden explained that nineteenth-century campaigning meant appealing to the young. Over and over Tilden hammered home three crucial points: politicians relied on young supporters, first-timers were most useful to parties out of power, and winning over young Americans was not that easy.

The "Sage" explained the need for young supporters in a pamphlet he circulated plotting the 1868 presidential campaign. Putting decades of experience into print, Tilden stressed that "*fresh* and unwearied *young* men, just coming upon the stage of action," made better campaigners than older partisans, who became demanding, expensive, and lazy as they aged.[5] Young partisans, Tilden found, brought "zeal, persevering and patient energy."[6]

Tilden spoke for the Democrats, but most organizations over the age of popular politics agreed on the need for youth. Politicians knew that bringing in first-timers was a better bet than luring unreliable independents with cash or beer. Most leaders preferred attracting young supporters to doling out "2 dollar bills to purchase floaters."[7] They all loudly proclaimed, usually with no evidence, that their movement was the true "party of young men."[8]

While all politicians agreed that they wanted young supporters, some were more desperate than others. Parties in power—the "Ins"—rarely bothered to reach beyond old allies to excited (but annoying) twenty-one-year-olds. Parties in opposition—the "Outs"—who were casting about for a path to victory were more likely to value young voters, and to incorporate young ladies as well, especially if they believed that the next election would bring them into office. Samuel Tilden understood how young men and women could help a rising opposition party. Acknowledging that in 1868 his Democrats had been "a long time out of power," the Sage of Gramercy declared, "We must ally the Democracy with the future. We must strike the roots of its growth into fresh soils."[9]

From the dawning of the age of popular politics until the 1880s, these "Ascendant Outs" made alternating bids for young voters. At first they treated young Americans as a useful device, a crowbar to help pry their rivals from office, lacking interests of their own. Parties only slowly learned to tailor their appeals to young people's specific needs. Instead, "Outs" often lectured young audiences about the corruption of those in power, surely the most common issue invoked in nineteenth-century elections.

This brings up the Sage of Gramercy's third insight. In an 1874 address to the Young Men's Democratic Club of New York—an elite group, toasting Tilden in Delmonico's grand dining room—the awkward politico told his audience about a conversation he had with an elder statesman of the party. The two leaders agreed that the Democrats should promote their most promising young members. Tilden then asked the politician to list his favorite new leaders. After listening to the roster of rising stars, Tilden informed the boss—in his cold and withering way—that everyone he named was middle-aged.[10] He scolded, "You are fifty, and I am fifty, and every one is fifty."[11]

Attracting young people was always a struggle. Elite leaders looked down at new generations from atop tall hierarchies, over which they had limited control. Nineteenth-century political parties were massive contraptions, not easily operated by deliberate leadership.[12] Despite the cliché, parties were not machines, and politicians were not mechanics; they could never really engineer millions of young people's intimate, disorganized political awakenings, driven by deeply personal motivations.

Not that politicians didn't try, desperately, to bring in new supporters. There was a sixty-year learning curve for politicians appealing to young voters. Unlike the twenty-one-year-olds who entered democracy in very similar ways from 1840 to 1890, politicians' tricks evolved over the age of popular politics. Because campaigners were so distant from the average young voter, however, their improvements did not change the nature of popular politics. Instead, each successive race displayed campaign architects' building awareness of young people's unique importance.

These alternating appeals sketch a survey of American political history. From the Whig "whirlwind" of 1840 to the Young American Democrats of the 1840s, the Wide Awake Republicans before the Civil War, and the rejuvenating Democrats in the 1870s, parties out of power demonstrated an ever-improving understanding of young Americans. These alternating parties built on previous tactics until something changed dramatically in the mid-1870s. For the rest of the century, Ins and Outs faced off in an increasingly fervent—and ultimately destructive—struggle to determine what role young people should play in democracy.

On the Advice of Our Elders

Getting around America in 1840 was not easy. The breakthrough technologies of the era were still fractured and disjointed. John Parsons—a witty, big-chinned graduate of the University of Virginia—learned this as he headed west on a postschool wander year. The first leg of John's trip, from Virginia to Baltimore, meant boarding three trains, two coaches, and a steamboat.[13] Getting out to his cousin in Indiana involved many more coal-chomping, soot-spewing vehicles. Along the way he encountered something as novel as all those chugging machines, observing a first in U.S. history: a nationwide populist political campaign, targeted especially toward young people, shouting at him from every junction and way station.[14]

John had just happened to wander into the Whig Party's Young Men's Convention in Baltimore. The rising movement had already nominated William Henry Harrison for president, but, convinced that 1840 would be their year, party leaders gathered their young supporters into a massive convention. John drifted through a fluttering sea of "10,000 handkerchiefs waved by the fair daughters of the city" and marveled at the complicated floats, the booming cannons, and the "parades of unmeaning contrivances." Political parties had kicked off campaigns with big rallies for decades, but this one was uniquely fixated on the young.[15] The president of the convention specifically called forth "the young men of half a continent," announcing, "The avalanche of the people is here."[16]

Campaigners seemed to chase Parsons west as he hopped from carriage to train to steamboat. On a stagecoach heading over the Appalachians, he happened to sit next to Whig congressman Robert P. Letcher. The fat-faced, long-haired Kentuckian was known for his common touch and skill with the fiddle, which he used to drown out rivals at debates. The jovial Letcher lectured John about William Henry Harrison, peppering him with arguments beginning and ending with "My young sir."[17]

Out in Indiana, the lobbying grew even more aggressive. An elderly preacher practically dragged Parsons to a "monster Whig barbecue," "young sir-ing" him all the way. At that rally Parsons watched farmers drain barrels of hard cider from shared tin cups and devour bubbling cauldrons of meaty, spiced burgoo stew. He also noted how unusually pushy politicians seemed that year. Even Indiana senator Albert S. White stooped to pandering, speaking from the back of a wagon before a crowd of "young boys who had left their games of marbles and mumble-peg to come to the meeting."[18]

The campaign that followed John Parsons west in the summer of 1840 was something genuinely new in American culture. Politicians had organized barbecues for ages, going back to an English tradition in which aristocrats treated local peasants to a feast.[19] But those events had affirmed the distance between the elites providing the food and the deferential commoners eating passively. As a newly democratic culture built up over the 1830s, parties experimented with rallying active young supporters. Nine years before John Parsons wandered through the Whigs' Young Men's Convention, for instance, another rally in Baltimore called forth young men, but they still justified their assembling "on the advice of our elders." They spent much of that rally debating whether they were "overstepping the modesty which befits our age" by actively campaigning.[20] Elite politicians were slowly beginning to see the utility of fiery young activists in the 1830s but still felt the need to justify their audacity. That would change, soon enough.

Before 1840, enthusiastic young partisans often struggled to assert their role in political life. In Philadelphia's black community—which had just lost the right to vote with a new Pennsylvania constitution in 1838—elders warned about overzealous youths. In such a crisis, Philadelphia's African Americans must not look to "inexperienced, hasty, immature" young men to determine "the destinies of our people," warned a letter in the *Colored American*.[21] Pushing back, a younger black writer pointed to all the threats facing their community and demanded to know why his peers should wait until they were forty or fifty to try to do something about them. Capturing the rising passions of young people in the later 1830s, the letter writer promised, "We will not be put down."[22]

Something changed around 1840. Politicians formerly accused of trying to "put down" young people began calling upon them to rise up instead. A population of young men and women had grown up watching the high-profile political battles of the 1830s and were ready to get involved. While earlier generations tended to see politics as an existential battle between good and evil, the young people socialized in the 1830s believed that democracy meant never-ending, always-entertaining competition.[23] And now members of a new party, the Whigs, felt confident that Democratic corruption and the gnawing depression would bring them victory.[24] Going into the 1840 election, with food prices skyrocketing and the Van Buren administration pilloried as a champagne-swilling old guard, the Whigs hoped these rising young voters would lift them up.[25]

To win in 1840, Whig leaders saw that they needed a united, excited campaign. For too long, Massachusetts congressman Leverett Saltonstall wrote to his wife, the party had attacked the Democrats individually, "*careening* upon their flanks, charging upon them with desperation but without system."[26] To unite against the Democratic Ins, Whigs launched a popular movement that would "bring out the hurra boys."[27] They put twenty-nine-year-old Horace Greeley in charge of their campaign publication, the *Log Cabin*, which reached 90,000 readers nationwide.[28] The brilliant, utopian, odd young editor "set the campaign to music" with catchy, funny, biting songs that enthralled a new generation expecting entertainment from politics.[29] With Greeley's help, the Whigs launched a race so loud that it set the tone for every political campaign since.

The race relied on many of the tricks that would drive youth politics for the next several decades. The Whigs organized a nationally coherent campaign, applying the same basic techniques from Massachusetts to Georgia to Ohio, creating the first election in which the presidential turnout exceeded the local vote.[30] They lobbied new voters with unprecedented confidence, reaching out to young Americans without apology. There was no more fear of "overstepping the modesty" expected of young people; instead parties began to speak directly to the concerns of rising generations. At one Philadelphia rally, speakers accused the Democrats of causing the depression and making it impossible for "young men to make an honest living."[31] Though vague, even this appeal represented a new way of viewing youth politics, by acknowledging that the young had their own interests.

The same principle that had Whig politicians pouring cider for John Parsons led to new roles for American women as well. Large numbers of young women marched in demonstrations—costumed as allegorical figures—or prepared banners, floats, and "collations" of cold foods (even then, barbecuing was a man's job). As rising Outs, the Whigs tried to bring in any unrealized advantages, part of their strategy of "keeping in play every mind and every hand," as Congressman Saltonstall told his wife.[32] Democrats denounced this as "the silliest political exploitation this country ever witnessed" and whined that campaigning distracted young women from their "sacred domestic routine" but tried to copy it nonetheless.[33]

Historians often point to the ironies of 1840. A party that had scoffed at democracy ran a wildly populist campaign. A movement that often preached temperance rolled out thousands of barrels of booze. The elite, aging William Henry Harrison attacked Martin Van Buren—younger, poorer, and the only president who spoke English as his second language—as the establishment candidate. Most ironic of all: the Whig whirlwind came to a terrible halt just thirty-one days after inauguration, when Harrison dropped dead. The vice president, "His Accidency" John Tyler, turned out to oppose most of the Whigs' big ideas.

Yet more than simple irony caused these odd results. These twists grew from the big change that the 1840 race heralded: politicians' ability to campaign had surpassed their ability to govern. It was easier, it turned out, to get up a wild political spectacle than it was to override a presidential

Political ribbons, a relatively new device in the 1840s, were aimed at young Americans. The first advertises the Young Men's National Whig Convention in Baltimore that John Parsons wandered through in 1840. The second promotes a young Whig convention in support of Henry Clay in 1844, relying on the Whigs' use of the raccoon as their mascot (partially because raccoons were scrappy survivors and partially in contrast to the Democrats' use of a fox as their mascot at the time). The third endorses the Native American Republicans' anti-immigration movement of 1844, appealing specifically to young voters by suggesting that only those with twenty-one years of citizenship deserved access to the ballot box. (From the Collections of the Division of Political History, National Museum of American History, Smithsonian Institution, Washington, D.C.)

veto. Just as the hard cider campaign marked the moment when national turnout surpassed local races, 1840 signaled the point when campaign fun outstripped government action, especially on the presidential level. By the same token, Whig politicians' use of young people against their enemies exceeded their ability to offer those new voters anything concrete in exchange. The elders who "young sir-ed" John Parsons with political arguments suggested little that might actually improve his life. The next step, after the breakthrough of 1840, was for a party to appeal to the real needs of young Americans.

Young America and Old Fogeys

Democratic leaders launched their own drive for youth in the mid-1840s, a political, cultural, and literary appeal they called "Young America." This new vision for American greatness stressed youth both literally, as an appeal to new voters, and figuratively, evoking a youthful, energetic nationalism to rival the hidebound regimes of "Old Europe."[34] Young America was primarily a metaphor, an "allusion to youth, purity, and freshness," an idealistic vision for a maturing nation.[35]

The new guard of Young Americans—men like Samuel Tilden, born during the 1812 war and rising to power in their thirties—saw themselves as incoming Outs, reclaiming their nation from the Whigs' phony populism. Their brief sojourn in opposition allowed them to reinvent themselves for a younger audience. John L. O'Sullivan, coiner of the phrase "Manifest Destiny," artfully compared his progressive movement to a snake. Time out of office had rubbed off the dead skin of backward-looking Democrats—old Jacksonians who picked unnecessary fights, seemed suspicious of the very idea of government, and rarely looked toward the future—so that a rising generation of "unsophisticated youth can come forward."[36]

So the Democratic Party, out of power for only a few years, borrowed from the Whigs' 1840 campaign and recast itself as the underdog looking to move forward. In 1844 the dark-horse candidate James K. Polk ran as "Young Hickory" and portrayed the oldest political party in the country as the rising "Young Democracy." In Ohio, Democrats claimed that the Whigs were "behind the age," while progressive Young Americans were "in keeping with the spirit of the times."[37] In Virginia, campaigners asserted that they represented "new youth," "new era," and "new life."[38] Even their campaign songs took on a youthful tempo: Democrats distributed lively "quicksteps" and "gallopades," unlike the plodding marches of their earlier campaigns.[39]

Democratic politicians fit their campaign into the youthful new culture of the "roaring forties." At a time of "go-ahead" young people, technological breakthroughs, and a new faith in national progress, Young Americans trumpeted the Democratic Party as "buoyant and bracing for the future."[40] They cast their Whig rivals as atavistic old Federalists, a zombie party refusing to die, the very embodiment of that new slight: Old Fogeys.[41]

Much of their talk was pandering, but Young Americans found something very concrete to offer young people: western lands. As president, Polk picked a fight with Mexico and ultimately won what would become

California, Nevada, Utah, Arizona, New Mexico, Colorado, and Wyoming. All that new territory let rootless young citizens envision the West as their birthright, an escape valve for when they felt trapped in the crowded East.[42] Though not initially intended for young people, the Democratic Party now had something real with which to entice all of those anxious youths stifled by the uncertainties of nineteenth-century life. It was the closest any party had gotten to a tangible offer to young people. Some prominent Young Americans even began to talk about free homes for settlers, a policy that would benefit rootless young people most of all.[43]

The Young America movement was not necessarily a movement of young Americans. Most of its leaders were in their thirties or forties—young for politicians but still twice the age of the average American. Some of its most prominent supporters were old frontier warriors, contemporaries of Andrew Jackson like Thomas Hart Benton and Sam Houston. The movement was always strongest as a political faction in Washington and as a literary movement in New York; it did not find much mention in the diaries of nineteen-year-olds across the country. Young America revitalized the Democratic Party and reached out to young people in innovative ways, bringing a progressive worldview and concrete offerings, but it did not establish the kind of campaign organizations, on the ground, that could continuously filter virgin voters into the party.

Republicans Wake Up

The first volley of youth-focused Outs—the Whigs of 1840—used young people's economic anxieties to overthrow the status quo. The second round—Democratic Young Americans—fired back with talk of progress, generation, and land. It was not until the third volley, a meteoric party rising in the 1850s, that a movement incorporated all of these tricks into the most successful bid for youth support.

The Republican Party was organized in 1854 and seized two branches of government within six years, rising so quickly that many forget it was ever a third party. During the unstable 1850s, the movement coalesced out of splinter groups and fading factions. These groups shared an opposition to the extension of slavery and a frustrated insistence that a southern conspiracy blocked the northern majority's rightful dominance. They hoped to leave behind old alliances and build a new movement among young voters. It is no coincidence that the best-organized bid for youth support came from this party rapidly rising from nonexistence to dominance.[44]

As their first presidential candidate, Republicans chose the adventur-ous John C. Frémont. The illegitimate son of a dashing French immigrant, Frémont gained national fame exploring the West and conquering Cali-fornia. He had eloped with the blue-eyed, raven-haired Jessie Benton, the brilliant and beautiful daughter of the tough old Jacksonian Thomas Hart Benton. Senator Benton raised his girl to speak five languages, attend cab-inet meetings, and orchestrate campaigns. The couple promised youth, vigor, Democratic connections, and romantic adventure.[45] The fact that Frémont was just forty-three and Jessie barely thirty further appealed to a new generation.[46]

Of all of Frémont's strengths as a candidate, Republican leaders consid-ered inexperience his most valuable asset. He was, the now-middle-aged Horace Greeley bragged, the "merest baby in politics," allowing the party to move beyond the vicious partisan battles of the last decade.[47] The lead-ers who guided the Republican Party made newness their watchword in 1856; like the Young Americans before them, they used "new" and "young" interchangeably. In their letters, prominent politicians all referred to Fré-mont as a "*new man*."[48] This young face might bring in young voters, an-other Republican newspaperman cheered; "a new man and a new party will take thousands!"[49]

Not only was John C. Frémont young and dashing, but his dramatic ca-reer summiting western mountains also allowed Republicans to cash in on a decade of expansionist Young American rhetoric. The *New York Times*—a stuffy paper read mostly by men who would hardly venture above Forty-Second Street, let alone across the Rockies—boasted that the intrepid explorer was the very "embodiement of the spirit of Young America."[50] Republicans distanced themselves from the Whigs' earlier caution about western expansion and even began to talk about free homes, a movement formerly associated with Democrats.[51] The Republicans' appropriation of the Young American rhetoric particularly spoke to youths "who are about to become voters" and might not remember a time when such appeals were distinctly Democratic.[52]

Unfortunately for Frémont, James Buchanan, perhaps the stodgiest president in American history (before Benjamin Harrison, at least), won a weak plurality and almost all electoral votes outside of the upper North. Republicans had been excited, but they lacked strong ground operations, while the Democrats benefited from established campaign techniques despite their dull candidate. A third organization, the nativist American Party, split the anti-Democratic popular majority. Having existed for only two years, the Republicans simply had not yet been able to thoroughly socialize enough young people to give their virgin votes to the new movement. Suffering from this lag time, the Republicans considered themselves lucky to achieve a "Victorious Defeat" and looked forward to 1860.[53]

Republican politicians had studied the previous round of rising Outs, borrowing the Young Americans' generational stirring and western expansion. Yet in their haste to learn from the Democrats, the Republican Party forgot many of the tricks the Whigs had debuted back in 1840. Reflecting on the 1856 defeat, one Massachusetts Republican wrote, "We were a sort of mob, unorganized, contending with a well drilled and bold enemy."[54] He sounded like the Whigs of the late 1830s who chastised their party for operating "with desperation but without system."[55] Finally in 1860, Republican politicians reached out to young men with both youthful rhetoric and a new type of "systematic organization."[56] Combining the lessons of two generations of rising Outs, the Republicans launched an unprecedented drive for young supporters.

It all began in the spring of 1860, when a few young clerks at Hartford's rifle factories started working as bodyguards for Republican speakers. When the brawling Kentucky emancipationist Cassius M. Clay spoke in town, one of his young guards supposedly used his torch to clobber a hostile Democrat. The story spread. Soon the group began holding rowdy meetings above a local drugstore, wearing shiny black capes to rallies, and calling themselves the "Wide Awakes." The strange club—made up of political novices in their early twenties—began to promote its movement through newspapers and pamphlets. In their circulars participants self-consciously sold themselves as rising young Outs, working to bring about Republican "ascendancy."[57]

The Wide Awakes incited political passions in an innovative way. Their torchlit demonstrations presented the dramatic image of hundreds of stern young men, clad in dark, shimmering uniforms, marching in unison to a stirring drumbeat. Instead of the "spontaneous hullabaloo" of the drunken Whigs of 1840, the militaristic Wide Awakes signaled a more serious young manhood, appealing to northerners who felt emasculated by years of submitting to the Slave Power.[58] They deliberately targeted young people, calling massive crowds of youths to "wake up" and helping to organize roughly 1,000 Wide Awake companies from Maine to San Francisco.[59] By the summer, most Americans believed—incorrectly—that there were at least 500,000 Wide Awakes in the nation.[60]

Their movement presented the Republican establishment with an unwieldy gift. The Wide Awakes debuted a bold campaign model that inspired new voters but also raised a new question: could party leadership collaborate with a grassroots movement led by a twenty-three-year-old? Republicans faced Samuel Tilden's challenge: were they dexterous enough to incorporate an excited, youthful movement into their existing hierarchy?

At first, many were hostile. The Wide Awakes had a bad habit of congregating, uninvited, before the homes of prominent Republicans late at night, waking leaders with brass bands, stinking torches, and unrehearsed serenades. Politicians disapproved. The gifted German stump speaker Carl Schurz, campaigning for the Republicans throughout the Midwest, complained to his wife that Wide Awake troops seemed to trail him from town to town, hollering outside whatever inn he was boarding at that night.[61] Lincoln's former rival William H. Seward was famously fond of a quiet cigar and a good night's rest. Beloved by the Wide Awakes, Seward frequently stuck his head out a window and begged noisy companies to "allow me to go to sleep."[62]

Yet top Republican organizers recognized that the Wide Awakes were a resource they could not afford to squander.[63] Thurlow Weed, the party's best strategist, called on his Republicans to remember that they were still the Outs and needed the support of young "Wide Awakes by the hundreds and thousands."[64] So Seward stopped shushing Wide Awakes and instead became their loudest supporter. In a late-summer speaking tour, Seward complimented massive crowds of youths in bustling cities and towns from Michigan to Kansas. He brought his fifteen-year-old daughter, Fanny, along; she was mesmerized by the crowds of uniformed young men.[65] In the past, such a movement was not possible, Seward shouted, but the Wide Awakes were rising and "none but Republicans will be born in the United States after the year 1860."[66]

No politician courted the young Wide Awakes with more enthusiasm than Charles Sumner. The crusading senator spoke to multiple Wide Awake companies each week in the final days of campaigning. Sumner made a particularly moving icon: the brutal beating he had suffered on the Senate floor in 1856 fed young northerners' frustrated desire to answer cowardly fire-eating Democrats. Sumner stoked their fury, goading young Wide Awakes to "leap forward in defense of Northern rights."[67] This appeal worked. When George Templeton Strong happened upon a Manhattan Wide Awake rally, he decided that "the North must assert its rights, now, and take the consequences" and walked away musing, "I think I'll vote the Republican ticket next Tuesday."[68]

While everything else about American politics seemed to be crumbling in 1860, the Wide Awakes established a model for youth-oriented campaigns that would be copied by most parties, in most major elections, over the next few decades. They blended the expectant anxiety of ascendant Outs with a militaristic organization and broad lessons drawn from past Whig and Democratic races. Observers constantly compared the 1860 campaign to "the good old days of 1840," and the election even topped 1840's record-breaking turnout rate, drawing 81.2 percent of eligible voters nationwide.[69] But the Wide Awakes also built on Democratic advances, appealing to the kind of generational excitement previously seen "in the anatomy of Young America."[70] Their iconography—an open eye, talk of throwing off past stupor—played on the same progressive notes with which Democrats had previously enchanted Young Americans. Replicating the success of the Wide Awakes became a goal that motivated politicos for the rest of the age of popular politics.

The Charm of Novelty

Seward's claim that "none but Republicans" would be born after 1860 turned out to be less ridiculous than it sounded. The upheavals of the Civil War threw off the wobbly cycle of party politics, attracting millions of young northerners and freed slaves to the Republican Party. Radicals' calls for a "hard war" on the Confederacy helped enforce the view—promoted by the Wide Awakes—that their party spoke for a vengeful northern masculinity. At the same time, the Union army served as a gigantic recruiting machine for the Republicans. Three out of every four Union soldiers who voted in 1864 supported Lincoln, and many put down lifelong roots in the Republican Party.[71] In addition, Reconstruction introduced millions of African American Republicans in states—South Carolina, Mississippi, Florida—where the party simply had not existed before.

The war and its aftermath caused an unusual period of one-party dominance. During the rest of the age of popular politics, control of the House of Representatives changed every three years on average. But from 1861 to 1875, the Republicans held the majority for fourteen years straight. And they occupied the White House from 1861 to 1885, excluding Andrew Johnson's accidental tenure after the assassination of Lincoln.

These years also marked, not coincidentally, William Dean Howells's rise to national prominence. Will moved to the heart of the American literary establishment in Boston. By 1871 he was actually editing the *Atlantic Monthly*, the publication he had idealized as an isolated, literary boy. He had made it. He grew a tired mustache, gained a respectable belly (expanding in each photograph), and published his best novels. And at each step along the way, politics helped.

It was not clear, when Will Howells's father was barely able to feed his family by printing a Republican paper in the 1850s, that they were joining a coming dynasty. To be a well-liked Ohio Republican in the Gilded Age was a bit like being a Virginia landowner in the Early Republic: it meant connections to the men who ran the nation. The Howellses did not have the wealth (nor certainly the slaves) of a Virginia planter, but they had the connections, and Will built on his father's ties. He assisted the careers of the men who won the presidency in each election from 1860 until 1884. As editor of the premier journal for educated Republicans, Howells was sought by Ulysses S. Grant, Rutherford B. Hayes, James A. Garfield, Edwin Stanton, Salmon Chase, and a host of other Buckeye Republicans for his counsel and friendship.[72]

As he aged, William Dean Howells experienced the petrifying of partisanship that often came with adulthood. His life affirmed the thinking of those campaigners who focused their efforts on virgin voters. Nothing, it seemed, could shift his stiff, tribal politics; no Democrat could change his vote. In his teens and twenties, Howells had viewed partisanship as subjective and silly, mocking the blinkered fanatics who gloried in minor victories but would "skim over that scrap" of unwelcome political news.[73] But by middle age, Will had become a stolid, uncritical Republican. He wrote a campaign biography for Ohio Republican presidential candidate Rutherford B. Hayes—a distant relative—totally devoid of independent journalistic inquiry. He even allowed the candidate's son to edit his phrasing, to make Hayes's Civil War experience sound sufficiently heroic. He refused to censure increasingly sleazy Republicans, shrugging, "A presidential candidate is always corrupt."[74]

Then Will took the final step into adulthood, passing down his politics to rising youth. When his son, John, turned sixteen, in the midst of a particularly crooked campaign, Will wrote to a friend musing over what "I will tell John."[75] He equivocated that there was nothing immoral about voting for a man merely "*accused* of bribery." In an expression of blind partisanship, Howells wrote, "Politician for politician, self-seeker for self-seeker, I prefer a Republican to a Democrat; and I would not vote a party into power which is composed of all that is retrograde and savage in our politics."[76] Decades into adulthood, Will Howells still believed, as his father had taught him, that Democrats were "enemies of the human race."[77]

And as he passed down his politics, Will still looked up to his father as his primary political informant. Even though he had the ear of presidents, after big elections Will Howells always wrote to his father to discuss the ups and downs for "people of our politics."[78]

One of those "enemies of the human race" was Samuel Tilden, Hayes's opponent in 1876, whom Will Howells hated with inexplicable zeal. When Howells considered the Sage of Gramercy winning the presidency, the irrationally panicked boy of his youth reemerged; the very idea was just "too nauseous." During the cliffhanger election in 1876, Will was unable to sleep, physically pained and "perfectly frantic" thinking about a Democratic president.[79] Hayes eventually "won" that race, but the era of Republican hegemony was coming to an end, in part because of Samuel Tilden's increasingly adept youth appeals. Though Will Howells saw Tilden as a nemesis, both were considering the same question: how to guide young people into politics.

While Will Howells enjoyed Republican rule in the 1860s and 1870s, Samuel Tilden's Democrats seemed stuck as archetypal Outs. Tilden's old allies had seceded, died, or converted to Republicanism. In the North, the organization stunk of treason; in the South, former Confederate Democrats were defeated and disillusioned. From his isolated perch in Gramercy Park, the Sage set about rebuilding his damaged party, turning to young voters to rejuvenate his movement.

Tilden and his ally Horatio Seymour responded with the "New Departure," a Democratic attempt at "burying out of sight all that is of the dead past."[80] Trying to move beyond their party's old fights over slavery and secession, the postwar Democrats focused on denouncing federal "centralism" and on stoking racial conflict. They redirected their efforts, abandoning old fire-eaters of the Deep South for a new generation of young white small farmers and wageworkers in the lower North. In many of these states, campaigners organized semisecret Jackson Clubs to "train up" new Democrats.[81]

By the 1870s, the Democrats' plan—bringing in young voters to raise up a struggling party—should have been strikingly familiar. In fact, Democratic presidential candidate Horatio Seymour's 1868 call for more Jackson Clubs sounds almost identical to Abraham Lincoln's plan to help struggling Whigs twenty years earlier. In 1848, Lincoln had hoped to organize clubs by gathering up "all the shrewd, wild boys around town," providing "an interesting pastime," and offering young Whigs importance in their communities.[82] Seymour expressed the same goals. Writing to Tilden, Seymour claimed that Jackson Clubs would offer young people a "motive as well as a method," provide a "charm of novelty," and give young Democrats "power in their towns."[83] Two politicians, representing two parties two decades apart, both looked to the same basic solution.

This solution highlights the cyclical nature of the Outs' reliance on the young. From the 1830s through the 1870s, diverse parties fell back on the same basic tactic: turning new voters against the corruption of the party in power. Though each wave innovated in some way—bringing in generational excitement, promising western land, or organizing uniformed marching clubs—they applied the same basic premise. As each generation of excited young campaigners grew up and burned out, another followed, raising a new movement with it.[84]

This cycle became so predictable that political families passed down the tactic. In October 1860, at the height of the Wide Awake movement, Illinois gubernatorial candidate Richard Yates stood before a sea of young Republicans and declared, "I love my wife first, my boy and little girl next, and after that the Wide Awakes."[85] A generation later, that boy whom Yates mentioned, Richard Yates Jr., gave a similar address. This time over Blue Points and roast quail, Richard Yates Jr. gave his own encouraging talk on "The Young Man in Politics."[86] Pandering to youth seemed timeless in the age of popular politics.

Chasing the High Tide

In the mid-1870s, the system dramatically changed. Politicians had come to rely on a predictable cycle in politics, as Ins consolidated their hold on power and Outs rallied youths. But the close races and attentive, organized campaigners of the Gilded Age broke this usual succession. Both parties began to make continuous bids for virgin voters. At first this competition positioned youths at the very center of American politics and pushed campaigns into a kind of frenzied overdrive. But, ultimately, the parties' competitive obsession with youth would wreck the entire system.

By the mid-1870s, many Americans began to lose interest in the debates of the Civil War era. Men and women born in the 1850s, who could barely remember Appomattox, let alone Fort Sumter, were rising as mature citizens—for them the long saga of slavery, secession, and Reconstruction seemed incredibly dated. Many young white Americans cared more about the interminable depression, partisan corruption, and their expanding nation (few African Americans, of course, had the luxury of losing interest in Reconstruction). Campaigners recognized that this rising cohort no longer cared about debating, as one comedian put it, "the cut of trousers that prevailed in 1861."[87] Even in the Deep South, where the Lost Cause flourished among veterans, some young Texans crassly wondered why they should bother "yelping about niggers and yanks to accommodate old suckers."[88]

Young Americans' fading interest in the Civil War upended the partisan status quo. Northern voters ceased to associate the Republicans with the victorious war or to see the Democrats as traitors. Why should young people care what the Democratic Party had done years before they were born?[89] Why should they support the Republican Party, which may have once stood for youth and progress but by the 1870s seemed to be made up of "rotten old hulks who monopolize the offices and dwell upon the past"?[90]

If the coming of the Civil War benefited the Republicans, its going worked in the favor of the Democrats. Helped by the "Long Depression" of 1873 and bitter Republican infighting, in 1874 the Democrats won control of the House for the first time in fourteen years, briefly grabbed the Senate in 1878, and won the presidency in 1884. Though aware that many voters were just "prattling infants when Lincoln was elected," old Republican stalwarts still clung to the past.[91] Perhaps they were too attached to their party's proudest era, or maybe they found it difficult to simultaneously pander to veterans and to young people, as those groups grew further apart. For whatever reason, the Grand Old Party grew grumpier as younger voters pushed for new issues. When a twenty-eight-year-old wrote to the *Boston Transcript* asking the paper to discuss topics other than the Civil War, its Republican editors angrily complained that "young men of this type have great political influence" but "should be handled as are—babies."[92]

The battle over the memory of the Civil War led the parties to broadly rethink the role of young people in politics. The war left a distinct marker in time, a "remember where you were" milestone, and highlighted just how rapidly generations age and new ones rise. Forward-looking politicians began see the decisive role that young voters played in American elections. Previously, young people were a temporarily useful bloc, sought by Outs but neglected by Ins. After the bitter, confused election in 1876, campaigners started to count the massive numbers of young people who determined increasingly close elections and concluded that new voters required their constant attention. As popular politics reached a fevered pitch in the 1880s, Democrats and Republicans realized what had been true, on the ground, all along: virgin voters decide victory.

This obsession with young voters took place during the high tide of political excitement. American democracy has never been more animated and intense than it was between 1876 and 1896. Voter turnout hit its peak in 1876, drawing even more voters than the 1860 campaign that sparked the Civil War. In hotly contested states like Indiana, more than 90 percent of eligible citizens turned out for five straight presidential contests stretching over twenty years. These Gilded Age elections were also the closest in American history. The popular vote between 1880 and 1888 was fourteen times closer than the average for the rest of the age of popular politics, with three elections in a row won by less than half a percentage point. Some races were decided by fewer than 2,000 votes—in a nation of 50 million—and others went to the loser of the popular ballot. Such razor-thin margins left both parties feeling like Outs. Many looked to young Americans for precious new votes.[93]

These competitive races threw fireworks into already blazing partisan bonfires. Evenly matched parties battled to turn out more marchers, louder bands, and tastier barbecues. A cottage industry grew up selling club uniforms and banners, with artists in such high demand that they frequently reused old flags, painting the face of the current year's candidate over the last year's, adding a mustache or muttonchops as needed.[94] Newspapermen churned out more partisan rags per person than at any other time in American history. By 1890 there were six times more papers in the nation than there had been in 1840, each shrieking their opinions as loudly as ever.[95] Historians tend to overlook these blustery Gilded Age campaigns because they did not represent major innovations, as in 1840, or deal with slavery and Civil War, like in 1860. But to an excited seventeen-year-old with no memory of those races, politics had never roared louder.

Finally, in the 1880s, politicians situated young Americans at the center of their fevered political culture. Parties that could agree on little else recognized that victory depended upon wining over "1000s of budding youngsters."[96] Newspapers ran long articles declaring that virgin voters would decide a coming election. This awareness grew so commonplace that the *New York Times* could yawn, "Young voters will determine this election, as they have determined every election in this state and city for the last five years."[97]

Party leaders were thrilled. Many became fixated on calculating the exact number of young men attaining majority with every election. Earlier leaders had been satisfied with vague pronouncements that a large proportion of young people supported their cause; by the 1880s Republicans and Democrats printed elaborate statistics—many of them bogus—claiming that "the equivalent of a new state" would cast a first ballot every four years. Hopeful Gilded Age campaigners began to add youths to their balance sheets, operating like the era's booming railroads or factories, embracing the bureaucratizing era's fascination with the power of quantification.[98]

These numbers-obsessed partisans had no idea how close they were to a thrilling revelation. Over the nineteenth century, American women steadily limited how many children they had, cutting the number in half between 1800 and 1900. As a result of this demographic shift and because Americans were living longer, the median age was creeping up. The average American was around seventeen in 1840, by 1880 he or she was twenty and nine-tenths, and in 1890 that average person reached twenty-two. This means that during the high tide of popular politics in the 1880s, the average age finally met the voting age, then set at twenty-one.[99] Due to the immigration of so many European men, America was also becoming more white and more male. Suddenly, in the 1880s, virgin voters—most of them white men in their early twenties—were no longer a sideshow courted solely by striving parties. Politicians seemed to realize, without ever calculating this statistic, that virgin voters were now their biggest audience.

Campaigners fell all over themselves appealing to this decisive bloc. Previously, leaders often used the phrase "generous and unsophisticated" when describing young people's political contributions.[100] The idea was that young citizens were helpful in campaigning and liberal with their time but nonetheless mindless cogs in partisan hierarchies. By the 1880s campaigners stepped beyond this utilitarian view. In 1882 the *Washington Post* begged politicians to respect young activists and not make them "do all the work of the campaign."[101] Instead, during the political high tide of the 1880s, campaigners introduced a host of appeals designed to win over young voters, though most were blatantly desperate and contradictory.

At first campaigners revisited the logic of "virgin voters," stressing the importance of partisan monogamy. One's first ballot, they taught, meant a lifelong commitment. This was particularly popular in the negative form among panicked Republicans trying to dissuade young voters from experimenting with the Democrats. In a widely reprinted 1879 speech, part of his bid to become a senator, James A. Garfield addressed new voters who might consider joining the Democrats. Garfield's speech, quoted in Republican pamphlets long after his assassination, warned the virgin voter, "You are about to pitch your tent in one of the great political camps." He pointed to the Democracy's long list of skeletons, barely hidden in shallow graves, and declared, "Don't pitch your tent among the dead."[102] Republicans picked up on this ghastly imagery, warning virgin voters that one misguided vote might leave them forever "fastened to the festering corpse of a bogus Democracy."[103]

Yet alongside these ominous warnings of what would happen to insufficiently partisan young people, campaigners made phony paeans to the value of independence. In the 1880s, political independence was increasingly seen as a virtue—especially among the new, urban middle class—and campaigners paid desperate lip service.[104] Truly independent young citizens, they claimed, would examine both sides, then slavishly follow theirs. Democrats warned young men not to let "torch light processions influence your vote" but to objectively look at the records of the parties, particularly the heinous corruption of the Republicans.[105] The Republicans—even while hissing about "festering corpses"—claimed to want young voters to impartially evaluate the parties.[106] The nation's comedians mocked this facade, satirizing politicians who claimed, "I don't want to influence you, so long as you vote my ticket."[107]

More often than barking nasty threats about partisan monogamy or ridiculous claims to love independence, most campaigners simply idealized young Americans. Earlier leaders viewed young people as a useful but potentially dangerous force, helpful on the ground but in need of constant guidance from higher up. By the 1880s, bosses and intellectuals had come to view virgin voters as earnest and wholesome. They assured themselves that a man "never casts a purer ballot than when he votes for the first time" and that a young American growing up in the 1880s is "sure to be wiser than his father."[108] Parties imagined that this purity meant that young people might revolutionize politics, overthrowing the bosses and perfecting society.[109] Jaded machines quickly learned to parrot the idealism of liberal reformers, using this optimism to lure another generation into their organizations.

Joining the Sage

Those years of close elections and partisan pandering were also the peak of Samuel Tilden's power and influence. He ran for president, winning the popular vote in the confused, contested, and monumentally excited 1876 election but losing the disputed electoral vote process that followed. He finished major renovations of his Gramercy mansion and lived there as a partisan prophet, pondering campaign tactics.

His three insights about youth politics were never more true. All sides believed that young people were, as the rural Populists put it, "the most important animal upon the farm."[110] They all considered themselves the Outs, continuously looking to virgin voters to bring victory in the next close race. Most of all, they acknowledged, with their desperate and contradictory appeals, just how hard it was for politicians to systematically reach out to young Americans.

On a broader level, many Americans borrowed some of Tilden's characteristic introspection. Between 1876 and the end to the century, citizens began an increasingly thoughtful discussion about what a democracy should be, who should vote, and who should lead. After decades of seemingly perpetual and instinctual partisanship, ordinary citizens became noticeably self-aware in the 1880s and 1890s. In previous eras, only a handful of visionaries expressed a holistic understanding of their democracy, but in the 1880s hundreds of writers, publishing in dozens of journals, considered their entire system. The best articles on the role that young people played in politics were all written during the 1884 election, while the greatest book on the subject, Albion Tourgée's *Letters to a King*, came out four years later.[111] Far from the mechanistic and thoughtless Gilded Age politics often depicted by historians, a growing number of citizens experienced a dawning self-awareness during those years.

A number of factors, some of them unrelated to youth, contributed to this new thoughtfulness. The fading of the Civil War era, the string of close elections, the pervasive sense of political corruption, and a drumbeat of depressions all contributed. Massive numbers of workers and farmers felt increasingly distant from their supposed representatives. A growing electorate, brimming not just with twenty-one-year-olds but with millions of new immigrants, seemed disorganized and unpredictable.

Yet the usual dreary Gilded Age narrative does not explain this self-awareness. For all the impoverished workers raging against the railroads and the bosses, there were optimistic middle-class liberals, filled with a faith that they could improve long-flawed systems. A burgeoning population, ranging from businessmen and lawyers to clerks and schoolmistresses, reassessed their political structure with a confidence in the perfectibility of all institutions. Many burned with the belief that their democracy, like the rest of society, was malleable.[112] Unlike past generations over the age of popular politics, they had lost interest in partisan inheritance and sustainability. They wanted progress.[113]

These reformers had no idea that they teetered on the brink. The majority were still intensely partisan. Most simply wanted to fix the democracy so that their own right-thinking party could dominate it. Many hoped to throw immigrants, nonwhites, non-Protestants, and the poor off the voting rolls.[114] Almost none grasped the change their improvements would bring.

It was hard to see how fragile popular democracy was, because from the perspective of the 1880s, everything about politics was superlative. Americans lived with the highest turnouts, the closest elections, the wildest swindles, and the most young voters. Middle-class improvers could debate the latest magazine article on democracy from the privacy of their drawing rooms while their sons and daughters still went out to rallies—hollering, marching, flirting, and fighting. During this inundating high tide, public hoopla and private contemplation swirled together.

But Tilden was right: everyone *was* fifty. Even the political culture. As it neared the half-century mark in the late 1880s, popular politics began to show its age. Often, this meant that campaigners expressed an adult self-awareness of what had been happening, on the ground, for a lifetime. Politicos launched middle-aged attempts to coordinate what had come naturally in earlier years. They tried too hard. Over the next decade, their efforts to turn the convenient relationship between young Americans and political parties into something more systematic would cause an early death for the unique political culture.

Conclusion

Things Ain't What They Used to Be

Graziano's shoeshine stand in Manhattan's Tweed Courthouse seemed like the ideal compromise between public and private politics. The worn wood and cracked leather chairs resided within the halls of power but were still out in the airy seven-story rotunda, amid the judges and the janitors. So that was where George Washington Plunkitt, the perfect caricature of a nineteenth-century district boss, made his office for three decades.[1]

"Plunky" would storm in every day at ten. Graziano always had the boss's mail waiting. The tall, angular politico would hoist himself into a chair, plop his boots down on the brass shoe-stands, and hold court. His mustache waggled as he spoke; his cloudy blue eyes darted from face to face. Plunkitt was restless and jerky and loud. Even after a half century in politics, he never mastered the winks and nods of a close-mouthed city boss.[2]

Born in 1842 in a shantytown that would become part of Central Park, Plunkitt was a rough contemporary of Will Howells and Oscar Lawrence Jackson. Over the age of popular politics, Plunkitt came to embody the bombastic, youth-focused democracy of the time. He left school at eleven to work as a butcher's boy in the meatpacking district but dreamed of "winning fame and money in New York City Politics."[3] So he started to round up his voting-age friends—a cousin who didn't care about elections, neighbors who followed his lead—and formed the "George Washington Plunkitt Association." He then promised their votes (which he called "marketable goods") to a district boss in exchange for a political position.[4]

From there Plunkitt wormed his way into city politics, becoming an inescapable presence on the west side and in Albany between the 1860s and the 1900s. At one point he held four different positions, drawing three government salaries, simultaneously.[5] He made millions fleecing the booming city's construction projects, a theft he considered "honest graft."[6] He bragged about these deals to journalist William Riordan at Graziano's

George Washington Plunkitt, the Tammany Hall district boss and big-mouthed political sage, perches on his shoeshine throne in Manhattan's Tweed Courthouse. In the early twentieth century, as politics retreated from the public square and bosses worked to stay out of the papers, Plunkitt's opinionated, youth-focused style of politicking made him a relic of the dissipating age of popular politics. (Cover of William L. Riordan, *Plunkitt of Tammany Hall: A Series of Very Plain Talks on Very Practical Politics* [New York: McClure, Phillips, 1905]; author's collection)

stand, and in 1905 Riordan published a widely popular book of Plunkitt's "plain talks on practical politics."[7]

Plunkitt never forgot that young voters underwrote his wealth and power. He framed his lectures as advice for "young men who are goin' to cast their first votes."[8] When not hanging out at Graziano's, he spent his restless energy bouncing from boxing matches to fires to wakes, "holding his district" by mentoring its young people.[9] Plunkitt found these youths jobs or opportunities. Though he expected their votes, he did not like to trouble them with political arguments.[10]

Around 1900 the view from Graziano's stand began to dim. In his candid talks with Riordan, Plunkitt struck an ominous tone, worrying about "the change that had come over the young men."[11] As the oldest district leader in Tammany Hall, he noticed that young people seemed to have far less interest in parades, fireworks, and Election Day whiskey than they used to.[12] He blamed reformers' war on corruption, asking, "How are you goin' to interest our young men in their country if you have no office to give them?"[13] Reciprocity drove machine politics, and Plunkitt claimed that good government types were causing working-class young men to lose interest in politics and become anarchist terrorists.[14]

As usual, Plunkitt mixed self-serving nonsense with a trenchant insight. Civil service reform was not inspiring anarchist terrorism, but something was indeed changing among the young. The ranks of virgin voters, who for sixty years marched into public democracy, stopped turning out around 1900. Voter turnout fell 6 percent from 1896 to 1900, then 8 percent from 1900 to 1904, and it kept plummeting after that. By 1924 it was down to fewer than half of eligible voters, a low not seen for a hundred years.[15]

Young voters led the way. First-time voter turnout fell by more than 50 percent between 1888 and 1924 in the most populous parts of the country. While new voters used to be overrepresented at the polling place in the 1880s, by the 1920s virgin voters disproportionately stayed home.[16] Older partisans kept voting, as they were raised to do, but there were fewer first-timers at each election. By 1909, even the optimistic Jane Addams could mourn the unalterable fact that democracy "no longer stirs the blood of the American youth."[17]

What was wrong with the young? Though turnout numbers fell in the early twentieth century, the Americans who failed to vote in 1900 were born around 1880. Something happened to their socialization in the 1880s and 1890s to break the cycle of succession, causing them to mature without their predecessors' dedication to democracy. Once that first round lost interest, the "big fellow" failed to guide "the little fellow" into politics.[18]

Plunkitt was right to blame meddling elites—"dudes who part their name in the middle"—but wrong to think civil service reform was the culprit.[19] During the height of youth involvement, very few young Americans had actually gotten jobs or money from politics, especially outside of the big cities. It was something else—a new and hopeful interest in young Americans, among campaigners and other youths, that ended up stifling their political involvement.

Two simultaneous revolutions—one among partisans and one among the young—remade the political culture. First, wealthy Americans attempted to wrest control of democracy from working-class politicos like Plunkitt, creating new youth organizations that stressed rational, informed, sober political engagement.[20] Well-intentioned reformers succeeded, in one generation, in doing more than any other movement in American history to clean up their democracy. But good government killed popular politics, unbundling political life from social life. Few young Americans wanted part of such an isolated movement.

At the same time, a vital new youth culture was emerging in the 1890s, providing an alternative to political entertainment. American society was moving away from the age mixing that had introduced so many young people to politics in the previous decades. Youths now spent more time with their peers. They came to value relating to their generation above struggling for maturity.[21] Public politics—which lived on the blended social life of drugstore bars and town square barbecues—just seemed less useful in baseball leagues and dance halls.

For fifty years the system had thrived because young Americans and political parties were inadvertently useful to each other. Twin ironies unraveled this connection in the 1890s. Parties' intentional efforts to structure what had once happened by chance killed off what made democratic involvement so enticing. Meanwhile, the more confident the young became in their own positions—as individuals and as a generation—the less they needed politics. For those maturing in the 1890s, politics had less pull and society had less push.

These changes grew from a new impulse to sort America's institutions into their proper arenas. As the long cultural earthquake of the nineteenth century subsided, many began to do away with the mixed organizations that had been created to cope with instability. America's new "search for order" can be seen throughout the social innovations of the 1890s: in the emerging Progressive movement; in urban planning, education, professional associations, and business management; and also in the mounting eugenics movement and more structured racial segregation.[22] This sorting impulse would be very bad for the messy bundle of public affairs and personal aspirations that powered young people's politics. To many Americans after 1890, politics belonged with politics, and youth belonged with youth.

Not even Plunkitt's "office" could withstand the new neatness. In 1902 the bureaucrats who ran the courthouse decided to expel the crowd of favor-seekers forever swarming around Plunky's shoeshine throne. They ordered him to find a private office, announcing that "the reform broom will sweep Plunkitt out" and sparking a standoff breathlessly reported in the papers.[23] Plunkitt fought back, bringing in his biggest, meanest friends to guard the stand from the unlucky custodians ordered to remove it. Yet even he could not fight city hall. First, Plunkitt had to take down his portrait hanging over the stand. Then he allowed janitors to mop the floor around the platform, which after thirty years had accumulated thick strata of dried tobacco spit. Finally, poor Graziano had to move to a quieter corner of the building.[24]

Graziano had gotten his start as a young Italian immigrant and lived for decades under the protection of the bombastic, charming, corrupt Plunkitt.[25] But by the turn of the twentieth century, men like Plunkitt could no longer guide, or manipulate, younger generations as they once had. A new order—sorted, segmented, and rational—redefined politics. The forces that drove Plunkitt off, rising in the 1880s and dominant by 1900, highlight what had made politics so appealing to young men and women to begin with. They explain what had compelled Plunkitt, as a young butcher's boy, to put down his cleaver and start hustling voters and why fewer young Americans would follow his lead after 1890.

A Gentleman Never Votes

The fire of popular politics began to dim when the respectable classes took interest. The well-to-do had long tried to ignore the "stupid utterances" of "beardless boys" shouting at public events.[26] But when Gilded Age reformers began to pay attention, they brought habits and values that were powerfully unappealing to the young people who fueled popular democracy. Their preferred style of politics inadvertently cut the links between the stages of youth, making political socialization difficult. Before they could do so, though, they had to change their minds about the nasty business of campaigning.

The wealthy had never really fallen for popular democracy.[27] Though active in the deferential republicanism of the early Republic, the rise of democracy and the expansion of capitalism pointed the moneyed classes away from the polling booth in the 1840s.[28] Even when campaign excitement reached frenzied peaks, affluent professionals were often the least passionate. Though the upper classes frequently held office, they rarely dirtied their hands organizing the campaigns that got them there. Why set one's reputation out before the "fickle popular breath," to absorb the "monstrous vilifications" of campaign mudslinging?[29]

As self-made capitalism came to dominate American culture, the affluent began to view politics as an illegitimate route to power. For them, power came from money, and money came from business. The well-to-do snarled that politics represented an unfair shortcut around capitalism. Party activists were pathetic "merchants who have failed in everything but

Democracy," while elections caused an irritating "paralysis of business."[30] "Politics," to many, seemed to be "the business of holding back, and holding up, business."[31] What had made popular politics so enticing to struggling young Americans—that it had little to do with how much money one had—made it repellent to those with cash to spend.

"Young men of fortune" were the least excited.[32] Older gentlemen could afford to take risks, but young professionals rarely wanted to chance the "personal degradation" that came with losing a campaign.[33] In 1873, *Harper's Weekly* editor Whitelaw Reid told a graduating class at Amherst College that they were right to avoid politics, which were, at bottom, a "vulgar struggle of vulgar men through vulgar means."[34] Theodore Roosevelt's friends famously tried to dissuade him from running for office in the early 1880s. To go into politics, the scion of one wealthy Quaker family wrote, was to join "a degraded caste," something like "confessing a moral weakness." Politicians, to this youth, were a "shifty-eyed lot, dribbling tobacco juice, badly dressed, never prosperous."[35] Even turning out on Election Day brought some stain; as young professionals reminded each other, "A gentleman never votes."[36]

Elite politicians complained about their apolitical sons, concerned that they were less vigorous than the hodcarriers and longshoremen marching under their brownstones' windows. Prominent Republican George Boutwell published an essay in 1879 worrying that "young men of culture and ability" were no longer willing to take on "the honors or duties of public station."[37] Albion Tourgée agreed—in his landmark *Letters to a King* he argued that prosperous youths had begun to "avoid the responsibility of self-government" after the Civil War.[38] Tourgée wrote with force, mocking wealthy youths as "neuters who eschew politics." Such young men had no choice in the matter, he declared: "The citizen-king cannot abdicate. I mean that you are required to 'go into politics' whether you desire to do so or not."[39]

The professional classes articulated a resigned sense of being trapped in popular democracy. They dominated so many other aspects of the increasingly unequal society, but the workings of the parties seemed to grow more distant every year. For a time all they did was grumble about the seemingly indomitable political system, calling it "the most atrocious tyranny ever invented."[40] E. L. Godkin, editor of the *Nation* and exemplar of such urbane, liberal reformers, complained that there never was a system like American democracy, from which "there seemed so little prospect of escape." Popular politics loomed over America with "the majesty of doom."[41]

Until the 1880s these "men of culture" had been a grumbling minority. Youth politics had succeeded, for decades, in obscuring divisions among the majority of middling and working-class citizens. At deafening rallies, wrapped in flashy uniforms, backgrounds and assets were often hard to distinguish. In the Gilded Age, as income inequality exacerbated class divisions, wealthy reformers moved to reshape the way Americans experienced their democracy. First, as discussed before, the parties concluded that new voters decided close elections and tried to recruit young Americans with frenzied appeals and plenty of cash. At the same time, well-to-do reformers launched a crusade to retake democracy for the upper classes, working "to emancipate the respectable white man."[42]

Samuel Tilden knew what to do. The Sage of Gramercy had spent years rattling around his mansion, dreaming up political techniques. He stood at the nexus of all the forces aligning to alter youth politics. He was an unabashed party man, a lifelong Democrat who understood how to manipulate that sprawling apparatus. But his position in New York society also introduced him to the wealthy reformers who looked down on both parties. Tilden could get the two sides talking.[43] Like many of these reformers, Tilden disliked public campaign spectacle. As one journalist put it, the Sage of Gramercy "never believed in skyrocket and the Roman candle system. . . . As a rule he considered brass bands and orators a waste of money and time."[44] Many wealthy reformers were equally hostile to hoopla, disparaging parades, bonfires, and fireworks as expensive displays that did more to entertain the rabble than guarantee victory.[45]

So in his 1876 presidential run, Tilden set up a "Literary Bureau" in a Manhattan office and used it to distribute 27 million pieces of educational campaign literature.[46] This approach, which relied on ideological information distributed by a private office, presaged the more restrained campaigns of the early twentieth century. However, Tilden's foray into "educational campaigning" had little effect on the hugely popular 1876 race. It would take another decade for a critical mass of reformers and party men to appreciate his approach, heavy on information and light on fun.

The turning point came in 1887, a year after Tilden died, first showing itself in young men's political clubs. Such organizations had characterized every election since at least 1840, serving as a public nucleus to entertain and recruit. They offered the ideal structure for reformers to remake politics. The problem was that they were just too entertaining, "organized in a spirit of fun, simply for the pleasure they afford."[47] This fun helped draw in middling young men and women but repelled respectable youths. It also failed to inform voters. The "trouble" with clubs, complained one of the chief Democratic reformers, was that they involved a lot of "shouting and marching" but were not "associations intended for deliberation. The *better* class of people will not join 'clubs.'"[48]

So the Republican Party set out, in the run-up to the 1888 presidential campaign, to form clubs that were civil, centralized, and maintained "on a permanent basis."[49] The party was still reeling from its loss in the 1884 presidential race, a close campaign that marked the peak of youth-focused appeals. So in December 1887, fifteen hundred delegates met in New York to put their own sons forward, convening the National League of Republican Clubs.[50]

This "Republican League" stressed two points. First, the new clubs existed to organize the "beardless and boyish workers of the Republican party."[51] Second, the Republican League would follow the orders of national campaign headquarters. This meant less hollering in the streets and fewer community events. The league preferred a corporate model. One speaker reminded young Republicans of "the necessity of organization," shouting, "This is an age of activity and progress . . . parties are business organizations."[52] The clubs would act as their directors ordered, mostly distributing pamphlets about tariff reform.

Within four months, the Democrats set up their own centralized, permanent youth clubs.[53] Both sides told themselves that this model would be the best way to bring in respectable young voters. One of the founders of the Republican League dismissed all clubs dating back to 1840 as a "temporary effervescence" and claimed that "there can be no weighty objections" to the new model.[54]

In 1887, while some reformers were building permanent, centralized, businesslike political clubs, others focused on ballots themselves. The actual process of voting had long been both a climactic rite for virgin voters and an ideal opportunity for sleazy ballot tricks. Reformers initiated a nationwide shift to what were then called "Australian ballots": nonpartisan voting forms printed by official state institutions and cast in private. Between 1887 and 1896, thirty-nine of the forty-five states made the change.[55]

Two revolutions, one in clubs and the other in voting, outlined a new partisan landscape in 1887 in which democracy ceased to be "part of the every-day business of American life."[56] In so many subtle ways, wealthy reformers were beginning to sort out the messy political culture that had driven politics for nearly fifty years.

As optimistic campaigners tinkered with the fundamentals of politics, a new youth culture was emerging with far less interest in what democracy had to offer. Reforming campaigners did not realize that the young were not a static target. Instead, parties and young people began to shrink from each other, unintentionally separating youth culture and political culture into their own discrete realms. At first, few earnest reformers or exuberant seventeen-year-olds could feel the change. Most saw it only in retrospect.

Flocks and Swarms

Henry Seidel Canby never forgot the impact that getting a bicycle made on his social life. That contraption emancipated the aristocratic Delaware boy from a world of manicured, fenced-in lawns. Henry was suddenly free to roam the twilight streets of Wilmington amid "flocks of young people," so long as he could navigate the cobblestones. Looking back from decades later, he pinpointed that moment in the early 1890s as a taking-off point for a new youth culture. Those clusters of young riders, circling "past and past again the porches where the elders were sitting," meant a separate space for his age group. It was the "first breakaway from home, a warning of the new age."[57]

Gleaming bicycles were just one of the many changes to the relationship between young people and adults between 1880 and 1900. Transcending any single device, a parallel youth culture was beginning to emerge, causing many young people to value relating to their peers over mixing with other age groups. If the "problem of youth" for earlier young people was finding a path to maturity, the new "problem" (exaggerated but real) seemed to be keeping up with one's own generation.[58]

This worldview would be very bad for young people's politics, which had previously been premised on age mixing and aspirations of maturity. During the age of popular politics, many young people embraced a vertical model of adulthood, using politics as a scaffolding to climb toward maturity. The new culture was more horizontal. The young started to care more about relating to other young people. They still hoped to achieve adulthood but worried less about climbing upward. Maturing in a society with more stable institutions, better peer relations, more time in school, and fewer years of semidependence, many young Americans focused less on their path into adulthood and more on one another.[59]

Age separation began among the same well-off classes who had decided to reform American politics. In the decades after the Civil War, some elites began to worry that the casual mixing of age groups in America's schools, businesses, churches, and parties was having dangerous effects on young people. Many had made their fortunes managing the growing corporate bureaucracies of Gilded Age America, becoming increasingly fixated on the concepts of time and age in the process. The phrases "on time" and "ahead of time" entered popular speech in the 1870s, and in 1882 the railroads sliced the nation into time zones. An organized, systematic, reformist culture hoped to sort America's young just as neatly.[60]

Shifting demographics drove this change. As wealthy Americans had fewer children and assigned them less dangerous work, it became easy to idealize youths and make a fetish of their vulnerabilities.[61] Earlier generations believed young people had destructive energies they needed to expel, but Gilded Age parents concluded that their sons and daughters needed protection. In the decades before psychologist G. Stanley Hall's *Adolescence* made the case for allowing teens to mature in sheltering isolation, elites began to separate out their young people from the scrum of adult life.[62] One columnist writing in the *Ladies' Home Journal* joked that the safest way for a boy to mature was "to be buried when he was fifteen and not dug up again until after he was twenty."[63]

By the 1880s, elite parents could raise their children in a world bounded by age. Education, medicine, literature, and toys all treated wealthy young men and women as a separate population, surrounded by peers and expected only to "act their age." Authors of advice books and ladies' magazines opined on the "schedules of childhood."[64] One typical anthology of parenting articles from the *Ladies' Home Journal* demonstrated this. From the book's title—*Before He Is Twenty*—to its essays on when a boy should work, when he should socialize outside the home, and when a girl should marry (an unmarried twenty-two-year-old was "a recognized disgrace"), such parenting guides betrayed a fixation with chronological age foreign to the culture just a few decades before.[65]

At first, the ideal of age separation was nearly meaningless to the vast majority of laboring parents. Many depended on children for a big chunk of family income.[66] In a world where youths simply had to be "big enough" to work, worrying about whether they were "old enough" seemed ridiculous.[67] Slowly, though, the demographic changes that inspired age separation among the rich began to show themselves in the lives of average Americans. In addition to the falling birth rate, American women who had formerly spaced out pregnancies over many years began to clump births more closely together. Families now had children of roughly the same age. Even the age difference between brides and grooms fell. By the 1890s, young Americans were increasingly surrounded by their peers.[68]

Schools played a key role. The number of public schools increased 750 percent between 1880 and 1900, while spending jumped from $60 million in 1870 to over half a billion by 1915.[69] More Americans were attending school, and they spent a larger chunk of their time there, now that fewer lived on an agriculture schedule. These bigger schools outgrew the one-room schoolhouse model. Classes that once mixed seven-year-olds and twenty-year-olds in a single room divided pupils into grades. Some introduced kindergartens. A growing number of educators argued that children of different ages "should be isolated."[70]

Ironically, the growth of big, diverse cities also helped separate out the young. Urban kids simply saw their elders less. Agricultural life meant that children provided an extra pair of hands to help father or mother, but they were just less useful to parents who worked in factories or department stores. Parents who had labored at home or in nearby fields now took trains and trolleys to reach distant workplaces. Kid began to work less, too, their jobs slowly replaced by automation or taken by new immigrants.[71] Urban kids, when not in school, spent long afternoons loitering in front of their tenements in loose gangs, fighting turf wars with "other-streeters."[72] A railroad bull might chase them out of a train yard or a shopkeeper might break up a fight in front of her candy shop, but otherwise it was taken for granted that city kids of the same age "tend to stay together."[73]

With more school, more playmates, fewer chores, and fewer bossy adults, young Americans began to clump together in a parallel culture. When Henry James returned to New York in 1904, after decades away, the new age separation struck him immediately. On a trip to the Lower East Side, James complained of "a great swarming," especially by young Jewish immigrants, writing, "The children swarmed above all."[74] James had left in the early 1880s, as the new style was emerging; by the early 1900s it dominated both upper- and working-class life. The "flocks" of wealthy young Delaware cyclists, peddling with Henry Seidel Canby, were joined by "swarms" of lower-class immigrant children.

As young people separated off to socialize, they created a peer-focused entertainment culture. Jane Addams's long tenure helping youths at her settlement house taught her to observe, with humor and empathy, the "multitudes of eager young creatures" venturing out together in a "search for pleasure."[75] These youths gravitated to dance halls packed with other young people, a far remove from community dances where "all of the older people of the village participated."[76] Too often this new culture is depicted as the birth of young people's entertainment, as if earlier youths simply sat home, waiting for the rise of vaudeville or dance crazes. What really happened, between 1880 and 1900, was the emergence of a distinct entertainment culture designed specifically for young people. Eighteen-year-olds in 1900 did not necessarily have more fun than eighteen-year-olds in 1870; they simply had it surrounded by other eighteen-year-olds. As Addams put it, "Never before have the pleasures of the young and mature become so definitely separated."[77]

The new youth-focused entertainment culture was so enticing that even stuffy, nervous G. Stanley Hall smiled, "This is a good age to be young."[78] In cities, Addams wrote, new entertainment districts appealed to "all that is gaudy and sensual," with dance halls, gin palaces, vaudeville theaters, and cabarets, not to mention "the highly colored theater posters, the trashy love stories, the feathered hats, the cheap heroics of the revolvers displayed in pawn-shop windows."[79] Working girls went out at night, not escorted by family or beaux but in groups of other young women their age.[80] In the country, team sports—baseball especially—changed young people's social patterns, reorienting them from individual feats of daring to cooperative group fun.[81] Improved public transportation also made socializing with other young people possible. Harpo Marx recalled the liberation that came with hopping a train to go watch the New York Giants play baseball, freeing him from his isolated immigrant community. He was "no longer a prisoner of the neighborhood," Marx wrote; "my life had new horizons."[82]

Those new horizons appeared slowly. This youth culture is most often associated with the first decade of the 1900s. But, like young people's political involvement, it took years to incubate. The twenty-year-old factory girls who flocked to dance halls in 1900 were born in 1880. What they witnessed, over much of their childhoods, was not the technological breakthroughs of the early twentieth century but the model of socializing that preceded those material changes. Many pointed to a shift in lifestyle in the 1890s that enabled the new mass youth culture of the 1900s. What mattered was not the technology that created Henry Canby's bike but the mode of socializing that made him prefer racing over cobblestones with kids his age.

The new peer-focused culture led to a broad rethinking of the lines between age groups. Men and women maturing in the 1880s and 1890s began to view themselves as members of a common generation and to invest this new identity with pride. Before the 1880s, young Americans did not tend to harbor a shared generational identity; instead they often viewed their peers as cautionary examples, distractions, or "loafers."[83] When they discussed their generation, many worried about a tragic decline from the glory of the Founding Fathers.[84] Occasionally, political movements like the Young Americans or the Wide Awakes made use of generational rhetoric, but really they meant a far more particular group of like-minded partisans, not anyone of their age group.[85] Youth consciousness existed, but it was mostly expressed individually. More often, youth was viewed as a phase to be escaped, so few embraced it for any longer than they had to.

As they spent more time with their peers and less time with adults, young people began to adopt the concept of a shared generation in the 1890s. This was part of an international trend, seen in English, French, and German culture as well, but it was particularly heated in America.[86] Randolph Bourne, born in the 1880s but not expressing himself until 1911, wrote a spirited defense of his generation, not just as individual young people but as a collective identity shaped in response to the values of their parents.[87] Jane Addams agreed. Looking to the young people who flocked to Hull House over the decades, she saw an unmistakable trend, a craving, not to escape into maturity, but to revel in shared youth. "Nothing," she declared, "is more certain."[88]

The change showed itself in Americans' word choices. For one, use of the term "grown-up" took off in the mid-1890s, implying an increasing division between young people and adults. And young men began to refer to each other as "fellows," a habit peaking in the late 1890s, indicating a jaunty bond with contemporaries. Most tellingly, published use of the words "young" and "old" reached historic heights in 1900, not seen before or since.[89]

The new generational pride brought a growing ambivalence to older age groups. Long before the door-slamming battles between teenagers and their harrumphing parents in the twentieth century, the rising generations simply felt distant in the 1880s and 1890s. A didactic culture still expected deference that would feel foreign later, but in the final years of the century, age groups simply seemed to "misunderstand each other as they never did before."[90]

Henry Seidel Canby watched the changes in the decade after he got his first bicycle. By 1900 Henry was twenty-two, a Yale graduate, and a potential voter. What began with the twilight rides grew, through school and work and social life, into a gulf between young and old. Henry felt that the change was ubiquitous; at least among his class he knew "no intelligent family in our town where parents and children saw the same world or talked the same language." The generations were as distant, he claimed, as immigrants and their Americanized children. And that space would only build over the years, as the generation raised in the 1870s and before "dropped further and further behind the youths."[91]

The End of the Great Barbecue

In the 1890s—as boys were out riding bikes and factory girls were heading to dance halls, as party men were setting up banquets or lighting fireplaces in club headquarters—youth and politics were quietly untangling themselves. Prosperous Americans sometimes called their booming era "the Age of Confidence," and both political organizers and young people assumed there were "no weighty objections" to their new styles.[92] Campaigners could not imagine that their structured clubs would fail to attract new virgin voters. Young people could not anticipate that embracing their generation would somehow limit their interest in political maturity. But over the course of the 1890s, confident new methods would sort out the messy institutions that had brought young people into politics for half a century.

The new political clubs were the first to cause trouble. What looked like the associations' strengths—permanence, centralization, explicit organization—neglected the subtle power of the older youth clubs. The men who conceived of the Republican League and the National Association of Democratic Clubs did not fully appreciate the "temporary effervescence" of young people's political clubs from the 1840s through the 1880s.[93] That model provided a collapsible network of loose bonds, which could be reestablished and altered as the election required. Any historian trying to track young men's associations in the archives sees this: they appear and disappear every few years. Temporary clubs easily incorporated new members with each election. But the new organizations maintained the same aging rosters over decades, failing to bring in much new blood after the 1890s.[94] On top of this, the old model carefully balanced national campaigns with local social structures, granting distant federal races personal significance. Permanent clubs with headquarters in Washington, New York, and Chicago threw off that balance.[95]

The new model further isolated the already-drifting age groups. Though earlier club members had mostly been in their late teens or early twenties, a wide range of ages appeared in their rosters. Clubs always had a few fifteen-year-olds and a couple of fifty-year-olds. Their meetings allowed the generations to mix and adults to inspire ambitious youths. The new model of the 1890s and 1900s, though, endorsed the age separation of the era. Organizations established separate "Boys Clubs" for members under twenty-one, and adults began to simply donate a few dollars rather than turn up for a rowdy Tuesday night meeting. The Republican League used inspiring rhetoric, telling young partisans that they were casting off "the shackles of old fogeyism," but really it was denying younger members the benefits of adult socialization.[96]

Permanent youth organizations won out with the help of generous reformers and national party organizations. Clubs were suddenly major financial institutions. The Republican League in Ohio established a board of stockholders to oversee its operations.[97] Well-documented Republican clubs in Philadelphia bought ornate houses and set up growing budgets. Their meticulous records, from 1892 until 1912, demonstrate growing finances and changing values. One club brought in $5,293 in 1898, at a time when the national per capita income was around $200.[98] This club had a special committee for entertainment, spent over $1,000 on games and cigars, and even held a monthly "Ladies Night."[99]

The new clubs did not abandon entertainment; they just closed off their fun from the public. During the age of popular politics, clubs met in storefronts or schoolhouses, but the permanent clubs bought private homes. The shift shows the sorting impulse's effect on politics. Temporarily meeting in a drugstore or classroom implied that political life fit into the larger community, that such institutions had multiple uses, and that politics could appear nearly anywhere. The permanent clubhouses of the 1890s, on the other hand, stated that political action happened in one designated space.[100] Many permanent clubs even set up in hotel suites. There was little chance of a curious virgin voter happening by a meeting held on the top floor of a Chicago hotel.[101]

The very image of what campaigning looked like began to change. For decades, America's illustrated newspapers had published a predictable succession of thrilling illustrations each election. There was always a barbecue, a torchlight parade, a bonfire, and jollification. They were redundant but still exciting and public. In the fall of 1896, *Harper's Weekly* chose to bring their images inside as well. That year, many of their engravings depicted behind-the-scenes campaign headquarters, showing a few prominent organizers sitting around in wingback chairs. It sent a very different message from a boisterous main street packed with election night revelers.[102]

Likewise, campaigners ceased throwing big public barbecues, held in town squares and centered on a roast ox or hog, that had inspired social mixing among ambitious youths. Instead, parties preferred invitation-only banquets in private halls, where select guests enjoyed the era's fascination with French cuisine.[103] Meals hidden under silver domes replaced long, rustic tables laid out with chops and ribs. The *carte de menu* from one 1892 political banquet lists Consommé Souveraine, Turbotins of Bass à la Gutierrez, Potatoes Viennoise, Filet of Beef a l'Aquitane, Cromesquis of Sweetbread a l'Andalouse, and Fancy Ices.[104] Clearly, this was not the kind of shared meal that might inspire a new Oscar Lawrence Jackson to take up politics.

Young Americans were turning from shared barbecues as well. The new youth culture had less interest in free, public, partisan entertainment. Americans' social life increasingly centered on leisure, consumption, and the making or spending of money. Entertainment was to be bought, or at the very least earned. Boys who would have run errands for political bosses in 1870, accumulating political and social capital, focused their hustling on money-making schemes in 1900. Immigrant boys acted like "little businessmen," according to their sisters, and some adults could "detect only commercial values in the young," accused Jane Addams.[105]

Youth politics had been built on a different model. While nineteenth-century young people expected to make their own entertainment—building a bonfire or a sparking a riot—the young of the twentieth century increasingly bought their fun, created by professional entertainers and marketed by showmen, impresarios, or corporations.[106] Go-ahead nineteenth-century youths certainly cared about making money, but they did not tend to divide their world so neatly between labor and leisure. Many valued a third pursuit: a blend of self-improvement, unpaid work, and fun that showed itself in literary and debating societies, all of those bees (spelling bees, quilting bees, husking bees, logging bees), and especially political action. The new youth culture believed that fun was to be bought, and democracy had little to sell. So much of popular politics—the meetings, the rallies, all that "hurrahing"—looked like unpaid work to the children of the new era.[107]

It was not the death of party barbecues or the rise of vaudeville but a far more idealistic goal that may have done the most damage. Republican and Democratic organizers began to use their permanent clubs to present party policies in an enlightened, thoughtful manner. This "educational campaigning" came to dominate popular politics by 1892. It appealed to reformers' legitimate concerns about the miserably misinformed electorate and was cheaper and more refined than spectacular public rallies. Young partisans had a new job: to facilitate the "methodical dispensing of correct, practical political information."[108]

But educational campaigns, however well intentioned, failed to understand the nature of popular politics or youth culture. Human interaction and social aspiration drove young people's involvement; literature on the tariff did not.[109] Educational campaigners meant well, but the rallying cry of one organization hints at why they failed to excite many seventeen-year-olds. Instead of a catchy slogan or a mean rhyme, the Duluth Republican League called upon young Americans to "study dispassionately."[110]

Even more dispassionate: those new government-printed "Australian" ballots stifled the wild spectacle of nineteenth-century elections. Voting had been a thrilling confrontation and declaration of manhood, as a first-time voter braved challengers in front of the adult men in his community. After the 1890s, turning out on Election Day felt private, quiet, and cold. The ballot itself had been a totem of democracy, ornately designed, handed off by mature-seeming hustlers and clutched by excited voters. After the rise of the Australian ballot between 1887 and 1896, it was merely a complicated government document. Voting reform cleaned up elections and wrested the tools of democracy from the hands of hustlers but also altered the rite of passage that had drawn in so many virgin voters. It perfectly encapsulated the trade-off between popular politics and good government.[111]

Ballot reform had the same intention and impact as the permanent clubs, private banquets, and educational campaigns. The parties sought to bring young people into democracy but could not appreciate the benefits of existing mechanisms. For decades young people had gravitated toward popular politics, drawn by the casual, heterogeneous environment that promised introduction to elders, social mixing, public spectacle, and plenty of fun. Reformers who preferred a more systematic style ignored the strengths of the old system, cutting the strong but loose bonds of popular politics and replacing them with weak, stiff ties that offered neither maturity nor advancement.

By the mid-1890s, each stage of young people's political socialization was under attack. Age separation reduced the amount of time children spent mixing with partisan elders. Private clubs no longer invited many youths into party life. Those youths, for their part, had less desire to join middle-aged men to slosh beer, bellow slogans, and curse the other party.

Educational committees and government ballot-printers replaced young canvassers and hustlers. Even the climactic act of casting one's virgin vote took place behind closed doors.

As political institutions became less open and young people found other venues for their enthusiasm, adults seemed to forget how to win over the young. Thomas P. Ballard, an earnest Chicago Republican and Union League member, provided a perfect example. In 1896 Ballard confidently proposed "an excellent scheme" to appeal to young voters. "It has always seemed strange to me," Ballard told the Chicago *Inter Ocean*, "that we give no attention to young men when they mature and arrive at the age of manhood." He proposed a civic ceremony, overseen by the mayor and held at the Union League, in which all first-time voters in Chicago would gather for speeches on their public duty.[112]

Ballard was no villain. He wanted to create informed, independent young voters. Men like Ballard simply overlooked the customs that had already ushered virgin voters into manhood. American culture had rituals in place to celebrate the occasion, maintained by friends, parents, and activists, not by the mayor or the Union League. Such reformers had trouble seeing customs that were not sanctioned by official associations.[113] And Thomas Ballard's profession? He worked for Ginn and Company, owners of Athenaeum Press, selling tens of thousands of textbooks to new, age-graded schools nationwide.[114]

By 1900, optimistic reformers like Ballard were often replaced by shrugging politicians who felt increasing difficulty communicating to young Americans. Adult politicians sat through more lectures on the power of the young voters but spoke with fewer of them. Jane Addams noticed that politicians were failing to "keep in touch with the youth."[115]

Youths who used to marinate in popular politics for decades now only sipped at their democracy. To many citizens born around 1880 and maturing in the 1890s, democracy looked like "a trade, a profession, or a calling" practiced by an interested few in secluded offices and banquet halls.[116] Growing up with an isolated political culture and an embracing peer culture, members of this generation did not feel pushed into politics by their social lives or pulled in by campaigners. As they wandered from democracy, Jane Addams observed, the young took with them "the very stores of enthusiasm which are needed to sustain it."[117]

Democracy Goes Indoors

It is difficult to track the demise of a cultural practice. Among young people it is particularly hard to point to rites not passed. You only get one youth, so comparing it with that of past generations is always tricky. Few twenty-one-years-olds explained in their diaries why they chose not to cast their first ballot in 1900. Yet we know that the soaring plateau of popular politics began to crumble, that between the 1890s and the 1920s, voter turnout went from a practice of the vast majority of enfranchised Americans to an outlying activity ignored by most.[118] And we can see, from available statistics and from the larger culture, that young Americans led the way.

At first, changes in the media obscured young Americans' flagging interest. Beginning in the 1890s, newspapers that had documented political life in a dense, populist style shifted to human interest stories on individual "young men in politics."[119] Those "young men" were often career politicians in their thirties or forties. Theodore Roosevelt, William Jennings Bryan, Albert J. Beveridge, George McClellan Jr., and Richard Yates Jr. had all used their relative youth as a selling point in their public careers.[120] Though journalists had long joked about supposedly "young politicians" who were "bald and toothless," newspaper profiles allowed one prominent thirty-five-year-old to stand in for a hundred anonymous seventeen-year-olds.[121]

But no paper could hide the falling away of the public political spectacles that had defined American democracy since 1840. Without a steady flow of excited young marchers, rallies and processions withered and died within a few years. In 1892 permanent clubs began to dismiss the idea of holding public rallies, and by 1896 they were already ebbing. In the words of historian Michael McGerr, "Spectacular parades almost vanished in the first decade of the twentieth century."[122]

Even Will Howells turned his back on politics. The first break came in 1887, just as reformers introduced new clubs and new ballots. The Haymarket Affair—in which an unknown bomber killed seven Chicago police officers, and several prominent radicals were executed despite little evidence linking them to the crime—turned Will against the system of justice. Fifty-year-old Howells wrote public letters to the *New York Tribune* condemning the executions and their supporters in both parties, calling on readers to acknowledge "we had a political execution in Chicago yesterday. The sooner we realize this, the better for us."[123]

From there, Howells denounced the party that he came of age support-ing. The Republicans had deformed into "the party of industrial slavery," becoming "a lie in defamation of its past."[124] Like his father, four decades earlier, another nonconformist Howells ditched his political party. One wonders how his adolescent son, John, took the news. Will dabbled in supporting the Populists in the 1890s but mostly lost interest in democracy after that. Young Americans were not the only ones turning from elections and rallies: a pervasive disappointment with both parties accelerated the decline across the ages.

The new culture felt foreign to men like Howells. It moved too quickly, seeming to burn brighter all the time. After a year abroad in the 1880s, Will felt cut off from the nation he returned to. America, he wrote, "had grown more American" in his absence, "and I with my crimson opinions was scarcely more than a dull purple."[125] These were the years when How-ells shifted his literary focus to analyzing his own youth, returning over and over again to the muddy riverbank civilization of his boyhood.

Many older Americans buried themselves in reflection as well. Memoir-ists recounting their youths documented the changing attitudes toward popular politics. The phrases "virgin vote" and "maiden vote" actually peaked in publications between the late 1880s and 1915, written, not by thrilled first-time voters, but by older men and women reminiscing about their bygone mid-nineteenth-century youths.[126] And though most ap-preciated the cleaner, fairer democracy of the twentieth century, many complained that younger generations lacked their zeal for politics. Theo-logian Lyman Abbott's *Reminiscences* included letters he sent to his cousin as a twenty-year-old in the 1850s, discussing time spent hustling ballots at Brooklyn polling places and his near trampling by a stampeding Re-publican procession. Abbott concluded with the popular sentiment, "The conditions which I described to my cousin in 1856 could not be duplicated anywhere in America in 1913."[127]

The same change is clear in the American Life Histories interviews col-lected by the New Deal–era Federal Writers' Project. Though recorded well after the end of the age of popular politics, these interviews show that a long-lingering divide emerged in the 1890s on conceptions of public de-mocracy. Interviewees who mentioned casting their virgin vote almost all participated in nineteenth-century elections, supporting Lincoln or Grant or Cleveland. Those who voted for Taft, Wilson, or Coolidge rarely both-ered to mention it. Tellingly, most subjects who grew up during the age of popular politics reminisced about "elections" as public, social events, while those born after the 1870s mostly spoke about people who were "elected," as a past-tense granting of individual power.[128]

One subject in the American Life Histories, a German American born in 1870, recalled that "politics played a big part in the life of this town years ago" and even began to wax nostalgic about a particularly clever vote-buying "lad."[129] On the other hand, when an interviewer asked a subject, born in 1892, if he voted, the man replied, "No, ma'am, I don't never vote. I don't believe in association with folks that hang around the polls. That kind of trash don't suit me."[130]

Others mistakenly blamed new technologies. A number of older Americans felt that the cars, telephones, movies, airplanes, and other inventions booming in the first quarter of the twentieth century drove off public democratic culture. One elderly man pointed out that "back in the old days," rural Americans came together "from the outlying districts with their buggies—bring their lunches and spend the day in town on election day." "Now they all got cars," he complained, and "can dash in here and vote quick as anybody else."[131] An editorialist in San Jose worried about young people's fixation with technology, observing that "aeroplanes and gas engines" have "the effect of deadening interest in politics."[132] No one technology caused the shift away from political entertainment—in fact, most appeared well after democratic enthusiasm began to wane—but each invention put more distance between a young generation and the world that had inspired virgin voters.

Even the writer who worried about "aeroplanes and gas engines" knew his time had passed. He went on to grumble that, among the young, he was "liable to be considered an old fogey who wags his head and says: 'things isn't what they used to be.'" His concern, that adolescents fixated on the modern would not like being lectured about democracy, shows how finished the age of popular politics was. Young people began to use phrases like "old fogey," "old-time," and "old-fashioned" when talking about their democracy.[133]

This generational thinking turned out to be very bad for youth politics. The whole system was premised on a succession of striving young people passing down their excitement. Young people's identification as a distinct generation of peers, rather than as an unceasing "army of younger brothers," cut the circuit. And once it was up to individual generations, youth politics became inherently ephemeral, as every generation grows up. Youth is temporary, so young people's politics only worked when it was easily imparted and inherited.

At the same time, what once made youth politics so vital led to its undo-ing. Young people just kept coming, quickly distancing themselves from the old popular political culture. All it took was a few small changes over a few short years to break up the flow of young people into democratic life. Once it began, every twenty-one-year-old who did not vote inspired a sixteen-year-old not to read a newspaper and an eight-year-old not to sing campaign songs. Youth politics never roared louder than in 1884, but the children born that year would hardly know it by the time they could vote. The fundamentally social appeal of popular politics, which had made it so alluring and useful, now made it irrelevant. The young men and women who used to fuel their democracy drowned it instead.

By the 1910s and 1920s, young people rarely considered politics a venue for their social needs. The diary of Yvonne Blue offers a good example. The fourteen-year-old Chicago girl had many of the same concerns as fourteen-year-olds of previous eras, but she looked elsewhere for solu-tions. Instead of upcoming rallies, her friends talked about movies. When Yvonne's teacher assigned her Mary Boykin Chesnut's classic Civil War diary, she was shocked that someone would fill her private journal with public events. Yvonne puzzled, "My diary is not in the slightest degree of political interest. I'm not much on politics. My diary is of interest only to myself."[134] For the young people coming of age in the twentieth century, the world of politics and the world of the self rarely overlapped.

It was that personal appeal that had invited so many young people to participate in their democracy in the nineteenth century. For Sally Mc-Carty, the Virginia girl who stayed up late listening to her parents talk Whig politics in the 1840s, there was something powerfully unifying about how interest in politics "affected people as vitally as their own private af-fairs."[135] For Benjamin Brown Foster, the nervous phrenologist arguing "a boy's opinion" at Maine polling places, it was the way issues "not intimately concerning myself" could reinforce his vulnerable sense of importance.[136] And for Oscar Lawrence Jackson, shouting before an Ohio audience of friends and rivals, it was the attention, novelty, praise, and infamy of his democratic grandstanding that could "tickle my vanity and rouse the ambi-tion of anyone my age."[137]

Reformers unbundled politics from the other rites of youth, just at the moment when young people needed such assistance less. After the sorting out of political culture and youth culture, all that democratic participation had to offer was its official goals: governance, rational choice, and, worst of all, duty. The more reformers spoke about young people's responsibilities as citizens, the fewer seemed interested. The short article discussing Thomas P. Ballard's scheme to celebrate first-time voters used the word "duty" eleven times.[138] This new way of seeing voting as a solely civic act lowered young people's enthusiasm. Once politics was cut off from the rest of life, put in the realm of obligation rather than aspiration, it had little appeal.

George Washington Plunkitt saw the change unfold. As custodians moved Graziano's shoeshine stand, mopped up the mess his friends had left, and shushed the favor-seekers making a racket in the courthouse rotunda, the pompous boss noted the end of the system he had spent his life manipulating. He told a friend, "I have studied politics and men for forty-five years, and I see how things are driftin'. Sad indeed is the change that has come over the young." As the twentieth century dawned, young Americans were "beginnin' to look coldly" on partisan spectacle, and fewer saw the utility of parties in their own struggling and ambitious lives.[139]

"And why should they," Plunkitt asked, mixing the best and worst of the age of popular politics; "what is there in it for them?"[140]

Afterword

Twelve-year-olds can't hold their liquor like they used to. Americans tend to frown on paramilitary political clubs. Bring a live raccoon to a rally and someone will call Animal Control. Those looking to get young people more involved in politics today can't just borrow the best tricks of nineteenth-century b'hoys or bosses. History is not a dusty toolbox, packed with old instruments to bring back into use. Culture changes too much in between.

Yet the speechifying of Oscar Lawrence Jackson and the detective work of Susan Bradford stand as tantalizing reminders of how different our lives could be. There was a time when schoolchildren argued about their favorite candidate, political rallies were a place to flirt, and adults stood around listening (inattentively) to the soapbox diatribes of youths. One can't help but wonder how our nation might be different if this were the case today.[1]

The fantasy that we could repurpose the best techniques of the age of popular politics is hubris at best. It brings to mind a Jurassic Park of poll hustlers, with electioneers in ragged tweed ambushing potential voters in Target parking lots and thuggish b'hoys chasing off League of Women Voters volunteers with brickbats and saucy Victorian slang.

And besides, this book does not venerate a golden age. Virgin voters and young activists were motivated and involved, but they could also be selfish, bigoted, frequently violent, and gallingly ignorant. Higher rates of youth voting wouldn't be worth it, if it meant a return to "awlings" in the line to vote.

Yet the story of the virgin vote shows that the world we know is not the only option. An average of 45 percent of eligible eighteen- to twenty-nine-year-olds have turned out for presidential elections over the last several decades. The 2014 congressional election experienced the lowest youth turnout ever recorded in forty years of elections.[2] Baby boomers, for all their talk, were only marginally more likely to vote in their twenties. (Youth turnout is as bad in other Western democracies; in fact, it is sometimes lower in Canada and Great Britain.)[3] Though the numbers fluctuate, they tend to follow larger turnout trends; Americans under thirty have been roughly 20 percent less likely to vote for quite some time. These statistics illustrate a gnawing problem—not necessarily a crisis, just a steady stream of young Americans not living up to their political potential.[4]

None of this means that young people inherently care less about politics, always have and always will. Iron laws of human nature cannot be drawn from statistics complied since 1972. America has one of the oldest, largest, and certainly the noisiest democracies on the planet. Looking back we can find a time when young adults and even children took a passionate, driving interest in politics. We owe it to our present to explore this past.

There was an age when young people saw promise in their political system. And there could be another. Kindling a passion for democracy among today's young people would require more cultural work than legal reform. The laws that govern elections have changed since the age of popular politics, but not fundamentally. The big differences come from practice and custom. We use our democracy differently than we used to. There are reforms—same-day registration, accessible ID requirements, moving voting to weekends—which would get more young people involved, but most of the work would focus on reworking America's democratic culture.[5]

What would George Washington Plunkitt, the scheming boss, or George Washington Albright, the enslaved activist, advise? For the most part, a renaissance of youth politics would require changing the assumptions we make about how and when young people are introduced to politics. If there is one point most nineteenth-century Americans would agree upon, it is that voters are built, slowly, over many years and many stages.

The fundamental premise driving the virgin vote was that democracy is social. It has become popular to look to neurology, evolutionary theory, or big data to explain American politics, but these views all neglect what political scientists and educators (not to mention ward bosses) have known for quite some time: social environment has the greatest influence on political behavior.[6] The key to getting young people involved in politics, regardless of brain chemistry or shopping habits, is to raise them in a culture that cares. It remains true, some 170 years after Sally McCarty stayed up late listening to her elders talk politics, that involved parents, relatives, siblings, and teachers make young voters.

Young people are no longer bound to their parents' party as they were in the age of popular politics, but social, cultural, and economic backgrounds still determine their level of involvement. Education has an extremely clear influence: eighteen- to twenty-nine-year-olds with a college degree or higher actually vote on par with some nineteenth-century elections, while barely a quarter of young people without a high school degree usually turn out.[7] A wide array of social factors affect involvement: volunteering has a positive impact on voting; the divorce of one's parents has a small negative result.[8] Background can still trump ideology as well. Young African American men, for instance, are more likely to label themselves "conservative" than young white men but were twice as likely to vote for the Democrats in 2012.[9] Voters of all demographics still weigh background above beliefs.

The age of popular politics also incorporated young people by embracing the passionate ugliness of partisan conflict. When James Witham, heading west on his wander year, argued about economic justice with an older man on his train, it sparked a lifelong involvement. When Annie Youmans made flirtatious bets with rival partisans, and when Anna Ridgely attended Republican rallies despite coming from a strong Democratic family, they engaged in this same kind of open political debate.

This is not the case today. Democracy occupies a strangely fractured place in American culture. On the one hand, vocal partisans on either side have returned political conflict to the realm of entertainment since 2000 or so, zealously following the latest election or congressional battle. Forget the horse race; the dogfight mentality is back. But a large number of Americans have clung to the twentieth century's avoidance of open political disagreement, responding to the sins of specific elected officials by blaming all politics. Congress has become the easy punch line of late-night shows and eye-rolling small talk. The partisans join in, attacking ridiculous caricatures of the other side or holding unreasonably high hopes for their own candidates. The combination helps produce some of the worst attitudes about democracy: cynicism, apathy, the "they're all corrupt" rhetoric that lumps the public servants in with the demagogues.

Open partisanship, it turns out, is less harmful to young people than this lazy dismissal of democracy. Honest discussion of political disagreements has been shown to have a positive impact on voter turnout.[10] Political scientists find that citizens who spent their adolescence in politically competitive regions are more likely to vote as adults.[11] Open conflict, Lincoln and Tilden and Plunkitt could have told you, inspires activism; it is apathy that diminishes it.

Yet there are many forces making Americans too polite to teach these conflicts. Fewer than one-third of teachers think that parents would strongly support their decision to teach about a current election in class.[12]

One study found that racially diverse schools (not minority-majority schools, but genuinely multiracial environments) are actually less likely to openly discuss politics for fear of causing conflict among student populations.[13] In the meantime, the zealots are not sitting on the sidelines. We can see the harm the dogfight mentality did to nineteenth-century politics, putting victory ahead of reform for many decades, but avoidance of political debate can be just as dangerous. We need to teach young people the skills of contained, honest political conflict.

Perhaps the stages that structured young people's involvement in popular politics can offer some lessons today. The building political education that children received makes clear the long scope of civic education. Nineteenth-century parents and politicians were adept at layering, stage by stage, a sturdy political consciousness, so that by the time they could finally vote young Americans were devoted partisans. Bringing more young people into politics in the twenty-first century requires adults to talk to their children. Expecting political parties to automatically turn uninformed eighteen-year-olds into active voters is like expecting public schools to overcome poverty, crime, and problems at home. If young people aren't voting enough, the blame falls on their entire community.

While children received their parents' politics, "youths" made them useful in their own lives. Today's teenagers live in a very different world, with very different problems, but often feel the same desire for agency and importance. The stressors have changed, but the underlying human emotions are familiar. Just as joining a Catholic organization helped guide the "poor boy" Michael Campbell to the Democratic Party, or membership in the Union League helped get young African Americans voting during Reconstruction, participation in groups still guides adolescents toward political involvement. This is particularly important among poorer Americans, who are less likely to join clubs, churches, and unions, and for young men, whose community involvement and voting habits fall behind those of young women.[14] Get these adolescents into organizations at fourteen, and they will be more likely to vote at eighteen or twenty.

Can the ritual of the virgin vote be brought back? Is there a way to celebrate young men's and women's first ballot, à la Thomas Ballard's plan in 1896? I'm not sure. In the 2012 election, *Girls* creator Lena Dunham filmed an ad supporting Obama and aimed at young women. Titled "Your First Time," the video played on the very old idea of political virginity. It aired as I was still researching this book, and I held my breath; it was thrilling to see rhetoric from the 1850s reanimated, even if unknowingly. The ad was soon forgotten, but it shows how compelling the old logic of the virgin vote can be. Could we bring back its meaning as well, making one's first vote a declaration of adulthood, not just a civic duty?

This seems to be the hardest change to engineer. It may run against the tone of the era to expect eighteen-year-olds to look forward to participating in government or joining a party, especially compared with other rites of passage: it's hard to compete with drinking twenty-one shots. Is there a way to play on young people's combination of individualism and exhibitionism to get them to value this ritual that is at once personal and public?

Some of the greatest insights into modern youth politics can be found in the fourth stage, as young adults considered how to persuade one another to vote. Recent work on political influence has affirmed what country-store canvassers knew: the substance of a campaigner's message ("negative" or "positive," "partisan" or "nonpartisan") matters less than his or her relationship with the voter. Despite all the talk about new campaign technologies, face-to-face lobbying is by far the most effective form of influence.[15] Media can play a strong role, as long as it is sufficiently social: automated phone calls and mass emails can actually depress involvement.[16]

Persuading young people to vote is best done in person by relatable members of one's community. Celebrity appeals aimed at young people do not seem to have a statistically significant impact on young people's involvement.[17] The idea is more than a little condescending. In addition, not knowing how and where to register is often a significant deterrent for young people; nationwide appeals by celebrities in Hollywood cannot provide this specific information to young voters in their communities. If Rock the Vote and other organizations do help get young people voting, it may be their on-the-ground workers, not celebrity PSAs, that are effective.

Campaigners hoping to win over young voters might consider playing on the "quarter generation" logic from the age of popular politics. Democracy is social and voting is aspirational; using canvassers slightly older than the target audiences may be a successful tool. Adults often think that teenagers are interested only in their own age group, but many are fixated on taking their next step into adulthood. Maturity fascinates most young people more than youth does. Personal interaction with adult-seeming college students might stand a good chance of getting high schoolers excited about voting, in a way sixty-five-year-olds or celebrities cannot.

For political parties, challenges currently exist that did not present themselves in the nineteenth century. During the age of popular politics, campaigning was mostly a matter of rallying the faithful; young people usually followed their family's party, and there were few independents. Although each party claimed to be the favorite of virgin voters, young people were usually split fairly evenly. Partisanship was too tied to background; even if one party had a big year, there were still many sons of the other side aging into the system. The result was close elections and steady competition. Three-fifths of presidents elected in the age of popular politics did not win a majority of the popular vote (most won pluralities), and the big landslides in American history took place in the twentieth century.

Today one party, the Democrats, can honestly claim to have far more young people on its side. In 2012, Barack Obama won 60 percent of eighteen- to twenty-nine-year-olds; in 2008 he took 66 percent of that age group. This is an unusual and significant divide in American political history, and it is impossible to predict how long it will last. It cannot be easily explained by the old canard that young voters are inherently more liberal. Millions of virgin voters cast their first ballots for candidates allied with the Know Nothings and the Ku Klux Klan in the age of popular politics. Young people's current preference for the Democratic Party is not inherent or fixed. The question is simply what can the Republicans do about it?

The only advice nineteenth-century politicos might offer to today's Republicans is to remember the power of being the national Outs. Nothing better rallied young people, at least in their era, than coming together to "throw the bums out." Republicans have made halfhearted attempts at summoning up this rhetoric—like vice presidential candidate Paul Ryan's 2012 speech at the Republican National Convention in which he declared, "College graduates should not have to live out their twenties in their childhood bedrooms, staring up at fading Obama posters and wondering when they can move out"—but so far they have preferred to rally their aging base instead. Maybe the iron law of youth politics, that every generation grows up and new cohorts rise, will work in their favor eventually.

For the Republican Party, the Democratic Party, and all the activists, educators, and parents wishing to increase young Americans' involvement in politics, the simplest lesson is to think long-term. One election cycle is just not long enough to build the interest, the aspiration, and the need to vote. Like other adult positions in society—parent, spouse, employee—voters are formed over decades of experience. Nineteenth-century partisans saw this, ready to recruit "the boys from thirteen to seventeen . . . this army of younger brothers."[18] Smart campaigners often knew who had a younger sibling just reaching the age when he might become politically useful. To improve youth voter turnout, reformers should forget about "game changers" and think about sustainability.

Likewise, this story reminds us that youth politics are not necessarily generational politics. Since 1900, most Americans have seemed to believe that the two go hand in hand, but the decline of youth involvement in the 1890s showed that too much identification with one's peers can make it difficult to build long-term youth movements. The bursts of young people's politics, in the 1930s or the 1960s, proved to be just as ephemeral as those generations' youths. They could produce a sudden peak of interest but not the steady succession of children, youths, and young adults that sustained the plateau of nineteenth-century democracy. Focus on the virgin voters, passing down their excitement, and forget generations.

Finally, we should expect no more or less from young people than we would from older Americans. There is a tendency to idolize or demonize youth in politics. They are either dismissed as lazy and self-absorbed or held up as pure and guileless, rising to rescue our democracy. Young Americans' intense engagement in the age of popular politics teaches a far more complicated, human lesson. Those young men and women were just like everyone else—passionate and clever and selfish and shortsighted. Like all citizens, their political involvement grew from personal need.

Well-meaning reformers helped kill off popular politics in the 1890s by believing the clichés about purehearted virgin voters. They would not listen to what George Washington Plunkitt kept shouting: that everyone hopes to *get something* out of politics. The reformers believed that twenty-one-year-olds were so honest and true that they would turn out to hear dispassionate treatises on tariff reform. In the process they squelched the fun.

The opposite tendency prevails today. Teens and twentysomethings are constantly depicted as too narcissistic to care about government. The TV show *30 Rock* captured this perfectly when a young character quipped, "My generation never votes; it interferes with talking about ourselves all the time." The joke was funny, a gag on an age group seemingly obsessed with publicizing the private, but it speaks to exactly what we get wrong about youth politics, implying that public involvement and self-interest are mutually exclusive. It reminded me of Yvonne Blue, the Jazz Age girl shocked at a Civil War diary that discussed political, not just personal, affairs. When we set public politics against personal identity, politics will always lose. Young people simply won't vote if it feels distant from their present selves and from their hopes for the future.

Those who criticize today's young people for self-involvement are wrong to blame just one generation. Flip through Oscar Lawrence Jackson's diary, brimming with tickled vanity, or Mattie Thomas's impassioned letters, bundling her romantic yearning with partisan vitriol. Young people have long loved talking about themselves. Politics used to let them.

Appendix

Year Property Requirements for Voting Removed

State	Year	Phase
New Hampshire	1784	Revolutionary
Vermont	1786	Revolutionary
Georgia	1789	Revolutionary
Pennsylvania	1790	Revolutionary
Delaware	1792	Revolutionary
Kentucky	1792	Revolutionary
Maryland	1801	Revolutionary
Ohio	1802	New state
Indiana	1816	New state
Mississippi	1817	New state
Illinois	1818	New state
Alabama	1819	New state
Maine	1820	New state
Massachusetts	1821	Reforming state
Missouri	1821	New state
New York	1821	Reforming state
Tennessee	1834	Reforming state
Michigan	1835	New state
Arkansas	1836	New state
Florida	1838	New state
New Jersey	1844	Reforming state
Connecticut	1845	Reforming state
Louisiana	1845	Reforming state
Texas	1845	New state
Iowa	1846	New state
Wisconsin	1848	New state
California	1850	New state
Virginia	1850	Holdout
North Carolina	1854	Holdout
Rhode Island	In place in 1855	Holdout
South Carolina	In place in 1855	Holdout

Percentage of States with Property Requirements

Year	%
1790	76
1800	62
1810	53
1820	39
1830	33
1840	27
1850	13
1855	9

Source: Alexander Keyssar, *The Right to Vote: The Contested History of Democracy in the United States* (New York: Basic Books, 2009), tables A-1, 2, and 3.

Median Age of Americans, 1800–1990

Year	Median age
1800	16
1810	16
1820	16.7
1830	17.2
1840	17.8
1850	18.9
1860	19.4
1870	20.2
1880	20.9
1890	22
1900	22.9
1910	24.1
1920	25.3
1930	26.5
1940	29
1950	30.2
1960	29.5
1970	28.1
1980	30
1990	32.8

Source: Michael R. Haines and Richard H. Steckel, *A Population History of North America* (New York: Cambridge University Press, 2000), table A-4, 702–4.

Eligible Voter Turnout in Presidential Elections, 1824–2012

Year	National voter turnout (%)	Year	National voter turnout (%)
1824	26.9	1920	49.2
1828	57.6	1924	48.9
1832	55.4	1928	56.9
1836	57.8	1932	56.9
1840	80.2	1936	61.0
1844	78.9	1940	62.5
1848	72.7	1944	55.9
1852	69.6	1948	53.0
1856	78.9	1952	63.3
1860	81.2	1956	60.6
1864	73.8	1960	64.0
1868	78.1	1964	61.7
1872	71.3	1968	60.6
1876	81.3	1972	55.2
1880	79.4	1976	53.5
1884	77.5	1980	52.6
1888	79.3	1984	53.3
1892	74.7	1988	50.3
1896	79.3	1992	55.1
1900	73.2	1996	49
1904	65.2	2000	49.3
1908	65.4	2004	56.7
1912	58.8	2008	63
1916	61.6	2012	59

Source: John P. McIver, *Historical Statistics of the United States, Millennial Edition*, ed. Susan B. Carter and Scott Sigmund Gartner (Cambridge: Cambridge University Press 2006), series Eb62–113.

Notes

Introduction

1. Oscar Lawrence Jackson, *The Colonel's Diary: Journals Kept before and during the Civil War*, ed. David P. Jackson (Sharon, Pa.: Privately published, 1922), 27–28, 40; Charles H. Smith, *The History of Fuller's Ohio Brigade, 1861–1865* (Cleveland: Press of A. J. Watt, 1909), 352; John Brown, *History of Hocking Valley, Ohio* (Chicago: Inter-state Publishing, 1883), 887; "Great Republicans Barbeque at Logan," *Ohio State Journal*, October 9, 1860; Judith S. Manikas, *Logan and Hocking County, Images of America* (New York: Arcadia, 2011).

2. Jackson, *Colonel's Diary*, 9; Robert William Fogel, *Without Consent of Contract: The Rise and Fall of American Slavery* (New York: W. W. Norton, 1989), 141. Owing mostly to superior nutrition, northern white men like Oscar were slightly taller than southern white men, who were, in turn, slightly taller than African American southern men.

3. U.S. Census Bureau, "Mean Center of Population for the United States: 1790 to 2010," last modified April 19, 2013, http://www.census.gov/geo/reference/pdfs/cenpop2010/centerpop_mean2010.pdf.

4. Michael R. Haines and Richard H. Steckel, *A Population History of North America* (New York: Cambridge University Press, 2000), 702–4.

5. Jackson, *Colonel's Diary*, 9–10.

6. Ibid., 9–17.

7. Ibid., 16, 18–20, 34–36. For a useful study of such societies and their impact on young Americans' place in public discourse, see Carolyn Eastman, *A Nation of Speechifiers* (Chicago: University of Chicago Press, 2009).

8. Jackson, *Colonel's Diary*, 40.

9. Ibid., 30.

10. Ibid., 17–19. Oscar never married but continued to be an active courter for much of his life. When he returned to politics in the 1880s, serving as a representative from Pennsylvania, several newspapers reported on forty-six-year-old Oscar as one of the most eligible bachelors in Congress. After describing his dark beard and untamed hair, the correspondent noted that Oscar was already courting a young lady. "Bachelors in Congress," *North American*, March 12, 1886.

11. Jackson, *Colonel's Diary*, 31.

12. Ibid., 31–32.

13. "Great Republicans Barbeque at Logan"; Jackson, *Colonel's Diary*, 32, 34.

14. "Great Republicans Barbeque at Logan." Though the crowds in Logan believed that Cartter's vote "nominated Mr. Lincoln," in fact he only reported the shift of other members of the Ohio delegation to supporting Lincoln. See "The Four Votes," *Chicago Press and Tribune*, May 19, 1860.

15. "Great Republicans Barbeque at Logan."

16. Jackson, *Colonel's Diary*, 34.

17. "Great Republicans Barbeque at Logan"; Jackson, *Colonel's Diary*, 32, 34.

18. Jon Grinspan, "'Young Men for War': The Wide Awakes and Lincoln's 1860 Presidential Campaign," *Journal of American History* 96 (September 2009): 357–78.

19. William A. Alcott, *Familiar Letters to Young Men on Various Subjects: Designed as a Companion to "The Young Man's Guide"* (Buffalo: Geo. H. Derby, 1850), 16–8, 253; William Alcott, *The Young Man's Guide* (Boston: Lilly, Wait, Colman, and Holden, 1834).

20. Clay W. Anderson to William G. Beatty, June 24, 1856, in *Life and Letters of Judge Thomas J. Anderson and Wife*, ed. James House Anderson and Nancy Anderson (Cincinnati: Press of F. J. Heer, 1904), 475.

21. A total of 115,155,823 were recorded in presidential elections between 1840 and 1900. Of course, many of these votes were cast by the same individuals in successive elections. Statistics calculated based on Gerhard Peters and John Woolley, "Presidential Elections Data," *American Presidency Project*, University of California, Santa Barbara, http://www.presidency.ucsb.edu/elections.php (last accessed October 15, 2014).

22. Before the twentieth century, all democratic governments excluded large blocs of society from suffrage. The Athenians denied slaves, roughly half of their population, the vote. In nineteenth-century Britain, three major reform acts left 95 percent of the population voteless after 1832 and still denied the vote to 40 percent of men and all women in 1884. In the Netherlands, the reformist constitution of 1848 maintained very high property qualifications, though the 1887 revision reduced them significantly. Nineteenth-century America's closest democratic competitors were Switzerland, which introduced full male suffrage in 1848; the self-governing colonies of south Australia, which did so in the 1850s; and France, which extended the right to vote to all men in 1875. No state anywhere extended the full right to vote to women before New Zealand did so in 1893. By extending the vote to most classes of adult white males, the United States, despite racial and gender restrictions, still enfranchised a plurality of its adult population and a larger proportion than other democracies.

John A. Phillips and Charles Wetherell, "The Great Reform Act of 1832 and the Political Modernization of England," *American Historical Review* 100 (April 1995), 413–14; Colin Pilkington, *The Politics Today Companion to the British Constitution* (Manchester: Manchester University Press, 1999), 134; Jan Willem Sap, *The Netherlands Constitution, 1848–1998* (West Lafayette, Ind.: Purdue University Press, 2000); Peter McPhee, "Electoral Democracy and Direct Democracy in France, 1789–1851," *European History Quarterly* 16 (1986): 77–96; Australian Electoral Commission, "The Right to Vote in Australia," last modified January 28, 2011, http://aec.gov.au/Elections/Australian _Electoral_History/righttovote.htm; Daniel T. Rodgers, *Atlantic Crossings: Social Politics in the Progressive Age* (Cambridge, Mass.: Harvard University Press, 1998), 35–36.

23. Alexander Keyssar, *The Right to Vote: The Contested History of Democracy in the United States* (New York: Basic Books, 2009), 1; Sean Wilentz, *The Rise of American Democracy: Jefferson to Lincoln* (New York: W. W. Norton, 2005), 4.

24. A strong body of literature has pushed back against the notion that American democracy erupted, from nowhere, with Andrew Jackson or the surge in voter turnout after 1840. The best works, situated in heated state races, uncover a forgotten world of experimental, tentative democratic culture. What they do not show (and what is anachronistic to expect them to find) is the kind of nationwide, sustained political culture that balanced entertainment and government between 1840 and 1900. Nonetheless, their work tempers the more sudden explanations of the rise of American democracy proposed by some historians. David Waldstreicher, *In the Midst of Perpetual Fetes: The Making of American Nationalism, 1776–1820* (Chapel Hill: University of North Carolina Press, 1997); Daniel Peart, *The Era of Experimentation: American Political Practices in the Early Republic* (Charlottesville: University of Virginia Press, 2014); Jeffrey L. Pasley, Andrew W. Robertson, and David Waldstreicher, eds., *Beyond the Founders: New Approaches to the Political History of the Early American Republic* (Chapel Hill: University of North Carolina Press, 2004); Byron E. Shafer and Anthony J. Badger, eds., *Contesting Democracy: Substance and Structure in American Political History, 1775–2000* (Lawrence: University of Kansas Press, 2001); Gordon S. Wood, *The Radicalism of the American Revolution* (New York: Vintage Books, 1993); Wilentz, *Rise of American Democracy*; David Hackett Fischer, *The Revolution of American Conservatism: The Federalist Party in the Era of Jeffersonian Democracy* (New York: Harper and Row, 1969).

25. States removed their property requirements in four stages, beginning with the revolutionary constitutions in states like New Hampshire, Vermont, and Pennsylvania (between 1784 and 1801), followed by those of new states in the Midwest and Deep South (from 1802 to 1821), then by a series of reforming East Coast states like Massachusetts and New York (1821 to 1845), and finally by the conservative holdouts like Virginia, Rhode Island, and South Carolina (in the 1850s and 1860s). Keyssar, *Right to Vote*, tables A-1, 2 and 3. See Appendix.

26. Property requirements also acted as a de facto limit on young adults' participation, as most men who were otherwise eligible to vote did not accumulate enough property to participate until later in life. Corinne T. Field, *The Struggle for Equal Adulthood: Gender, Race, Age, and the Fight for Citizenship in Antebellum America* (Chapel Hill: University of North Carolina Press, 2014), 31.

27. Turnout statistics drawn from John P. McIver, *Historical Statistics of the United States, Millennial Edition*, ed. Susan B. Carter and Scott Sigmund Gartner (Cambridge: Cambridge University Press 2006), series Eb62–113.

28. The idea of a prolonged political period running from the antebellum era through the Gilded Age is not new. Michael McGerr calls this a period of "popular politics," Morton Keller refers to it as the "Party-Democratic Regime," and Joel Silbey labels the specific period from 1838 to 1893 the "American political nation." Scholars of youth and aging, including Joseph Kett, Steven Mintz, and David Hackett Fischer also see similar patterns for youth from the 1840s at least through the 1880s. Michael E.

McGerr, *The Decline of Popular Politics: The American North, 1865–1928* (Oxford: Oxford University Press, 1986); Morton Keller, *America's Three Regimes* (New York: Oxford University Press, 2007), 67–200; Joel Silbey, *The American Political Nation, 1838–1893* (Stanford: Stanford University Press, 1994); Joseph Kett, *Rites of Passage: Adolescence in America, 1790 to the Present* (New York: Basic Books, 1977), 5; Steven Mintz, *Huck's Raft: A History of American Childhood* (Boston: Belknap Press of Harvard University Press, 2006), 75–200; David Hackett Fischer, *Growing Old in America* (New York: Oxford University Press, 1977).

29. Morton Keller, *Affairs of State* (Cambridge, Mass.: Belknap Press of Harvard University Press, 1977), 241.

30. French visitor Michael Chevalier noted the absence of a folk culture in the United States in the 1830s but added that American democracy was, slowly, beginning "to create everything afresh." Looking back from the 1920s, Charles Murdock agreed. He reflected that as a boy in the 1840s, "holidays were somewhat infrequent" and "there were no distractions in the way of professional football or other games," so he found his entertainment in the excited campaigns of the era. Michael Chevalier, *Society, Manners and Politics in the United States* (Boston: Weeks, Jordan, 1839), 316; Charles A. Murdock, *A Backward Glance at Eighty* (San Francisco: P. Elder, 1921), 6–7.

31. There were different regional political cultures within this larger national scene. On average, voter turnout was highest in the Mid-Atlantic, Midwest, and Upper South and lowest in the West, New England, and especially the Lower South. Regions with more cultural diversity and multiparty competition usually had the highest turnouts and the most intense popular enthusiasm. McIver, *Historical Statistics of the United States*, series Eb62–113.

32. Rutherford B. Hayes, January 6, 1838, *Diary and Letters of Rutherford Birchard Hayes*, ed. Charles Richard Williams (Columbus: Ohio State Archaeological and Historical Society, 1922), 17.

33. W. J. Rorabaugh, *The Alcoholic Republic: An American Tradition* (New York: Oxford University Press, 1979), 232–36.

34. John R. William to William Thomas, November 10, 1895, in *The Welsh in America: Letters from the Immigrants*, ed. Alan Conway (Minneapolis: University of Minnesota Press, 1961). British readers were often treated to reports of crazed American campaigns. Frances Anne Kemble, October 1832, *Journal of Frances Anne Butler*, vol. 1 (Philadelphia: Carey, Lea and Blanchard, 1835); Charles Dickens, *American Notes for General Circulation* (London: J. M. Dent, 1907), 75.

35. Richard L. Rapson, "The American Child as Seen by British Travelers, 1845–1935," *American Quarterly* 17 (Autumn 1965): 520–34; Kenneth D. Rose, *Unspeakable Awfulness: America through the Eyes of European Travelers, 1865–1900* (New York: Routledge, 2014), 159–62.

36. Field, *Struggle for Equal Adulthood*, 53.

37. Kett, *Rites of Passage*; Howard Chudacoff, *How Old Are You? Age Consciousness in American Culture* (Princeton: Princeton University Press, 1989); Howard Chudacoff, *The Age of the Bachelor* (Princeton: Princeton University Press, 1999); Mintz, *Huck's Raft*. Corinne T. Field's article "Are Women . . . All Minors? Women's Rights and the Politics

of Aging in the Antebellum United States," *Journal of Women's History* 12 (Winter 2001): 113–37, also argues for the voting age as a rare (and exclusively male) dividing line between age groups.

38. "Political Indifference," *Daily Inter Ocean*, June 18, 1892.

39. Field, *Struggle for Equal Adulthood*.

40. On top of this, the new voting laws of Reconstruction enfranchised whole communities at a time, so black men of all ages won the right simultaneously. While campaigners lobbying white voters often focused on twenty-one-year-olds aging into the system, electioneers hoping for black first-timers appealed to adults. "The First Vote," *Harper's Weekly*, November 16, 1867; Dorothy Sterling, ed., *The Trouble They Seen: The Story of Reconstruction in the Words of African Americans* (New York: Da Capo Press, 1976), 100–105; John Roy Lynch, *The Reminiscences of an Active Life: The Autobiography of John Roy Lynch*, ed. John Hope Franklin (Chicago: University of Chicago Press, 1970), 59–61; Edward S. Redkey, ed., *A Grand Army of Black Men: Letters from African-American Soldiers in the Union Army, 1861–1865* (Cambridge: Cambridge University Press, 1992), 205–29; Daniel R. Biddle and Murray Dubin, *Tasting Freedom: Octavius Catto and the Battle for Equality in Civil War America* (Philadelphia: Temple University Press, 2010), 421–41; John I. Young, interviewed by Henry Muir, Montgomery County, Ohio, Works Progress Administration, Ex-Slave Narratives, Ohio Historical Society, "The African-American Experience in Ohio, 1850–1920," http://dbs.ohiohistory.org/africanam/page.cfm?ID=13937&Current=001&View=Text (last accessed December 21, 2013); Steven Hahn, *A Nation under Our Feet* (Boston: Belknap Press, 2003); Ned Cobb, *All God's Dangers: The Life of Nate Shaw*, compiled by Theodore Rosengarten (Chicago: University of Chicago Press, 1974).

41. And, by our twenty-first-century expectations, white Americans made up a truly surprisingly majority of the population. Nationwide the percentage of white Americans hovered between 85.6 percent and 87.9 percent between 1840 and 1900, and outside of the slave states, the nation was 98.8 percent white in 1860. A tiny proportion of the population identified as neither white nor black. In an era before the Great Migration of African Americans to the North or of the emigration of large numbers from Latin America and Asia in the twentieth century, most of the country (particularly the more populous middle and northern regions) experienced little racial diversity. Though I have incorporated the voices of young nonwhite Americans where I could, my sources often represent these different demographics. Haines and Steckel, *Population History of North America*, 702–4; Gary W. Gallagher, *The Union War* (New York: Harvard University Press, 2011), 42.

42. Paul Kleppner, *Who Voted? The Dynamics of Electoral Turnout, 1870–1980* (New York: Praeger, 1982), 34; "Young Men in Council: The Conference of Young Republicans," *Boston Daily Advertiser*, August 27, 1878; George Boutwell, "Young Men in Politics," *North American Review* 129, no. 277 (December 1879): 537–51; Albion Winegar Tourgée, *Letters to a King* (Cincinnati: Cranston and Stowe, 1888), 49, 58.

43. Jackson, *Colonel's Diary*, 28, 17, 27. As William Allen White similarly wrote about the Young Republican clubs of his Kansas boyhood, "Youth pretends that it is organizing to reform the world, as a matter of fact, it is organizing politically to

get jobs." William Allen White, *The Autobiography of William Allen White* (New York: Macmillan, 1947), 91.

44. Young people expressed hostility toward a collective youth identity, emphasizing that they had no intention of "obtruding upon the public in collectively protesting, and calling upon the young men." *Nominating Rally for Delegates to National Convention of Young Men, National Republican Party* (Baltimore: Sand and Neilson, 1831); *Young Men of Boston! Broadside for Charles Wells as Boston Mayor*, 1832, Printed Ephemera Collection, Library of Congress; Frederick Von Raumer, *America and the American People* (New York: J. and H. G. Langley, S. Astor House, 1841), 353; *Young Men! Vote for Edgar Tehune for Congress* (Chicago, 1886), broadside in Printed Ephemera Collection, Library of Congress.

45. Haines and Steckel, *Population History of North America*, 702–4.

46. Mrs. Charley Huyck (first name unknown), interviewed by Harold J. Moss, January 24, 1939, American Life Histories Interviews.

47. "Young Men to the Front," *Wheeling (W.Va.) Register*, March 26, 1880; James S. Clarkson, "The Politician and the Pharisee," *North American Review* 152, no. 414 (May 1891): 613–23.

48. The two greatest books on the centrality of parties in nineteenth-century America are Silbey's *American Political Nation*, which details the scale and significance of parties over roughly six decades, and Richard Franklin Bensel's *The American Ballot Box in the Mid-Nineteenth Century* (Cambridge: Cambridge University Press, 2004), which makes the structural power of parties clear on the individual level on election day.

49. Roughly 91 percent of voters chose the same party between 1840 and 1852, and that number jumped to 95 percent from 1860 to 1892. Voters backed a single organization in almost every contest; 91.8 percent voted a straight one-party ticket from 1880 to 1896. Partisans maintained these bonds over decades. Thomas B. Alexander's fascinating study of partisan "consistency" from 1840 and 1860 found that during what is widely considered the most tumultuous period in American political history, the Democratic Party's share of the presidential vote shifted by less than half a percentage point. Kleppner, *Who Voted?*, 26; Mark Lawrence Kornbluh, *Why America Stopped Voting: The Decline of Participatory Democracy and the Emergence of Modern American Politics* (New York: New York University Press, 2000), 36; Thomas B. Alexander, "The Dimensions of Voter Partisan Consistency in Presidential Elections from 1840 to 1860," in *Essays on American Antebellum Politics, 1840–1860*, ed. Stephen E. Maizlish (College Station: Texas A&M University Press, 1982), 75.

50. Lydia Maria Child to Sarah Blake Sturgis Shaw, October 27, 1856, in *Letters of Lydia Maria Child*, ed. Wendell Phillips (Boston: Houghton Mifflin, 1882), 85; John Worrell Northrop, May 1861, in *Chronicles from the Diary of a War Prisoner in Andersonville* (Wichita: J. W. Northrop, 1904); Tourgée, *Letters to a King*, 49; Charles Nordhoff, *Politics for Young Americans* (New York: Harper and Brothers, 1875), 35. Switching parties, according to the Reverend John Mather Austin, "betrays an entire destitution of moral principle and rectitude," while the youth advice author Charles Nordhoff railed, "A non-partisan government is the dream of weak and amiable men." Reverend

John Mather Austin, *A Voice to Youth: Addressed to Young Men and Young Ladies* (Utica: Grosh and Hutchinson, 1839), 230.

51. Parmenas Taylor Turnley, *Reminiscences of Parmenas Taylor Turnley: From the Cradle to Three-Score and Ten* (Chicago: Donohue and Henneberry, 1892), 23.

52. William Dean Howells, *Years of My Youth* (New York: Harper and Brothers, 1916), 160. For speeches going unheard, through poor acoustics or lack of interest, also see Joseph J. Mersman, *The Whiskey Merchant's Diary*, ed. Linda A Fisher (Athens: Ohio University Press, 2007), 137; Lyman Abbott, *Reminiscences* (Boston: Houghton Mifflin, 1914), 107–10; William L. Riordan, *Plunkitt of Tammany Hall: A Series of Very Plain Talks on Very Practical Politics* (New York: E. P. Dutton, 1963), 7–10; and Rachel Sheldon, *Washington Brotherhood: Politics, Social Life, and the Coming of the Civil War* (Chapel Hill: University of North Carolina Press, 2013).

53. "Political Indifference."

54. For examples of the assumption that new voters were young voters, see "To the Young Men Who Will Cast Their First Vote," *Washington Daily National Intelligencer*, January 17, 1844; "The Next Presidency," *New York Herald*, May 28, 1844; "To the Young Voters," *New York Times*, September 10, 1876; "The Mothers Vote This Year," *Salt Lake Tribune*, June 26, 1884; and "A New Crop of Republicans for 1888," *Grand Forks Herald*, September 28, 1886. Likewise, an analysis of rosters of "new voters clubs" shows that 86 percent of native-born first-time voters were under thirty years old and that the large majority of older voters were born overseas. See "Their First Vote," *Milwaukee Sentinel*, July 29, 1888; "Campaign Uniforms," *Milwaukee Daily Journal*, September 15, 1888; "Campaign Clubs," *Milwaukee Journal*, May 26, 1892; and "The Independent Twenty-Onesters," *San Francisco Daily Evening Bulletin*, August 17, 1869.

55. William E. Gienapp, "Politics Seem to Enter into Everything: Political Culture in the North, 1840–1860," in *Essays on American Antebellum Politics, 1840–1860*, ed. Stephen E. Maizlish (College Station: Texas A&M University Press, 1982), 54–56.

56. "Political Indifference."

57. Abraham Lincoln to William H. Herndon, June 22, 1848, *Abraham Lincoln: The Collected Works*, 9 vols., ed. Roy P. Basler (New Brunswick: Rutgers University Press, 1953), 1:491.

58. "People of the State of Illinois versus Peachy Quinn Harrison, Indictment for Murder," August 31, 1859–September 3, 1859, Circuit Court of Sangamon County, Lincoln Legal Papers, Abraham Lincoln Presidential Library, Springfield, Ill., p. 33; Abraham Lincoln to P. Quinn Harrison, November 3, 1859, *Abraham Lincoln*, 3:492.

59. "A Triumph of Young America," *Milwaukee Daily Sentinel*, May 14, 1867; "The Grand Army Anniversary," *Philadelphia Inquirer*, August 5, 1891. For further examples of adult campaigners' criticisms of young partisans, see Raumer, *America and the American People*, 353; "State Legislature Remarks"; Edward Everett Diary, October 20, 1853, Everett Papers, Massachusetts Historical Society, Boston; "Letter by Charles E. Coffin," *American Economist* 9, no. 18 (May 5, 1893): 164; Andreas Ueland, *Recollections of an Immigrant* (New York: Minton, Balch, 1929), 50; and Glenn Wallach, *Obedient Sons: The Discourse of Youth and Generations in American Culture, 1630–1860* (Amherst: University of Massachusetts Press, 1997), 75–76.

60. This debate has defined the last several decades of nineteenth-century political scholarship. In the 1980s and 1990s, William Gienapp, Jean Baker, Joel Silbey, and
Michael McGerr stressed the centrality and accessibility of democracy in American
life. Glenn Altschuler and Stuart Blumin pushed back in 2000 with *Rude Republic*,
challenging this rosy view of American democracy and arguing that a small number of
party activists foisted popular politics on an ambivalent and poorly informed public.
In the 2000s, historians Mark Summers and Richard Bensel implicitly supported *Rude
Republic* by highlighting the ways party activists manipulated voters. The supporters
of the popular politics school lashed out at Altschuler and Blumin in a number of re-
views and articles (my own included). In 2005 Mark E. Neely attempted to bridge this
divide, attacking Altschuler and Blumin's dismissals of popular interest but acknowledging that "politics did not enter into everything." Instead he portrayed uneven
boundaries between politics and American life as "more like a beach than a sea-wall."
This project attempts to expand upon Neely's middle ground. I endorse the earlier
historians' work on the intense interest in politics in American life but challenge their
(occasional) assumptions that this involvement meant a "deeper understanding" of
the issues. While I consider Altschuler and Blumin's work misguided on the question
of popular interest in politics, I have concluded that *Rude Republic* was nonetheless a
convincing, insightful, and badly needed exploration of the superficiality often un-
derpinning nineteenth-century democracy. I embrace their argument—supported
by Richard Bensel—that "party loyalty, for some . . . served as an alternative to a
thoughtful absorption in public affairs." The two sides seem to be talking past each
other; this study attempts to show that, for young people in particular, politics could
be popular and poorly informed at the same time. Glenn C. Altschuler and Stuart M.
Blumin, *Rude Republic: Americans and Their Politics in the Nineteenth Century* (Princeton: Princeton University Press, 2000), 2, 5; Gienapp, "Politics Seem to Enter into
Everything"; Jean H. Baker, *Affairs of Party: The Political Culture of Northern Democrats
in the Mid-Nineteenth Century* (Ithaca: Cornell University Press, 1982); Silbey, *American
Political Nation*; McGerr, *Decline of Popular Politics*; Mark Wahlgren Summers, *Party
Games: Getting, Keeping, and Using Power in Gilded Age Politics* (Chapel Hill: University
of North Carolina Press, 2004); Bensel, *American Ballot Box*; Mark E. Neely Jr., *The
Boundaries of American Political Culture in the Civil War Era* (Chapel Hill: University of
North Carolina Press, 2005), 21.

61. "Great Republicans Barbeque at Logan"; Jackson, *Colonel's Diary*, 32, 34.

62. Jackson, *Colonel's Diary*, 34, 32.

63. Almost all studies of youth tend to fall back on a belief in segmented generations, but young people's sustained involvement in politics over sixty years makes it
impossible to think in such tidy blocks. Generations do exist, as blurry overlapping
blobs, but too many young people, over too long a period, dove into public democracy for historians to hope to isolate any one block as uniquely invested in politics.

64. "Young Reformers Club," *American Reformer*, November 8, 1884, 364.

65. I came to this sense after publishing a study of the Wide Awake clubs that
ignited the 1860 campaign. I was certain that the Wide Awakes made up an entirely
unprecedented movement. But as I read more about the campaigns that preceded

1860, and those that followed, I realized that many trends stretched across decades. As I examined campaign materials in the collections of the Smithsonian's National Museum of American History, or read diaries extending over lifetimes, or flipped through engravings of rallies and barbecues, or saw the way Republicans reused appeals from William Henry Harrison's 1840 election in his grandson's campaign, forty-eight years later, a larger era of shared behaviors emerged. Each campaign was unique, but each was designed, deliberately, to follow similar trends. As Mark Wahlgren Summers cleverly put it, "The 1868 presidential campaign was beyond all question the most venomous, scurrilous, and misleading—since the last one." Or, in the even more apt words of Finley Peter Dunne's Mr. Dooley, a comic persona capable of sparking wisdom, "I see gr-reat changes takin' place ivry day, but no change at all ivry fifty years." While making note of the many real changes taking place across the age of popular politics, this book represents a larger effort to avoid the tendency to trumpet "game changers" and instead examines the power of culture to replicate itself, even in tumultuous times. Grinspan, "'Young Men for War,'" 360; Mark Wahlgren Summers, *The Press Gang* (Chapel Hill: University of North Carolina Press, 1994), 43; Finley Peter Dunne, *Dissertations by Mr. Dooley* (New York: Harper and Brothers, 1906), 271; Michael F. Holt, "Change and Continuity in the Party Period: The Substance and Structure of American Politics, 1835–1885," in *Contesting Democracy: Substance and Structure in American Political History, 1775–2000*, ed. Byron E. Shafer and Anthony J. Badger (Lawrence: University of Kansas Press, 2001), 93–115; Silbey, *American Political Nation*; Alexander, "Dimensions of Voter Partisan Consistency."

66. This steadiness helps explain why nineteenth-century democracy often failed to bring about progressive social, economic, or racial change. American voters did not usually look to their political system for radical reform; they wanted the very opposite from politics. What historians see as inertia, shaken and striving young people saw as an inviting permanence. Because of this satisfaction with the status quo, those who wanted to see major changes—abolitionists, secessionists, women's rights activists, labor organizers, socialists—all had to look outside the political system. This helps define "politics," as nineteenth-century Americans would, as a culture bounded by the interests of the political parties and the issues they were willing to address.

67. Mark Twain, December 21 1901, *Selected Mark Twain—Howells Letters, 1872–1910* (Cambridge, Mass.: Belknap Press of Harvard University Press, 1967), 348; Susan Goodman and Carl Dawson, *William Dean Howells: A Writer's Life* (Berkeley: University of California Press, 2005), xvi.

68. William Dean Howells's autobiographies also seem to be quite trustworthy, consistently returning to the same events and emotions over many decades. His literary commitment to realism, small domestic dramas, and opposition to sentimentalism make his autobiographies clean and reliable, as many scholars of Howells have noted. Even his writings as a youth, in his many diaries and early short stories from the 1850s, express similar views to those that appear in his autobiographies from 1890 or 1916. See William Dean Howells, *The Early Prose Writings of William Dean Howells, 1853–1861*, ed. Thomas Wortham (Athens: Ohio University Press, 1990); William Dean Howells, "1852 Diary and Spanish Exercises," Houghton Library, Harvard Special Collections,

Cambridge, Mass.; and Rodney D. Olsen, *Dancing in Chains: The Youth of William Dean Howells* (New York: New York University Press, 1991).

69. W. D. Howells, *Years of My Youth*, xii.

70. Kleppner, *Who Voted?*, 68–69.

Chapter 1

1. Joseph D. Cushman Jr., introduction to *Through Some Eventful Years* by Susan Bradford Eppes (Macon, Ga.: J. W. Burke, 1926), ix–xxvi.

2. "Diary of a Trip to Florida," January 5, 1855, Diary of an unknown traveler in Florida, Florida State University Strozier Library Special Collections, Tallahassee.

3. Susan Bradford Eppes, *Through Some Eventful Years* (Macon, Ga.: J. W. Burke, 1926), 55.

4. Ibid., 61.

5. Ibid.

6. Ibid., 55–56.

7. Ibid., 64.

8. Ibid., 56.

9. Ibid., 62.

10. Ibid., 56; Catherine Elizabeth Havens, *The Diary of a Little Girl in Old New York* (New York: Henry Collins Brown, 1919), 72–80.

11. Authors of child-rearing literature debated the topic, with some writers endorsing an early and enthusiastic partisan education and others largely denouncing popular politics. For the former, see Reverend John Mather Austin, *A Voice to Youth: Addressed to Young Men and Young Ladies* (Utica: Grosh and Hutchinson, 1839), and Albion Winegar Tourgée, *Letters to a King* (Cincinnati: Cranston and Stowe, 1888). For a more censorious tone, see William A. Alcott, *The Young Man's Guide* (Boston: Lilly, Wait, Colman, and Holden, 1834); William A. Alcott, *Familiar Letters to Young Men on Various Subjects: Designed as a Companion to the Young Man's Guide* (Buffalo: Geo. H. Derby, 1850); and Augustus Woodbury, *Plain Words for Young Men* (Concord: McFarland and Jenks, 1858).

12. Sally McCarty Pleasants, *Old Virginia Days and Ways: Reminiscences of Mrs. Sally McCarty Pleasants* (Menasha, Wis.: George Banta, 1916), 6.

13. Elizabeth Varon, "Tippecanoe and the Ladies, Too: White Women and Party Politics in Antebellum Virginia," *Journal of American History* 82 (September 1995): 494–521.

14. Pleasants, *Old Virginia Days and Ways*, 10.

15. For strong studies of what it meant to be a Democrat, see Sean Wilentz, *The Rise of American Democracy: Jefferson to Lincoln* (New York: W. W. Norton, 2005); Jean H. Baker, *Affairs of Party: The Political Culture of Northern Democrats in the Mid-Nineteenth Century* (Ithaca: Cornell University Press, 1982); Harry Watson, *Liberty and Power: The Politics of Jacksonian America* (New York: Hill and Wang, 2006); and Lee Benson, *The Concept of Jacksonian Democracy: New York as a Text Case* (Princeton: Princeton University Press, 1961).

16. Daniel Walker Howe, *The Political Culture of American Whigs* (Chicago: University of Chicago Press, 1984); Michael F. Holt, *The Rise and Fall of the American Whig Party* (New York: Oxford University Press, 1999).

17. For a brief survey of glaring errors and willful ignorance, see Lester Ward, *Young Ward's Diary*, ed. Bernhard J. Stern (New York: G. P. Putnam's Sons, 1935), 39; John Parsons, *A Tour through Indiana in 1840: The Diary of John Parsons of Petersburg, Virginia*, ed. Kate Milner Rabb (New York: R. M. McBride, 1920), 5; William Dean Howells, *Years of My Youth* (New York: Harper and Brothers, 1916), 160; Alcott, *Familiar Letters to Young Men*, 253–60; William L. Riordan, *Plunkitt of Tammany Hall: A Series of Very Plain Talks on Very Practical Politics* (New York: E. P. Dutton, 1963), 8; Bayard Taylor, *El Dorado; or, Adventures in the Path of Empire*, vol. 2 (London: Henry G. Bohn, 1850), 189; and Edward Beck, "Diary," in *"A Funnie Place, No Fences": Teenagers' Views of Kansas, 1867–1900*, ed. C. Robert Haywood and Sandra Jarvis (Lawrence: University of Kansas, Division of Continuing Education, 1992).

18. Joseph Kett, *Rites of Passage: Adolescence in America, 1790 to the Present* (New York: Basic Books, 1977), 4.

19. For the best examples of the ethnocultural interpretation of nineteenth-century politics, see Benson, *Concept of Jacksonian Democracy*; Michael F. Holt, *Forging a Majority: The Formation of the Republican Party in Pittsburgh, 1848–1860* (New Haven: Yale University Press, 1969); and Joel Silbey, *The American Political Nation, 1838–1893* (Stanford: Stanford University Press, 1991). For more intimate studies of how family influenced individual party identity, see J. Baker, *Affairs of Party*, and Richard Franklin Bensel, *The American Ballot Box in the Mid-Nineteenth Century* (Cambridge: Cambridge University Press, 2004).

20. David Ross Locke, *Nasby: Divers Views, Opinions and Prophecies of Petroleum V. Nasby* (Cincinnati: R. W. Carroll, 1867), 2; Mary Ryan, *Civic Wars* (Berkeley: University of California Press, 1998), 142.

21. The 1876 election, disastrous for the democracy, was probably the best thing that ever happened to the name Rutherford. Census data drawn from *HeritageQuest Online*, http://persi.heritagequestonline.com (last accessed June 14, 2013).

22. Frances Anne Kemble, *Journal of Frances Anne Butler*, vol. 1 (Philadelphia: Carey, Lea and Blanchard, 1835), 112; Charles Plummer Diary, September 1, 1840, Historical Society of Pennsylvania, Philadelphia; J. Parsons, *Tour through Indiana in 1840*, 26; Emily Chubbuck Judson, *The Life and Letters of Mrs. Emily C. Judson* (New York: Sheldon, 1860), 101.

23. Lydia Maria Child to Sarah Blake Sturgis Shaw, October 27, 1856, in *Letters of Lydia Maria Child*, ed. Wendell Phillips (Boston: Houghton Mifflin, 1882), 86.

24. Eliza Frances Andrews, *The War-Time Journal of a Georgia Girl, 1864–1865*, ed. Spencer B. King Jr. (New York: Appleton-Century-Crofts, 1908), 308. Also see Anna Ridgely, May 20, 1860, "A Girl in the Sixties," ed. Octavia Roberts Corneau, *Journal of the Illinois State Historical Society* 2 (October 1929): 9–11, and Sarah Ida Fowler Morgan Dawson, June 1862, *A Confederate Girl's Diary* (Boston: Houghton Mifflin, 1913), 79–81.

25. Andrew Dickson White, *Autobiography of Andrew Dickson White* (New York: Century, 1904), 1:45.

26. Ibid., 52. In Kansas, William Allen White similarly admitted that he had spent his youth knowing that "I was for Horace Greeley, though I hadn't the faintest idea who Horace Greeley was, nor what 'bein' for him" implied." Greeley had been dead for several years by the point in his autobiography that White claimed to have supported him. William Allen White, *The Autobiography of William Allen White* (New York: Macmillan, 1947), 9.

27. A. D. White, *Autobiography*, 52.

28. Quoted in Ned Cobb, *All God's Dangers: The Life of Nate Shaw*, compiled by Theodore Rosengarten (Chicago: University of Chicago Press, 1974), 42–44.

29. Ibid.

30. Ibid.

31. Kett, *Rites of Passage*, 14. For examples of political socialization by older siblings, see Charles Plummer Diary; David Schenck Papers, Southern Historical Collection, University of North Carolina, Chapel Hill, N.C.; Frances E. Willard, *Glimpses of Fifty Years: The Autobiography of an American Woman* (Chicago: Women's Temperance Publication Association, H. J. Smith & Co., 1889), 69; and Benjamin Brown Foster, *Downeast Diary*, ed. Charles H. Foster (Orono: University of Maine at Orono Press, 1975).

32. Annie Youmans, November 1868, *Diary of Annie L. Youmans Van Ness, 1864–1881* (Alexandria, Va.: Alexander Street Press, 2004); Willard, *Glimpses of Fifty Years*, 69; Rolf Johnson, *Happy as a Big Sunflower: Adventures in the West, 1876–1880*, edited by Richard E. Jensen (Lincoln: University of Nebraska Press, 2000), 31–33; Rutherford B. Hayes, *Diary and Letters of Rutherford Birchard Hayes*, ed. Charles Richard Williams (Columbus: Ohio State Archeological and Historical Society, 1922), 17.

33. W. D. Howells, *Years of My Youth*, 73.

34. William Dean Howells, *A Boy's Town: Described for "Harper's Young People"* (New York: Harper and Brothers, 1890), 4; W. D. Howells, *Years of My Youth*, 13, 19.

35. W. D. Howells, *Years of My Youth*, 15, 73; Susan Goodman and Carl Dawson, *William Dean Howells: A Writer's Life* (Berkeley: University of California Press, 2005), 15–17.

36. W. D. Howells, *Years of My Youth*, 16.

37. W. D. Howells, *Boy's Town*, 1, 129–36; Goodman and Dawson, *William Dean Howells*, 26; William Dean Howells, "1852 Diary and Spanish Exercises," Houghton Library, Harvard Special Collections, Cambridge, Mass.

38. Goodman and Dawson, *William Dean Howells*, 12–15; W. D. Howells, *Years of My Youth*, 23.

39. W. D. Howells, *Boy's Town*, 131.

40. Ibid., 126–28.

41. Ibid., 228.

42. Ibid., 131.

43. W. D. Howells, *Years of My Youth*, 3.

44. Pleasants, *Old Virginia Days and Ways*, 13.

45. Dawson, May 1862, *Confederate Girl's Diary*, 53; Annie Burnham Cooper, October 18, 1888, in *Private Pages: Diaries of American Women, 1830s–1970s*, ed. Penelope Franklin (New York: Ballantine Books, 1986), 173; Amanda McDowell Burns, May 6, 1861, *Fiddles in the Cumberland*, ed. Amanda McDowell and Lela McDowell Blanken-

ship (New York: Richard R. Smith, 1943); Charlotte Howard Conant, November 4, 1880; November 11, 1883; June 1, 1884, *A Girl of the Eighties at College and at Home*, ed. Martha Pike Conant (Boston: Houghton Mifflin, 1931), 261.

46. On maternal political instruction, see Ronald J. Zboray and Mary Saracino Zboray, *Voices without Votes: Women and Politics in Antebellum New England* (Durham: University of New Hampshire Press, 2010); Elizabeth R. Varon, *We Mean to Be Counted: White Women and Politics in Antebellum Virginia* (Chapel Hill: University of North Carolina Press, 1998); J. Baker, *Affairs of Party*; and Rebecca Edwards, *Angels in the Machinery: Gender in American Party Politics from the Civil War to the Progressive Era* (New York: Oxford University Press, 1997). For examples of mothers guiding their sons' views, see John Albee, *Confessions of Boyhood* (Boston: Gorham Press, 1910), 259, and Isaac Stephenson, *Recollections of a Long Life, 1829–1915* (Chicago: Privately published, 1915), 152.

47. "The Mothers Vote This Year," *Salt Lake Tribune*, June 26, 1884; "A New Crop of Republicans," *Grand Forks Daily Herald*, September 28, 1886.

48. Almira Heard to J. Theodore Heard, October 2, 1855, Letters of J. Theodore Heard, University of Virginia Special Collections, Charlottesville.

49. Bradford Eppes, *Through Some Eventful Years*, 125.

50. Ibid.

51. Ibid., 126

52. Ibid.

53. Kett, *Rites of Passage*, 11–12; Jacob Heffelfinger Diary, December 8, 1859, in Letters of J. Theodore Heard.

54. Historians have long believed that "Americans did not learn their partisanship in school," basing this misconception on a reading of nineteenth-century educational theory. Beyond those dusty primers, a wild world hollered from America's schoolyards. J. Baker, *Affairs of Party*, 28. Glenn C. Altschuler and Stuart M. Blumin, *Rude Republic: Americans and Their Politics in the Nineteenth Century* (Princeton: Princeton University Press, 2000), 11, 91. Baker's book is still the best work on political socialization and should be commended for its honesty, freely acknowledging that politics did not enter into everything. Baker's argument that America's schools overtly taught republicanism is indisputable. The point here is that Baker and many others privilege written literature on educational theory over the daily socialization that was at work in American schools. Baker does highlight the overt education American children received on the subject of republicanism but misses the unofficial initiation into partisanship.

55. Paul Kleppner, *Who Voted? The Dynamics of Electoral Turnout, 1870–1980* (New York: Praeger, 1982), 36; Steven Mintz, *Huck's Raft: A History of American Childhood* (Boston: Belknap Press of Harvard University Press, 2006), 197.

56. Julian A. Selby, *Memorabilia and Anecdotal Reminiscences of Columbia, South Carolina* (Columbia: R. L. Bryan, 1905), 127; Frederick M. Culp, *Gibson County, Past and Present* (Paducah, Ky.: Turner, 1961), 41; Art Shields, *My Shaping-Up Years: The Early Years of Labor's Great Reporter* (New York: International, 1983); Louis Beauregard Pendleton, *Alexander H. Stephens* (Philadelphia: George W. Jacobs, 1907), 44; Charles Waddell

Chesnutt, *The Journals of Charles W. Chesnutt*, ed. Richard Brodhead (Durham: Duke University Press, 1993), 152.

57. W. D. Howells, *Boy's Town*, 127.

58. Martha Farnsworth, *Plains Woman: The Diary of Martha Farnsworth, 1882–1922*, ed. Marlene Springer and Haskell Springer (Bloomington: Indiana University Press, 1986), 19. Also see Bettie Ann Graham Diary, October 27, 1860, University of Virginia Special Collections, Charlottesville; John M. Roberts, *Buckeye Schoolmaster: A Chronicle of Midwestern Rural Life, 1853–1865*, ed. J. Merton England (Bowling Green, Ky.: Bowling Green State University Popular Press, 1996), 224; Stephenson, *Recollections of a Long Life*, 152; and W. White, *Autobiography of William Allen White*, 31.

59. W. White, *Autobiography of William Allen White*, 9.

60. *Newark Evening News*, October 10, 1884. The context of this quote makes an even stronger case, promising, "Go to any schoolhouse during a national campaign, and it will be a safe venture that you will find the great majority of children violent little partisans, ready to do valorous battle for the candidate upon whom their infantile affections are centered and firmly convinced that the diminutive adherents of the opposing faction are both conspirators in pinafores and traitors in short pantaloons." This poetic, hyperbolic view acknowledges that most children's enthusiasm far outpaced their knowledge.

61. Willard, *Glimpses of Fifty Years*, 155.

62. Steven Hahn, *A Nation under Our Feet* (Boston: Belknap Press, 2003), 278; James M. McPherson, *The Abolitionist Legacy: From Reconstruction to the NAACP* (Princeton: Princeton University Press, 1975), 143; Dorothy Sterling, ed., *The Trouble They Seen: The Story of Reconstruction in the Words of African Americans* (New York: Da Capo Press, 1976), 301. Schoolhouses, often the only public building in a community, served as makeshift political spaces for some white communities as well. Campaigners located public debates in classrooms, and partisan clubs sometimes turned schools into headquarters. In 1868 one angry young Indiana Republican could barely contain his outrage when he lamented that the Democrats were using the local schoolhouse to organize a "young men's *demicratic* association." Moses Puterbaugh to Uriah Oblinger, June 26, 1868, Uriah W. Oblinger Family Collection, Nebraska State Historical Society, Lincoln.

63. Theodore Sutton Parvin, *The Life and Labors of Theodore Sutton Parvin*, ed. Joseph E. Morcombe (Clifton, Iowa: Allen, 1906), 26.

64. Over the century teaching became increasingly professionalized and the number of amateur young male teachers fell, replaced by trained female educators. It is possible that this demographic change meant fewer politically zealous young male schoolteachers, contributing to the falling interest in partisanship among young people in the early twentieth century. See David Nasaw, *Schooled to Order: A Social History of Public Schooling in the United States* (New York: Oxford University Press, 1979); Darrel Drury and Justin Baer, *The American Public School Teacher: Past, Present, and Future* (Cambridge, Mass.: Harvard Education Press, 2011); and Paul H. Mattingly, *The Classless Profession: American Schoolmen in the Nineteenth Century* (New York: New York University Press, 1975).

65. "Pedagogues and Presidents," *St. Louis Globe-Democrat*, October 23, 1881, 4.

66. Ward, *Young Ward's Diary*, 20. Conveniently, Ward turned out to be a gifted scholar and became an influential sociologist.

67. Jacob Heffelfinger Diary, December 8, 1859, in Letters of J. Theodore Heard.

68. Farnsworth, *Plains Woman*, 6.

69. Jacob Frey, *Reminiscences of Baltimore* (Baltimore: Maryland Book Concern, 1893), 48; James Witham, *Fifty Years on the Firing Line: My Part in the Farmers' Movement* (Chicago: Privately published, 1924), 2.

70. David Beardsley, "Birthday Commentaries on His Life," in *Visions of the Western Reserve*, ed. Robert A. Wheeler (Columbus: Ohio State University Press, 2000), 186.

71. Richard L. Rapson, "The American Child as Seen by British Travelers, 1845–1935," *American Quarterly* 17 (Autumn 1965): 520–34; Richard L. Rapson, ed., *The Cult of Youth in Middle-Class America* (Lexington, Mass.: Heath, 1971), 16.

72. W. D. Howells, *Boy's Town*, 65.

73. Ibid., 66.

74. Johan Huizinga, *Homo Ludens: A Study of the Play Element in Culture* (Boston: Beacon Press, 1955), 12.

75. E. Anthony Rotundo, *American Manhood: Transformations in Masculinity from the Revolution to the Modern Era* (New York: Basic Books, 1993), 31.

76. W. D. Howells, *Boy's Town*, 65.

77. Edward Bok, "The Boy in the Office," in *Before He Is Twenty: Five Perplexing Phases of Boyhood Considered: Essays from "Ladies' Home Journal,"* ed. Edward Bok (New York: F. H. Revell, 1894), 55; Kett, *Rites of Passage*; Mary Ryan, *Cradle of the Middle Class* (Cambridge: Cambridge University Press, 1981), 165; Walter Licht, *Getting Work: Philadelphia, 1840–1950* (Cambridge, Mass.: Harvard University Press, 1992).

78. Rapson, "American Child as Seen by British Travelers," 520–34.

79. Rotundo, *American Manhood*, 39.

80. This gendered difference also has roots in Americans' fear of the destructive capabilities of young men, which they hoped a few years of play might exorcise. Girls, supposedly less dangerous to society, were offered less independence. See Bok, "Boy in the Office," 55; G. Stanley Hall, *Youth: Its Education, Regimen, and Hygiene* (New York: D. Appleton, 1907), 207; Howard Chudacoff, *The Age of the Bachelor* (Princeton: Princeton University Press, 1999); Karen Halttunen, *Confidence Men and Painted Women: A Study of Middle-Class Culture in America, 1830–1870* (New Haven: Yale University Press, 1983); Rodney Hessinger, *Seduced, Abandoned, and Reborn: Visions of Youth in Middle-Class America, 1780–1850* (Philadelphia: University of Pennsylvania Press, 2005); and Rotundo, *American Manhood*. For a counterpoint, see Anne Scott MacLeod, "The Caddie Woodlawn Syndrome: American Girlhood in the Nineteenth Century," in *The Girls' History and Culture Reader: The Nineteenth Century*, ed. Miriam Forman-Brinell and Leslie Paris (Urbana: University of Illinois Press, 2011), 199–221, and Anya Jabour, *Scarlett's Sisters: Young Women in the Old South* (Chapel Hill: University of North Carolina Press, 2007).

81. J. Frank Kernan, *Reminiscences of the Old Fire Laddies and Volunteer Fire Departments of New York and Brooklyn* (New York: M. Crane, 1885).

82. Bok, *Before He Is Twenty*.

83. R. Johnson, *Happy as a Big Sunflower*, 67–92; David Schenck Papers.

84. W. D. Howells, *Boy's Town*, 67, 72.

85. Michael Feldberg, *The Philadelphia Riots of 1844* (Westport, Conn.: Greenwood Press, 1975), 109; Iver Bernstein, *The New York City Draft Riots: Their Significance in American Society and Politics in the Age of the Civil War* (New York: Oxford University Press, 1990), 30; W. T. Ellis, *Memories: My Seventy-Two Years in the Romantic County of Yuba, California* (Eugene: University of Oregon Press, 1939), 6.

86. Kernan, *Reminiscences of the Old Fire Laddies*; W. D. Howells, *Boy's Town*, 17.

87. George Templeton Strong, *Diary: Young Man in New York, 1835–1849*, ed. Allan Nevins and Milton Halsey Thomas (New York: Macmillan, 1952), 8. That phrase comes from Allan Nevins's editorial notes.

88. Frey, *Reminiscences of Baltimore*, 89. For more detail on fires in urban America, see Amy S. Greenberg, *Cause for Alarm: The Volunteer Fire Department in the Nineteenth-Century City* (Princeton: Princeton University Press, 1998), and Mark Tebeau, *Eating Smoke: Fire in Urban America, 1800–1950* (Baltimore: Johns Hopkins University Press, 2003).

89. Frey, *Reminiscences of Baltimore*, 49.

90. B. Foster, *Downeast Diary*; W. D. Howells, *Boy's Town*, 127–40; Lyman Abbott, *Reminiscences* (Boston: Houghton Mifflin, 1914), 33–36.

91. Frey, *Reminiscences of Baltimore*, 53.

92. W. D. Howells, *Years of My Youth*, 160, 130; Frey, *Reminiscences of Baltimore*, 52; William Fletcher King, *Reminiscences* (New York: Abingdon Press, 1915), 52; "The Village Election," *Milwaukee Daily Sentinel*, May 14, 1867.

93. W. D. Howells, *Boy's Town*, 128; Jackson A. Graves, *My Seventy Years in California* (Los Angeles: Times Mirror Press, 1927), 33; Mrs. Charley Huyck, interviewed by Harold J. Moss, Lincoln, Neb., January 24, 1939, American Life Histories Interviews; "The Rival Bonfires," *Youth's Companion*, October 16, 1884, 57, 387.

94. Harpo Marx, *Harpo Speaks!*, ed. Rowland Barber (New York: : Bernard Geis Associates, 1961), 27.

95. Ibid., 47–49.

96. Frank Leach, *Recollections of a Newspaperman; A Record of Life and Events in California* (San Francisco: S. Levinson, 1917), 11.

97. Ellis, *Memories*, 6.

98. Bettie Ann Graham Diary, October 27, 1860.

99. Pleasants, *Old Virginia Days and Ways*, 6.

100. Frey, *Reminiscences of Baltimore*, 53. Frey also said that rallies were "calculated to catch the eye of a boy of nine years of age." Realistically, children just on the cusp of adolescence, between twelve and fifteen, seem to have been the target audience.

101. W. D. Howells, *Boy's Town*, 130; William Dean Howells, *Imaginary Interviews* (New York: Harper and Brothers, 1910), 260. The growing genre of juvenile literature often printed stories about young boys and girls at such events. "The Rival Bonfires," 57, 387; Mary Densel, "The Grand Procession," *Harper's Young People*, November 9, 1880; Matthew White, "The Roverings and the Parade," *Harper's Young People*, No-

vember 16, 1880; Henry Liddell, *The Evolution of a Democrat: A Darwinian Tale* (New York: Paquet, 1888).

102. Andrew Dickson White, *Autobiography*, 1:48; King, *Reminiscences*, 51–52; Robert Gray Gunderson, *The Log Cabin Campaign* (Lexington: University Press of Kentucky, 1957); Frey, *Reminiscences of Baltimore*, 53; Mrs. Charley Huyck interview; Harry Germaine, "A Campaign Club's Equipment," *Daily Inter Ocean*, May 31, 1896; "The Making of Campaign Banners," *Harper's Weekly*, September 10, 1892; "In a Campaign Banner Factory," *Rocky Mountain News* (Denver, Colo.), August 23, 1896.

103. W. D. Howells, *Boy's Town*, 130.

104. Ibid., 127–28.

105. W. D. Howells, *Years of My Youth*, 3.

106. Riordan, *Plunkitt of Tammany Hall*, 19.

107. James Michael Curley, *I'd Do It Again* (New York: Arno Press, 1976), 46.

108. Ibid.; Joseph F. Dineen, *Ward Eight* (New York: Harper and Brothers, 1936); Alice Stone Blackwell, *Growing Up in Boston's Gilded Age* (New Haven: Yale University Press, 1990).

109. "Pebbles," *New York Independent*, March 30, 1911, 70, 672; Curley, *I'd Do It Again*, 22; "Reported by Police," *Boston Daily Advertiser*, November 10, 1884, 8; "A Fine Old Bostonian," *New York Times*, August 15, 1933, 16.

110. Curley, *I'd Do It Again*, 22.

111. According to James Michael Curley, Sodekson's mother had fled with Nathan after pogroms in their hometown of Preinai, Lithuania, then part of Russia. Curley, *I'd Do It Again*, 23–25.

112. Bosses commonly assigned this unwanted task to boys. George Washington Plunkitt had this same job four decades earlier, tracking down voters "who had jags on" and helping them to the polls. Riordan, *Plunkitt of Tammany Hall*, 19; Curley, *I'd Do It Again*, 23–25.

113. Curley, *I'd Do It Again*, 23; Robert W. Bruére, "A Newsboys' Labor Union," *Outlook*, December 1906, 287; "To Newsboys," *American Federationist* 9 (January 1902): 11.

114. Jack Beatty, *The Rascal King: The Life and Times of James Michael Curley* (Boston: Da Capo Press, 1992), 61.

115. George Washington Albright, interviewed by Elizabeth Lawson for Federal Writers' Project, Mississippi Slave Narratives, not published in collection; printed in the *New York Daily Worker*, June 18, 1937, and the *New York Daily World*, July 11, 1975; accessed through Mississippi Slave Narratives, http://msgw.org/slaves/albright.pdf, December 20, 2013.

116. George Washington Albright, Mississippi Slave Narratives, 18.

117. Bradford Eppes, *Through Some Eventful Years*, 119; George Washington Albright, Mississippi Slave Narratives, 11.

118. George Washington Albright, Mississippi Slave Narratives, 12; James West Davidson, *They Say: Ida B. Wells and the Reconstruction of Race* (New York: Oxford University Press, 2007), 21; Hahn, *Nation under Our Feet*, 87.

119. George Washington Albright, Mississippi Slave Narratives, 12. For strong accounts of slave life and physical descriptions of the region in which Albright lived,

see the slave narratives of Callie Gray and Aaron Jones. Callie Gray, transcribed by Ann Allen Geoghegan, *Mississippi Narratives Prepared by the Federal Writers' Project of the Works Progress Administration for the State of Mississippi*, http://msgw.org/slaves/gray-xslave.htm (December 20, 2013); Aaron Jones, transcribed by Ann Allen Geoghegan, *Mississippi Narratives*, http://msgw.org/slaves/jones-aaron-xslave.htm, December 20, 2013.

120. "Loyal League Disclosure," *Hinds County (Miss.) Gazette*, July 10, 1868; "The Loyal League: A Peep into the Midnight Radical Conclaves," *Charleston Courier*, July 23, 1867; Davidson, *They Say*, 21; Hahn, *Nation under Our Feet*, 87.

121. George Washington Albright, Mississippi Slave Narratives, 13. Also see Callie Gray, *Mississippi Narratives*, and Aaron Jones, *Mississippi Narratives*.

122. Albright, Mississippi Slave Narratives, 11–12.

123. Alcott, *Familiar Letters to Young Men*, 253.

Chapter 2

1. Benjamin Brown Foster, *Downeast Diary*, ed. Charles H. Foster (Orono: University of Maine at Orono Press, 1975), 140.

2. Ibid.

3. Ibid., 102, 124, 76.

4. Ibid., 146.

5. Ibid., 217, 107, 97.

6. Ibid., 7, 38.

7. Ibid., 149, 31.

8. Ibid., 140–41.

9. Ibid.

10. Ibid., 69, 141.

11. Ibid., 76.

12. Lester Ward, *Young Ward's Diary*, ed. Bernhard J. Stern (New York: G. P. Putnam's Sons, 1935), 8, 25; Amanda McDowell Burns, July 5, 1861, in *Fiddles in the Cumberland*, ed. Amanda McDowell and Lela McDowell Blankenship (New York: Richard R. Smith, 1943); Jacob Heffelfinger Diary, June 12, 1858, in Letters of J. Theodore Heard, University of Virginia Special Collections, Charlottesville; David Schenck Papers, Southern Historical Collection, University of North Carolina, Chapel Hill, N.C. For a brilliant study of failure in America, see Scott A. Sandage, *Born Losers: A History of Failure in America* (Cambridge, Mass.: Harvard University Press, 2005).

13. Rolf Johnson, *Happy as a Big Sunflower: Adventures in the West, 1876–1880*, ed. Richard E. Jensen (Lincoln: University of Nebraska Press, 2000), 160–96.

14. Charles W. Plummer Diary, September 27, 1840, Historical Society of Pennsylvania, Philadelphia.

15. Stanley Lebergott, *The Americans: An Economic Record* (New York: Norton, 1984), 66; Thomas Weiss, "U.S. Labor Force Estimates and Economic Growth," in *American Economic Growth and Standards of Living before the Civil War*, ed. Robert E.

Gallman and John Joseph Wallis (Chicago: University of Chicago Press, 1992), 22; Paul Boyer, et al., *The Enduring Vision* (New York: Wadsworth, 2003), 544.

16. William Fletcher King, *Reminiscences* (New York: Abingdon Press, 1915), 64. For more on the uncertain process of aging, see William Quesenbury Claytor, January 1, 1849, *Diary of William Claytor, 1849–1896* (Alexandria, Va.: Alexander Street Press, 2002); Parmenas Taylor Turnley, *Reminiscences of Parmenas Taylor Turnley: From the Cradle to Three-Score and Ten* (Chicago: Donohue and Henneberry, 1892), 24–25; James Silk Buckingham, *America, Historical, Statistic, and Descriptive*, 2 vols. (New York: Harper and Brothers, 1841), 1:120.

17. Charles G. Sellers, *The Market Revolution* (Oxford: Oxford University Press, 1991), 12.

18. This process began in the eighteenth century and built momentum exponentially over the decades. These changes, some argue, peaked in the 1820s but were still avoidable until midcentury. For further studies of the "market revolution" and Americans' growing focus on social and economic progress, see Sellers, *Market Revolution*; Daniel Walker Howe, *What Hath God Wrought* (Oxford: Oxford University Press, 2007); Mary Ryan, *Cradle of the Middle Class* (Cambridge: Cambridge University Press, 1981); Paul E. Johnson, *A Shopkeeper's Millennium* (New York: Hill and Wang, 1978); and Alan Taylor, *William Cooper's Town* (New York: Alfred A. Knopf, 1995).

19. David Herbert Donald included this quote in his famous "Excess of Democracy" explanation for the coming of the Civil War, arguing that the social unravelings of the antebellum era brought about the conflict. Some historians, like Allan Nevins, have claimed that the Civil War reversed this trend, introducing an "organizational revolution," but this shift was largely limited to a small core of industrialists. For most Americans, the years after the Civil War brought as much social change as did the decades leading up to it. David Herbert Donald, "An Excess of Democracy," in *Lincoln Reconsidered: Essays on the Civil War Era* (New York: Vintage Books, 2001), 56; Allan Nevins, *The War for Union*, vol. 3, *The Organized War, 1863–1864* (New York: Charles Scribner's Sons, 1971).

20. Ellen K. Rothman, *Hands and Hearts: A History of Courtship in America* (New York: Basic Books, 1984); Howard Chudacoff, *The Age of the Bachelor* (Princeton: Princeton University Press, 1999).

21. Steven Mintz, *Huck's Raft: A History of American Childhood* (Boston: Belknap Press of Harvard University Press, 2006), 151–80; Walter Licht, *Getting Work: Philadelphia, 1840–1950* (Cambridge, Mass.: Harvard University Press, 1992), 1–17; James Schmidt, *Industrial Violence and the Legal Origins of Child Labor* (Cambridge: Cambridge University Press, 2010).

22. The "go-ahead principle" was a popular shorthand for young nineteenth-century Americans' striving ambition, as in "Not content with going ahead personally, we have infused the go-ahead principle into the very foundations of the republic." *The American Review: A Whig Journal* (New York: E. N. Grossman Printer, 1849), 4:287. Also see the infamous minstrel routine *Zip Coon on the Go-Ahead Principle* (Boston: L. Deming, 1832), and Timothy Templeton, *The Adventures of My Cousin Smooth* (New York: Miller, Orton, and Mulligan, 1855), 2.

23. Joseph Kett, *Rites of Passage: Adolescence in America, 1790 to the Present* (New York: Basic Books, 1977), 11–13; E. Anthony Rotundo, *American Manhood: Transformations in Masculinity from the Revolution to the Modern Era* (New York: Basic Books, 1993), 7, 56.

24. William Fletcher King, *Reminiscences* (New York: Abingdon Press, 1915), 64.

25. Kett, *Rites of Passage*, 11–14; Schmidt, *Industrial Violence*; Howard Chudacoff, *How Old Are You? Age Consciousness in American Culture* (Princeton: Princeton University Press, 1989); Frances B. Cogan, *All-American Girl: The Ideal of Real Womanhood in Mid-Nineteenth-Century America* (Athens: University of Georgia Press, 1989), 63–135.

26. Reverend John Mather Austin, *A Voice to Youth: Address to Young Men and Young Ladies* (Utica: Grosh and Hutchinson, 1839), 3; William A. Alcott, *Familiar Letters to Young Men on Various Subjects: Designed as a Companion to the Young Man's Guide* (Buffalo: Geo. H. Derby, 1850), 78; James Isaac Vance, *The Young Man Foursquare* (New York: F. H. Revell, 1894), 41; Junius Henri Browne, *The Great Metropolis: A Mirror of New York* (Hartford, Conn.: American Publishing, 1869), 73; L. K. Washburn, "A Lecture to Young Men," *Boston Investigator*, October 3, 1888; Karen Halttunen, *Confidence Men and Painted Women: A Study of Middle-Class Culture in America, 1830–1870* (New Haven: Yale University Press, 1982).

27. Roy F. Nichols discussed the structural implications of this never-ending campaign cycle, but its personal impact on the lives of young Americans is just as important. Roy F. Nichols, *The Disruption of American Democracy* (New York: Macmillan, 1948), 21.

28. William L. Riordan, *Plunkitt of Tammany Hall: A Series of Very Plain Talks on Very Practical Politics* (New York: E. P. Dutton, 1963), 13. For other examples of adult politicians inviting young people into politics, see Lew Wallace, *An Autobiography* (New York: Harper and Brothers, 1906), 1:203–5; C. S. Bundy, *Early Days in the Chippewa Valley* (Menomonie, Wis.: Flint Douglas, 1916), 6–11; and Abraham Lincoln to P. Quinn Harrison, November 3, 1859, *Abraham Lincoln: The Collected Works*, 9 vols., ed. Roy P. Basler (New Brunswick: Rutgers University Press, 1953), 3:492.

29. Quoted in Edwin Arnold, *Seas and Lands* (London: Longmans, Green, 1894), 78.

30. David Reynolds, *Walt Whitman's America* (New York: Knopf, 1995), 100–101.

31. Anna Ridgely, May 20, 1860, "A Girl in the Sixties," ed. Octavia Roberts Corneau, *Journal of the Illinois State Historical Society*, 2 (October 1929), 6–9.

32. Martha Farnsworth, *Plains Woman: The Diary of Martha Farnsworth, 1882–1922*, ed. Marlene Springer and Haskell Springer (Bloomington: Indiana University Press, 1986), 54. On the use of kazoos in political events in the 1880s, see Mark Wahlgren Summers, *Party Games: Getting, Keeping, and Using Power in Gilded Age Politics* (Chapel Hill: University of North Carolina Press, 2004), 5.

33. Ridgely, April 8, 1860, and June 24, 1860, "Girl in the Sixties." As Anna grew older, the Civil War destroyed her earlier life. Her two most serious suitors died in the Union army, leading Anna into the ranks of the Peace Democratic movement. By 1864, she was no longer hurrahing Lincoln but rather calling for an "uprising of the people" against the Republican Party.

34. Historians studying this period tend to agree on a basic model of courtship

running from the Jacksonian era until the 1890s. Rothman, *Hands and Hearts*; Chudacoff, *Age of the Bachelor*; Stephanie Coontz, *Marriage, a History: From Obedience to Intimacy* (New York: Viking, 2005); Karen Lystra, *Searching the Heart: Women, Men, and Romantic Love in Nineteenth-Century America* (New York: Oxford University Press, 1992); Cogan, *All-American Girl*, 101–75.

35. Eugene Virgil Smalley, "Indiana Mass Meeting," *New York Tribune*, September 23, 1876.

36. For further reading on these bachelor communities, see Chudacoff, *Age of the Bachelor*.

37. For every 100 fifteen- to nineteen-year-old women in Nevada there were 218.7 men of the same age, while in Louisiana 100 young women had only 89.12 young men to choose from. Campbell Gibson and Kay Jung, *Historical Census Statistics on Population Totals by Race, 1790 to 1990* (Washington, D.C.: U.S. Census Bureau, Population Division, 2002).

38. Ridgely, July 29, 1860, "Girl in The Sixties."

39. Michael R. Haines and Richard H. Steckel, *A Population History of North America* (New York: Cambridge University Press, 2000), 702–4.

40. Carroll Smith-Rosenberg, "Sex as Symbol in Victorian Purity: An Ethnohistorical Analysis of Jacksonian America," in *Turning Points: Historical and Sociological Essays on the Family*, ed. John Demos and Sarane Spence Boocock (Chicago: University of Chicago Press, 1978), 212–47.

41. John D'Emilio and Estelle B. Freedman, *Intimate Matters: A History of Sexuality in America*, 3rd ed. (Chicago: University of Chicago Press, 2012), 55–202; Rotundo, *American Manhood*; Lystra, *Searching the Heart*; Cogan, *All-American Girl*, 101–75.

42. Marriage age in the twentieth century can be graphed as a reverse check mark, slowly dropping from 1890 to lows during the Cold War and rising rapidly for the last four decades. Chudacoff, *Age of the Bachelor*, 48.

43. Ridgely, March 11, 1860, "Girl in the Sixties," 7.

44. Cogan, *All-American Girl*, 101–75; Beth L. Bailey, *From Front Porch to Back Seat: Courtship in Twentieth-Century America* (Baltimore: Johns Hopkins University Press, 1988).

45. For particularly good examples of the challenges of courting in this shaken society, see Farnsworth, *Plains Woman*, 19, 24, 44–66, and letters of Mattie V. Thomas and Uriah W. Oblinger, 1864–1869, Uriah W. Oblinger Family Collection, Nebraska State Historical Society, Lincoln.

46. "Grant and Colfax," *Des Moines Daily State Register*, October 27, 1868; "Saturday's Local the News of a Day in the Capital City," *Bismarck Daily Tribune*, September 29, 1889.

47. Charlotte Howard Conant, September 19, 1888, *A Girl of the Eighties at College and at Home*, ed. Martha Pike Conant (Boston: Houghton Mifflin, 1931), 261.

48. Ward, *Young Ward's Diary*, 6–35.

49. "The Political Arena. Democrats Discussing the Convention of Monday," *Knoxville Journal*, November 29, 1893.

50. Steven Hahn, *A Nation under Our Feet* (Boston: Belknap Press, 2003), 228.

51. Ronald J. Zboray and Mary Saracino Zboray, *Voices without Votes: Women and Politics in Antebellum New England* (Durham: University of New Hampshire Press, 2010), 98–102; "Multiple News Items," *Portland Morning Oregonian*, November 2, 1894.

52. Lili (full name unknown) to Mattie Thomas, December 19, 1864, in Uriah W. Oblinger Family Collection.

53. Anne L. Youmans Van Ness, January 1868; September 1868; November 1868, *Diary of Annie L. Youmans Van Ness, 1864–1881* (Alexandria, Va.: Alexander Street Press, 2004).

54. Letters from Clay W. Anderson to William G. Beatty, October 27, 1855; June 24, 1856; September 18, 1856, in *Life and Letters of Judge Thomas J. Anderson and Wife*, ed. James House Anderson and Nancy Anderson (Cincinnati: Press of F. J. Heer, 1904), 473, 475, 476.

55. Historians Mary Zboray and Ronald Zboray disagree, rightly pointing out that many women fell back on a "rhetoric of diffidence," feigning political ignorance in the presence of men. While there are a significant number of examples of young women who did this, many others made deliberate use of their political knowledge. Zboray and Zboray, *Voices without Votes*, 12.

56. Alice Bradley Haven criticized this belief that women should avoid talking politics amongst themselves, writing to her sister, "You laugh at my interests in politics . . . and you ask me to write to you whether Millard Filmore or Fillard Milmore is President. . . . I understand what your affectation of ignorance implies. Do not be afraid of my knowing too much even to please you, who have such a horror of women dabbling in politics." Alice Bradley Haven, *Cousin Alice: A Memoir of Alice B. Haven*, ed. Cornelia Richards (New York: D. Appleton, 1868), 135–37. Other examples of women discussing politics with men but avoiding it with women can be found in Susan Hale to Alexander Hale, November 1, 1848, in *Letters of Susan Hale*, ed. Caroline P. Atkinson (Boston: Marshall Jones, 1918); Blanche Butler Ames to Sarah Hildreth Butler, January 7, 1861, in *Chronicles from the Nineteenth Century: Family Letters of Blanche Butler and Adelbert Ames*, comp. Blanche Butler Ames, vol. 1 (Clinton, Mass.: Privately published, 1957), 63; Cornelia Oatis Hancock, November 14, 1864, in *Letters of a Civil War Nurse: Cornelia Hancock, 1863–1865*, ed. Henrietta Stratton Jaquette (Lincoln: University of Nebraska Press, 1998); and Isabella Maud Rittenhouse Mayne, January 1882, in *Maud*, ed. Richard Lee Strout (New York: Macmillan, 1939), 48–52.

57. Young men had significantly higher rates of relocation than young women and also traveled in a less structured manner. When women relocated, they tended to have a specific destination, often with a relative, and they were more likely to travel in groups, rely on paid transportation, and stay in lodgings along the way. Young men were far more likely to set off on a wander year with little money or direction and to simply meander on foot across multiple states. An illuminating comparison can be seen in two accounts of trips, one by a young man and the other by a young woman, taken across the Midwest in 1840: John Parsons, *A Tour through Indiana in 1840: The Diary of John Parsons of Petersburg, Virginia*, ed. Kate Milner Rabb (New York: R. M. McBride, 1920), and Elize R. Steele, *Summer Journey in the West* (New York: John S. Taylor, 1841).

58. Alcott, *Familiar Letters to Young Men*, 141.

59. Merle Curti, *The Making of an American Community: A Case Study in Democracy in a Frontier County* (Stanford: Stanford University Press, 1959), 68. For similar urban statistics, see Stephan Ternstrom and Peter R. Knights, "Men in Motion: Some Data and Speculations about Urban Population Mobility in Nineteenth-Century America," *Journal of Interdisciplinary History* 1 (Autumn 1970): 7–35.

60. Marcus Pomeroy, *Reminiscences and Recollections of "Brick" Pomeroy* (New York: Advance Though, 1890), 19.

61. Rhody Holsell, *Born in Slavery: Slave Narratives from the Federal Writers' Project, 1936–1938, Missouri Narratives*, 10:191; William Wheeler to Theodosia Davenport Wheeler, February 14, 1860, *Letters of William Wheeler of the Class of 1855, Y.C.* (Cambridge: Privately published, 1875), 46; J. Parsons, *Tour through Indiana in 1840*.

62. Oscar Lawrence Jackson, *The Colonel's Diary: Journals Kept before and during the Civil War*, ed. David P. Jackson (Sharon, Pa.: Privately published, 1922), 28.

63. Richard Bensel offers a thorough study of colonization in *The American Ballot Box in the Mid-Nineteenth Century* (Cambridge: Cambridge University Press, 2004), 159–64, as does Mark W. Summers in *The Plundering Generation: Corruption and the Crisis of the Union, 1849–1861* (New York: Oxford University Press, 1987), 54–58.

64. "Districting Middlesex for Representatives," *Lowell Citizen and News*, August 1, 1857. Supreme Court justice Joseph Story worried about this practice, noting "the habits of our people, compared with many other nations, are migratory," and proposed structures to help mobile young men orient themselves politically. Joseph Story, "Domicil," in *Encyclopaedia Americana*, vol. 3, ed. Francis Lieber (Philadelphia: Lea and Blanchard, 1844), 58.

65. Lyman Abbott, *Reminiscences* (Boston: Houghton Mifflin, 1914), 98; Andreas Ueland, *Recollections of an Immigrant* (New York: Minton, Balch, 1929), 38; Nils Haugen, *Pioneer and Political Reminiscences* (Evansville, Wis.: Antes Press, 1930); Isaac Stephenson, *Recollections of a Long Life, 1829–1915* (Chicago: Privately published, 1915); Bundy, *Early Days in the Chippewa Valley*; Franklin A. Buck, *A Yankee Trader in the Gold Rush: The Letters of Franklin A. Buck*, comp. Katherine A. White (Boston: Houghton Mifflin, 1930).

66. James Witham, *Fifty Years on the Firing Line: My Part in the Farmers' Movement* (Chicago: Privately published, 1924), 2.

67. Ibid., 1–12.

68. Charles A. Murdock, *A Backward Glance at Eighty* (San Francisco: P. Elder, 1921), 10; John M. Roberts, *Buckeye Schoolmaster: A Chronicle of Midwestern Rural Life, 1853–1865*, ed. J. Merton England (Bowling Green, Ky.: Bowling Green State University Popular Press, 1996), 224; William Dean Howells, *Years of my Youth* (New York: Harper and Brothers, 1916), 108; Mayne, January 1862, *Maud*, 48–52; Charles W. Plummer Diary, September 1, 1840.

69. Frederick Law Olmstead, *Journeys and Explorations in the Cotton Kingdom* (London: S. Low, 1862); Abbott, *Reminiscences*, 98; Jackson, *Colonel's Diary*, 9. Also see Eric Foner, *Free Labor, Free Soil, Free Men* (Oxford: Oxford University Press, 1970), for a strong portrayal of northern travelers' perspectives on the South.

70. The memoirs of Scandinavian immigrants in the Upper Midwest are particularly rich in stories of work-camp political socialization, as are reminiscences from the California frontier. See Ueland, *Recollections of an Immigrant*, 38; Haugen, *Pioneer and Political Reminiscences*; Stephenson, *Recollections of a Long Life*; Bundy, *Early Days in the Chippewa Valley*; and Buck, *Yankee Trader in the Gold Rush*.

71. Witham, *Fifty Years on the Firing Line*, 9; Jackson, *Colonel's Diary*, 27.

72. L. K. Washburn, "A Lecture to Young Men," *Boston Investigator*, October 3, 1888. For a thorough examination of the dangers faced during the late teenage years and some progressive solutions, see the essays in Edward Bok, ed., *Before He Is Twenty: Five Perplexing Phases of Boyhood Considered: Essays from "Ladies' Home Journal"* (New York: F. H. Revell, 1894).

73. Rotundo, *American Manhood*, 20; Kett, *Rites of Passage*, 173; Amy S. Greenberg, *Manifest Manhood and the Antebellum American Empire* (Cambridge: Cambridge University Press, 2005); Gail Bederman, *Manliness and Civilization* (Chicago: University of Chicago Press, 1995).

74. Burns, May 1861, *Fiddles in the Cumberland*; Haven, February 1852, *Cousin Alice*, 135–37; Ellen Tucker Emerson to Addie Manning, September 8, 1856, *The Letters of Ellen Tucker Emerson*, vol. 1, ed. Edith W. Gregg (Kent: Kent State University Press, 1982), 118–20; Eliza Frances Andrews, May 1865, *The War-Time Journal of a Georgia Girl, 1864–1865*, ed. Spencer B. King Jr. (New York: Appleton-Century-Crofts, 1908).

75. Michael F. Campbell Diary, December 30, 1881, Sterling Library, Yale Special Collections, New Haven, Conn.

76. Ibid., May 7, 1881.

77. Ibid.

78. "Business Cycle Expansions and Contractions," *National Bureau of Economic Research*, last modified January 4, 2009, http://www.nber.org/cycles/cyclesmain.html.

79. Michael F. Campbell Diary, May 7, 1881.

80. Ibid., May 7, 1878.

81. Looking back on the 1884 campaign, a San Francisco newspaperman sighed, "Cleveland's head and neck have occupied a large place in the past campaign." See "The Physical and Phrenological Differences between the Presidential Candidates," *St. Louis Globe-Democrat*, November 1, 1884; "Heads and Necks in Congress, Senators and Representatives with Thick Necks," *San Francisco Daily Evening Bulletin*, December 27, 1884; "The Heads of Great Men," *Galveston Daily News*, September 10, 1893; Brooklyn Young Republican Club, *Young Republican Campaign Song Book*, comp. Henry Camp (Brooklyn: Harrison and Morton, 1888); Michael F. Campbell Diary, May 7, 1881.

82. Michael F. Campbell Diary, May 7, 1881.

83. Schmidt, *Industrial Violence*, 1–40. Also see Farnsworth, *Plains Woman*, 7.

84. Michael F. Campbell Diary, November 20, 1879; March 5, 1881; March 17, 1881; May 7, 1881.

85. Richard J. Carwardine, *Evangelicals and Politics in Antebellum America* (New Haven: Yale University Press, 1993); Rodney Hessinger, *Seduced, Abandoned, and Reborn: Visions of Youth in Middle-Class America, 1780–1850* (Philadelphia: University of Pennsylvania Press, 2005).

86. Horace Greeley's *New York Tribune* politicized more young Americans than any other paper. Its mass availability, its focus on societal progress, and Greeley's deliberate appeals to the young made it an unparalleled tool for recruiting Whigs and Republicans. The Democratic Party never fielded a publication of similar power. For examples of young readers politicized by the *Tribune*, see Ward, *Young Ward's Diary*, 74; B. Foster, *Downeast Diary*, 110; Witham, *Fifty Years on the Firing Line*, 6; and Rasmus Bjorn Anderson, *Life Story of Rasmus Bjorn Anderson* (Madison, Wis.: Privately published, 1915), 40.

87. Michael F. Campbell Diary, October 31, November 1, 1880.

88. The Know Nothings' calls for a twenty-one-year waiting period for immigrants to be naturalized demonstrate this sense that foreign-born voters were skipping ahead of native-born virgin voters. Tyler Anbinder, *Nativism and Slavery: The Northern Know Nothings and the Politics of the 1850s* (New York: Oxford University Press, 1992), 138. Also see Albion Winegar Tourgée, *Letters to a King* (Cincinnati: Cranston and Stowe, 1888), 43, and Vance, *Young Man Foursquare*, 69–70.

89. J. Roberts, *Buckeye Schoolmaster*, 53; Charles W. Plummer Diary, May 30, 1844; Clay W. Anderson to William G. Beatty, October 27, 1855, in *Life and Letters of Judge Thomas J. Anderson and Wife*; George Templeton Strong, *Diary: Young Man in New York, 1835–1849*, ed. Allan Nevins and Milton Halsey Thomas (New York: Macmillan, 1952), 94; Young Men's Fillmore and Donelson Association, "An Address from the Young Men's Fillmore & Donelson Association of Boston to the Young Men of Massachusetts," 1856, Printed Ephemera Collection, Library of Congress; "Young America," *Semi-Weekly Raleigh Register*, August 16, 1856.

90. Michael F. Campbell Diary, August 24, 1880.

91. For examples of campaign handbooks, see The Unexcelled Campaign Fireworks Company's *Illustrated Campaign Handbook Manual of Arms and Tactics* (New York, 1888) and *A Red-Hot Campaign for 1880! Great Sale: Fine Art Campaign Pictures!*, both in the Political Campaign Collections, Smithsonian Institution, National Museum of American History, Washington, D.C. For examples of the most uniform-obsessed movement of the era—the Wide Awake clubs of 1860—see Julius G. Rathbun, "'The Wide Awakes': The Great Political Organization of 1860," *Connecticut Quarterly* 1 (October 1895): 327–35; Henry T. Sperry, *The Republican Wide-Awakes of Hartford, Organized March 3, 1860* (Hartford, 1860), pamphlet, Connecticut Imprints, Connecticut Historical Society, Hartford; and B. F. Thompson, "The Wide Awakes of 1860," *Magazine of History with Notes and Queries* 10 (November 1909): 293. For the most thorough study of torches, see Herbert R. Collins, "Political Campaign Torches," *Contributions from the Museum of History and Technology* (Washington, D.C.: Smithsonian Press, 1966), 1–44.

92. Michael F. Campbell Diary, August 27, 1880, and September 4, 1880. Information on the James E. English House, a New Haven architectural icon designed by the famous Henry Austin, was drawn from Henry Austin Papers, Beinecke Rare Book Library, Yale University, New Haven, Conn.; and from discussion with the house's extremely helpful current occupants, the owners of the Maresca Funeral Home. Michael McGerr makes excellent use of this meeting between Michael Campbell and

James English in *The Decline of Popular Politics* to show the relatively accessible style of popular politics during its height. His impressive work does not, however, situate this meeting in the context of Michael Campbell's larger insecurities and ambitions. Not only did Campbell win a surprising degree of access to Governor English, as McGerr shows, but he did so because of the youthful uncertainties that bedeviled the rest of his life. Michael E. McGerr, *The Decline of Popular Politics: The American North, 1865–1928* (Oxford: Oxford University Press, 1986), 12–22.

93. Michael F. Campbell Diary, August 23, 1880.

94. Ibid., June 29, 1881.

95. W. D. Howells, *Years of My Youth*, 57.

96. Chudacoff, *How Old Are You?*, 117.

97. Chloe Bridgman Conant Bierce, *Journal and Biological Notice of Chloe B. Conant Bierce* (Cincinnati: Elm Street Printing, 1869), 98; Susan Allibone, July 1835, *A Life Hid with Christ in God* (Philadelphia: J. B. Lippincott, 1856), 46–49; Ella Gertrude Clanton Thomas, April 1852, in *The Secret Eye: The Journal of Ella Gertrude Clanton Thomas, 1848–1889*, ed. Virginia Ingraham Burr (Chapel Hill: University of North Carolina Press, 1990), 103; Charlotte L. Forten Grimké, August 1854, *The Journals of Charlotte Forten Grimké*, ed. Brenda Stevenson (Oxford: Oxford University Press, 1988), 96.

98. Susan Goodman and Carl Dawson, *William Dean Howells: A Writers Life* (Berkeley: University of California Press, 2005), 26. Howells wrote thoughtfully, decades later, about his "very morbid boyhood." W. D. Howells, *Years of My Youth*, 19.

99. William Dean Howells to Victoria Howells, October 27, 1857, *Selected Letters of William Dean Howells*, ed. George Arms (Boston: Twayne, 1979), 1:14; Howells to Dune Dean, September 9, 1857, ibid., 1:10.

100. Goodman and Dawson, *William Dean Howells*, 14–16; William Dean Howells, *My Year in a Log Cabin* (New York: Harper and Brothers, 1893).

101. Goodman and Dawson, *William Dean Howells*, 14; William Dean Howells, *A Boy's Town: Described for "Harper's Young People"* (New York: Harper and Brothers, 1890), 20.

102. W. D. Howells, *Years of My Youth*, 77, 105.

103. Ibid., 72–75; William Dean Howells, August 1852, "1852 Diary and Spanish Exercises," Houghton Library, Harvard Special Collections, Cambridge, Mass.

104. Howells to Dune Dean, September 9, 1857, *Selected Letters*, 1:10.

105. W. D. Howells, *Years of My Youth*, 73, 90, 150.

106. Ibid., 151.

107. Goodman and Dawson, *William Dean Howells*, 20

108. W. D. Howells, "1852 Diary and Spanish Exercises."

109. W. D. Howells, *Years of My Youth*, 124.

110. Howells to Victoria Howells, October 27, 1857, *Selected Letters*, 1:14; Howells to Dune Dean, September 9, 1857, ibid., 1:10; W. D. Howells, *Years of My Youth*, 125.

111. Howells to Victoria Howells, October 27, 1857, *Selected Letters*, 1:14.

112. W. D. Howells, *Years of My Youth*, 125.

113. Ibid., 153, 110.

114. Charles W. Plummer Diary, March 29, 1842.

115. Michael F. Campbell Diary, May 7, 1881; J. Roberts, *Buckeye Schoolmaster*, 93.

116. W. D. Howells, *Years of My Youth*, 153.

117. Tourgée, *Letters to a King*, 13, 36, 34.

Chapter 3

1. John J. McCarthy, "When I First Voted a Democratic Ticket," collected by Bessie Jollensten, October 19, 1938, American Life Histories Interviews.

2. Ibid.

3. Robert R. Mahnken, "Ogallala—Nebraska's Cowboy Capital," *Nebraska History* 28 (April–June 1947): 85–109; *Compendium of History, Reminiscence, and Biography of Western Nebraska* (Chicago: Alden, 1909).

4. McCarthy, "When I First Voted a Democratic Ticket"; *Ogallala Reflector*, November 4, 1884.

5. McCarthy, "When I First Voted a Democratic Ticket"; John J. McCarthy, "A Speech Made by J. J. McCarthy at Kearney, Nebraska," collected by Bessie Jollensten, October 19, 1938, American Life Histories Interviews.

6. McCarthy, "When I First Voted a Democratic Ticket."

7. "The Independent Twenty-Onesters," *San Francisco Daily Evening Bulletin*, August 17, 1869; Albion Winegar Tourgée, *Letters to a King* (Cincinnati: Cranston and Stowe, 1888), 37.

8. Charles G. Leland, *Memoirs* (London: William Heinemann, 1894), 13.

9. Charles G. Leland, *Pipps among the Wide Awakes* (New York: Wevill and Chapin, 1860), 1.

10. For more on the history of American facial hair, see Gerald Carson, "Hair Today, Gone Tomorrow," *American Heritage* 17 (February 1966): 45, and especially Adam Goodheart's clever take in *1861: The Civil War Awakening* (New York: Alfred A. Knopf, 2011), 111–13.

11. "State Legislature Remarks," *Raleigh Register, and North-Carolina Gazette*, February 24, 1843; "Riot," *Liberator*, December 20, 1850; "Political Painters," *St. Louis Globe-Democrat*, January 12, 1876; "The Ball Opens," *St. Louis Globe-Democrat*, June 20, 1876; "Latent Forces and How to Develop Them," *Independent*, February 14, 1895.

12. Glenn Wallach, *Obedient Sons: The Discourse of Youth and Generations in American Culture, 1630–1860* (Amherst: University of Massachusetts Press, 1997), 65.

13. "To Anti-gang Democrats," *Daily Inter Ocean*, March 26, 1893; James S. Clarkson, "The Politician and the Pharisee," *North American Review* 152, no. 414 (May 1891): 618.

14. "About Facial Foliage," *Daily Inter Ocean*, July 16, 1893.

15. Lester Bodine, *Off the Face of the Earth* (Omaha: Festner, 1894), 101.

16. This quote, and the claim that young men's political interests peaked during their "hair-oil period of existence," comes from a story titled "The Magic Mirror," published in the *Bangor Daily Whig and Courier*. Even though the story described the experiences of a twenty-one-year-old prince in Persia, he nonetheless casts his virgin

vote. Apparently, the experience of voting was considered so ubiquitous that even young men ruled by the Qajar dynasty practiced the rite. "The Magic Mirror," *Bangor Daily Whig and Courier*, May 13, 1868.

17. "The young man who deposited his maiden vote on Nov. 7 was easily recognized," *Milwaukee Daily Sentinel*, December 11, 1876.

18. Leland, *Pipps among the Wide Awakes*, 10.

19. Frances E. Willard, *Glimpses of Fifty Years: The Autobiography of an American Woman* (Chicago: Women's Temperance Publication Association, H. J. Smith and Co., 1889), 69–70.

20. Ella Gertrude Clanton Thomas, November 1852, in *The Secret Eye: The Journal of Ella Gertrude Clanton Thomas*, ed. Virginia Ingraham Burr (Chapel Hill: University of North Carolina Press, 1990), 117.

21. Sarah Ann Ross Pringle, interviewed by Effie Cowan, McLennan County, Texas (undated), American Life Histories Interviews.

22. "Young Voters at Cleveland's Home," *San Francisco Daily Evening Bulletin*, September 6, 1884.

23. "Classified," *New York Times*, November 4, 1864.

24. "Their First Vote," *Milwaukee Sentinel*, July 29, 1888; "Campaign Uniforms," *Milwaukee Daily Journal*, September 15, 1888; "Campaign Clubs," *Milwaukee Journal*, May 26, 1892.

25. George Templeton Strong, *Diary: Young Man in New York, 1835–1849*, ed. Allan Nevins and Milton Halsey Thomas (New York: Macmillan, 1952), 151; William Saunders Brown Diary, October 30 through November 10, 1844, University of Virginia Special Collections, Charlottesville; John Hunton Diary, September 5, 1880, University of Virginia Special Collections Charlottesville; Emil R. Kaiser, interviewed by Francis Donovan, Thomaston, Conn., December 15, 1938, American Life Histories Interviews.

26. Strong, *Diary*, 94.

27. Ibid.,151.

28. Ibid., 160.

29. William Dean Howells, *A Boy's Town: Described for "Harper's Young People"* (New York: Harper and Brothers, 1890), 77.

30. Rodney D. Olsen, *Dancing in Chains: The Youth of William Dean Howells* (New York: New York University Press, 1991), 121.

31. William Dean Howells, *The Early Prose Writings of William Dean Howells, 853–1861*, ed. Thomas Wortham (Athens: Ohio University Press, 1990), 102.

32. James Michael Curley, *I'd Do It Again* (New York: Arno Press, 1976), 44–47.

33. Newtown Township Poll Books, Camden County, New Jersey, November 4, 1856, March 11, 1857, March 10, 1858, November 6, 1860, Historical Society of Pennsylvania, Philadelphia; "Lincoln Wide Awakes," *Daily Cleveland Herald*, May 26, 1860; "Wide-Awakes," *Daily Cleveland Herald*, May 29, 1860; "Their First Vote," *Milwaukee Daily Sentinel*, July 29, 1888.

34. Drums were used to particularly loathsome effect by white southerners during Reconstruction as an advance warning to would-be black voters. Older Democrats

even moved to suppress their use by excited young Redeemers. U.S. Senate, *Recent Election in Mississippi*, 44th Cong., 2nd sess., 1877.

35. Carl Schurz, *The Reminiscences of Carl Schurz* (New York: McClure, 1907), 2:194; August Segerberg, September 28, 1884, in *Letters from the Promised Land: Swedes in America, 1840–1915*, ed. H. Arnold Barton (Minneapolis: University of Minnesota Press, 1975), 194; Emil R. Kaiser interview; Sally McCarty Pleasants, *Old Virginia Days and Ways: Reminiscences of Mrs. Sally McCarty Pleasants* (Menasha, Wis.: George Banta, 1916), 6; Anna Ridgely, April 8, 1860, in "A Girl in the Sixties," ed. Octavia Roberts Corneau, *Journal of the Illinois State Historical Society*, 2 (October 1929): 40–46; letters from Clay W. Anderson to William G. Beatty, October 27, 1855, in *Life and Letters of Judge Thomas J. Anderson and Wife*, ed. James House Anderson and Nancy Anderson (Cincinnati: Press of F. J. Heer, 1904), 473.

36. For information on the rise of campaign slogans in the 1840 race, see Robert Gray Gunderson, *The Log Cabin Campaign* (Lexington: University Press of Kentucky, 1957), 123. For other nasty slogans, see F. A. Wagler, *Govr. Polk's March and Quick Step* (Baltimore: Geo. Willis Jr., 1844); A. Tennessean, *Hickory Waltz and Gallopade* (New York: John F. Nunns, 1844); John F. Goneke, *James K. Polk's Grand March and Quick Step* (Philadelphia: G. Willis, 1844), all from the collection Music for the Nation: American Sheet Music, ca. 1820–1860, Library of Congress, http://www.loc.gov/collection/american-sheet-music-1820-to-1860/about-this-collection, and Brooklyn Young Republican Club, *Young Republican Campaign Song Book*, comp. Henry Camp (Brooklyn: Harrison and Morton, 1888).

37. Brooklyn Young Republican Club, *Young Republican Campaign Song Book*, 34.

38. See Newtown Township Poll Books, November 4, 1856, March 11, 1857, March 10, 1858, November 6, 1860; U.S. House, *Digest of Election Cases*, 47th Cong., 2nd sess., 1879, Miscellaneous Document No. 35; U.S. Senate, *Recent Election in Mississippi*, 44th Cong., 2nd sess., 1877; Sarah Ann Ross Pringle interview; Douglas Egerton, *The Wars of Reconstruction: The Brief, Violent History of America's Most Progressive Era* (New York: Bloomsbury, 2014), 286.

39. Richard Franklin Bensel, *The American Ballot Box in the Mid-Nineteenth Century* (Cambridge: Cambridge University Press, 2004), 22.

40. Nathaniel Parker Willis, "Letter from N. P. Willis about the Presidency," *New York Evening Post*, October 4, 1856.

41. Child went on: "What a Rip! To lie sleeping fifty years, dreaming of kid gloves, embroidered vests, and perfumed handkerchiefs, taking it for granted that his country was all the while going forward in a righteous and glorious career. Isn't it too bad that such parasol-holders should have the right to vote, while earnest souls like you and me must await the result in agonizing inaction? Things look squally; don't they, dear?" Lydia Maria Child to Sarah Blake Sturgis Shaw, October 27, 1856, in *Letters of Lydia Maria Child*, ed. Wendell Phillips (Boston: Houghton Mifflin, 1882), 85.

42. Carroll Smith-Rosenberg, "Sex as Symbol in Victorian Purity: An Ethnohistorical Analysis of Jacksonian America," in *Turning Points: Historical and Sociological Essays on the Family*, ed. John Demos and Sarane Spence Boocock (Chicago: University of

Chicago Press, 1978). The censorious rhetoric could be very different from the actual realities of premarital sex for many young Americans. See Helen Lefkowitz Horowitz, *Rereading Sex: Battles over Sexual Knowledge and Suppression in Nineteenth-Century America* (New York: Knopf Doubleday, 2003), and Patricia Cline Cohen, Timothy J. Gilfoyle, and Helen Lefkowitz Horowitz, *The Flash Press: Sporting Male Weeklies in 1840s New York* (Chicago: University of Chicago Press, 2008).

43. Walter Marion Raymond, *Rebels of the New South* (Chicago: Charles H. Kerr, 1905), 151; "The First Vote," *Vermont Patriot*, August 11, 1860; "Young Men!," *Daily Cleveland Herald*, July 3, 1860; "The First Vote—Young Men, Start Right," *Daily Ohio Statesman*, September 13, 1860.

44. "What Is Democracy? To the Young Voters of the United States," *Pomeroy's Democrat*, June 3, 1876.

45. John Worrell Northrop, May 1861, in *Chronicles from the Diary of a War Prisoner in Andersonville* (Wichita: J. W. Northrop, 1904); Lydia Maria Child to Sarah Blake Sturgis Shaw, October 27, 1856, in *Letters of Lydia Maria Child*, 8; Tourgée, *Letters to a King*, 49.

46. Robert Bryant, Herculaneum, Missouri, *Born in Slavery: Slave Narratives from the Federal Writers' Project, 1936–1938, Missouri Narratives*, 10:69.

47. In cartoons, the mere act of casting a vote seemed to physically inflate a young man, and one political satire—*Solid for Mulhooly*—played with the idea of weighty partisans. Rufus Edmonds Shapley, *Solid for Mulhooly* (New York: G. W. Carleton, 1881).

48. "The Young Man's First Vote," *Rocky Mountain News* (Denver, Colo.), November 1, 1890.

49. Anonymous, *Maidenhead Stories, Told by a Set of Joyous Students* (New York: Erotica Biblion Society, 1897); Howard Chudacoff, *How Old Are You? Age Consciousness in American Culture* (Princeton: Princeton University Press, 1989), 62.

50. For formal investigations into virginity and nineteenth-century sexuality, see John D'Emilio and Estelle B. Freedman, *Intimate Matters: A History of Sexuality in America*, 3rd ed. (Chicago: University of Chicago Press, 2012), 55–202; Karen Lystra, *Searching the Heart: Women, Men, and Romantic Love in Nineteenth-Century America* (New York: Oxford University Press, 1992); and Frances B. Cogan, *All-American Girl: The Ideal of Real Womanhood in Mid-Nineteenth-Century America* (Athens: University of Georgia Press, 1989), 101–75.

51. Michael F. Holt, "The Election of 1840, Voter Mobilization, and the Emergence of the Second Party System," in *A Master's Due: Essays in Honor of David Herbert Donald*, ed. John McCardell (Baton Rogue: Louisiana State University Press, 1985), 16.

52. "Hurrah for the Young Democracy," *Weekly Ohio Statesman*, May 29, 1844. For more on "renunciation meetings," see "Our Glorious Hickory Club," *Ohio Statesman*, November 29, 1843; "A Movement among the Young Men," *Chillicothe Scioto Gazette*, September 26, 1844; "Wm. A. Neil, Esq.," *Daily Ohio Statesman*, October 2, 1850; "Young Men Who Will Cast Their First Vote," *Memphis Enquirer*, December 28, 1843; and "Taking the Right Side," *Weekly Raleigh Register, and North-Carolina Gazette*, March 8, 1844.

53. "The Young Men," *Pittsfield (Mass.) Sun*, October 30, 1856.

54. "Young Men!," *Daily Cleveland Herald*, November 3, 1856.

55. "Is Chicago Republican?," *Daily Inter Ocean*, October 25, 1879; "To the Young Men of Orleans Co.," *Vermont Patriot*, July 13, 1840; "First Vote," *North American and United States Gazette*, September 17, 1868; "Are the Young Men of West Virginia in Favor of Constitutional Government?," *Wheeling Register*, April 3, 1880; "Voting," *Salt Lake Tribune*, October 30, 1880; "Every Young Man," *Puck*, April 27, 1881.

56. James Witham, *Fifty Years on the Firing Line: My Part in the Farmers' Movement* (Chicago: Privately published, 1924), 21.

57. Bensel, *American Ballot Box*, 20, 58; Harpo Marx and Rowland Barber, *Harpo Speaks!* (New York: Bernard Geis Associates, 1961), 48; Emil R. Kaiser interview; Don Powers and Susie Powers, interviewed by John William Prosser, Columbia, S.C., February 6, 1939, American Life Histories Interviews.

58. Bensel's *American Ballot Box* includes the best investigation of the process of challenging voters. See 93–106.

59. Digest of Election Cases, Cases of Contested Elections in the House of Representatives, from 1865 to 1871 Inclusive, 38th Cong., 2nd Sess., Misc. Document No. 152 (1870), 620.

60. This unique demand—that a young man be able to know and somehow verify his age—sets voting apart from almost all other rituals in nineteenth-century America. Howard Chudacoff has cleverly pointed out the culture's general lack of interest in age separation during this period, but political participation runs against this trend. Chudacoff, *How Old Are You?* Corinne T. Field makes this same point in her article "Are Women . . . All Minors? Women's Rights and the Politics of Aging in the Antebellum United States," *Journal of Women's History* 12 (Winter 2001): 113–37.

61. Andrew Dickson White, *Autobiography of Andrew Dickson White* (New York: Century, 1904), 1:74.

62. *Contested Election, McClure against Gray, Proceedings of the Committee Appointed upon the Petitions of Citizens of the 4th Senatorial District, Contesting the Election of Henry W. Gray* (Philadelphia: J. B. Lippincott, 1872), 11.

63. Leland, *Pipps among the Wide Awakes*, 15.

64. Robert M. Howard, *Reminiscences* (Columbus, Ga.: Gilbert, 1912), 7; Leland, *Pipps among the Wide Awakes*, 14; Lyman Abbott, *Reminiscences* (Boston: Houghton Mifflin, 1915), 111. The added fact that many of these claims came from places, like rural Alabama and Georgia, where there were hardly any Irish people casts further doubt on such stories.

65. Michael W. Fitzgerald, *The Union League Movement in the Deep South: Politics and Agricultural Change During Reconstruction* (Baton Rogue: Louisiana State University Press, 1989), 9.

66. Ibid., 66; James West Davidson, *They Say: Ida B. Wells and the Reconstruction of Race* (New York: Oxford University Press, 2007), 21; Steven Hahn, *A Nation under Our Feet* (Boston: Belknap Press, 2003), 87; U.S. House, *Digest of Election Cases*, 47th Cong., 2nd Sess., 1879, Miscellaneous Document No. 35; U.S. Senate, *Recent Election in Mississippi*, 44th Cong., 2nd Sess., 1877; Sarah Ann Ross Pringle interview.

67. Bensel, *American Ballot Box*, 83–96; Diary of an Unknown Resident of Madison County, Virginia, 1852, University of Virginia Special Collections, Charlottesville.

68. Leander Stillwell, *The Story of a Common Soldier of Army Life in the Civil War, 1861–1865* (Kansas City, Mo.: Frank Hudson, 1920), 96. Diaries and memoirs by many underage soldiers recount voting illegally, and none articulate a sense of shame in doing so. Many Union prisoners of war even held mock contests on northern election days from Andersonville or other southern prisons, and they observed no age restrictions. In some cases, Confederate prison guards even facilitated these contests, though they were often chagrined when Lincoln won. Warfare, particularly fought by citizen-soldiers, has always helped enfranchise young men and question age-based voting restrictions. William Bircher, November 1864, *A Drummer-Boy's Diary* (St. Paul: St. Paul Book and Stationery Co., 1889), 199; Sim Moak, *The Last of the Mill Creeks* (Chico, Calif.: Privately published, 1923); Northrop, November 1864, in *Chronicles from the Diary of a War Prisoner in Andersonville*, 228; Michael Dougherty, November 1864, *Prison Diary of Michael Dougherty* (Bristol, Pa.: C. A. Dougherty, Printer, 1908), 128; Thomas W. Springer Diary, November 8, 1864, University of Virginia Special Collections, Charlottesville; Wendell W. Cultice, *Youth's Battle for the Ballot* (New York: Praeger, 1992).

69. Bayard Taylor, *El Dorado; or, Adventures in the Path of Empire*, vol. 2 (London: Henry G. Bohn, 1850), 189; Erastus Flavel Beadle, *Ham, Eggs, and Corn Cake: A Nebraska Territory Diary*, ed. Ronald Naugle (Lincoln: University of Nebraska Press, 2001), 76; C. S. Bundy, *Early Days in the Chippewa Valley* (Menomonie, Wis.: Flint Douglas, 1916), 6.

70. White males ages fifteen to twenty-nine made up 53.29 percent of California residents in 1850. Campbell Gibson and Kay Jung, *Historical Census Statistics on Population Totals by Race, 1790 to 1990*, Working Paper Series No. 56 (Washington, D.C.: U.S. Census Bureau, Population Division, 2002).

71. James G. Blaine, *Life and Public Services of Hon. James G Blaine*, ed. James P. Boyd (Philadelphia: Publishers Union, 1893), 240. State politicians often introduced liberal voting laws in a bid to attract migrants. In the years after America's conquest of California, many local Mexicans were also encouraged to vote, "to give this primitive people their first lesson in the mysteries of American citizenship." Horace Bell, *Reminiscences of a Ranger: Early Times in Southern California* (Los Angeles: Yarnell, Caystile and Mathes, Printers, 1881), 73; B. Taylor, *El Dorado*, 189.

72. Enos Christman, *One Man's Gold: The Letters and Journal of a Forty-Niner*, ed. Florence Morrow Christman (New York: Whittlesey House, 1930), 117. Also see Moak, *Last of the Mill Creeks*; David R. Leeper, *The Argonauts of 'Forty-Nine: Some Recollections of the Plains and of the Diggings* (South Bend, Ind.: J. B. Stoll, 1894), appendix 4; and Bell, *Reminiscences of a Ranger*.

73. Leeper, *Argonauts of 'Forty-Nine*, appendix 4.

74. Beadle, *Ham, Eggs, and Corn Cake*, 76.

75. B. Taylor, *El Dorado*, 189.

76. McCarthy, "When I First Voted a Democratic Ticket."

77. Beadle, *Ham, Eggs, and Corn Cake*, 102.

78. W. D. Howells, *Early Prose Writings*, 102; Susan Goodman and Carl Dawson, *William Dean Howells: A Writers Life* (Berkeley: University of California Press, 2005), 37.

79. William Dean Howells, *Years of My Youth* (New York: Harper and Brothers, 1916), 136.

80. Lew Wallace, *An Autobiography*, vol. 1 (New York: Harper and Brothers, 1906), 205.

81. Leland, *Pipps among the Wide Awakes*, 16.

82. Ibid.

83. Bircher, November 1864, *Drummer-Boy's Diary*, 199; Charles G. Hampton, "Twelve Months in Rebel Prisons," in *War Papers Read before the Michigan Commandery of the Loyal Legion of the United States* (Detroit: James H. Stone, 1898), 2:242.

84. Anne L. Youmans Van Ness, July 28–30, 1869, *Diary of Annie L. Youmans Van Ness, 1864–1881* (Alexandria, Va.: Alexander Street Press, 2004), 432–35.

85. Emily Hawley Gillespie, April 1859, *A Secret to Be Buried: The Diary and Life of Emily Hawley Gillespie* (Iowa City: University of Iowa Press, 1989), 19–20; Phebe M. Hallock Irish, March 25, 1866, in *Diary* (Philadelphia: Thomas William Stuckey, 1876), 66–67.

86. Youmans Van Ness, November 8, 1864, *Diary of Annie L. Youmans Van Ness*, 39.

87. Ibid., November 8, 1864, and November 3–4, 1868, 39, 355–58.

88. Field, "Are Women . . . All Minors?," 113–37; Corinne T. Field, *The Struggle for Equal Adulthood: Gender, Race, Age, and the Fight for Citizenship in Antebellum America* (Chapel Hill: University of North Carolina Press, 2014).

89. The general trend that most women's politics remained interpersonal, while most men's became an internal identity, can be seen in the far greater presence of political discussions in women's letters than in their diaries. Women's politics were mostly about influence and usually reached their greatest expression in correspondences, not personal reflections. Susan Hale to Alexander Hale, November 1, 1848, *Letters of Susan Hale*, ed. Caroline P. Atkinson (Boston: Marshall Jones, 1918); Blanche Butler Ames to Sarah Hildreth Butler, January 7, 1861, *Chronicles from the Nineteenth Century: Family Letters of Blanche Butler and Adelbert Ames*, comp. Blanche Butler Ames, vol. 1 (Clinton, Mass.: Privately published, 1957), 63; Charlotte Howard Conant, October 19, 1880, and September 19, 1888, *A Girl of the Eighties at College and at Home*, ed. Martha Pike Conant (Boston: Houghton Mifflin, 1931), 261; Cornelia Oatis Hancock, November 14, 1864, *Letters of a Civil War Nurse: Cornelia Hancock, 1863–1865*, ed. Henrietta Stratton Jaquette (Lincoln: University of Nebraska Press, 1998); Isabella Maud Rittenhouse Mayne, January 1882, *Maud*, ed. Richard Lee Strout (New York: Macmillan, 1939), 48–52; Ronald J. Zboray and Mary Saracino Zboray, *Voices without Votes: Women and Politics in Antebellum New England* (Durham: University of New Hampshire Press, 2010).

90. Willard, *Glimpses of Fifty Years*, 69–70; Frances E. Willard, "Address at Washington Meeting of National Council of Women, 1888," extract in *Glimpses of Fifty Years*, 593.

91. Mayne, November 4, 1885, and November 1, 1882, *Maud*, 361, 136–42.

92. Leland, *Pipps among the Wide Awakes*, 1, 7, 15.

93. Theodore Sutton Parvin, *The Life and Labors of Theodore Sutton Parvin*, ed. Joseph E. Morcombe (Clifton, Iowa: Allen, 1906), 17.

94. Ibid., 64.

95. "Editorial Notes," *Arizona Weekly Journal-Miner*, October 12, 1892.

96. Bensel, *American Ballot Box*, 3.

97. B. Taylor, *El Dorado*, 2:189. Over the course of the age of popular politics, this rejection of the familial party became more common until the movement for independent voting really took off in the 1880s. Augustus Woodbury, *Plain Words for Young Men* (Concord: McFarland and Jenks, 1858), 157; "Radical Amendment," *Harrisburg Weekly Patriot and Union*, October 31, 1867; "The Young Voters," *Cleveland Gazette*, September 27, 1884; "Young Men Should Be Independent," *Kansas City Evening Star*, August 1, 1884; "Garfield to Young Voters. Do Not Pitch Your Tent in the Camp of the Dead. Come into the Camp of Glory and Life," *Daily Inter Ocean*, November 5, 1888.

98. Wallace, *Autobiography*, 203.

99. John Herbert Claiborne, *Seventy-Five Years in Old Virginia* (New York: Neale, 1904), 132.

100. William E. Gienapp, "Politics Seem to Enter into Everything: Political Culture in the North, 1840–1860," in *Essays on American Antebellum Politics, 1840–1860*, ed. Stephen E. Maizlish (College Station: Texas A&M University Press, 1982), 54–56.

101. John Pope, interviewed by Irene Robertson, Biscoe Ark., *Born in Slavery: Slave Narratives from the Federal Writers' Project, 1936–1938, Arkansas Narratives*, vol. 2, part 5, 360.

102. William Saunders Brown Diary, November 4, 1844.

103. Ibid., November 5, 1844.

104. Ibid., November 9–10, 1844.

105. Ibid., November 10, 1844.

106. *Report of the Committee of the Senate upon the Relations between Labor and Capital, and Testimony Taken by the Committee* (Washington, D.C.: Government Printing Office, 1885), 131.

107. Jared Benedict Graham, *Handset Reminiscences: Recollections of an Old-Time Printer and Journalist* (Salt Lake City: Century, 1915), 105.

108. "Harrison Men of '40," *Republican Magazine*, 1, 1892; John Albee, *Confessions of Boyhood* (Boston: Gorham Press, 1910), 259; Charles Francis Adams Jr., *The Forum*, vol. 13 (New York: Forum, 1892); John M. Roberts, *Buckeye Schoolmaster: A Chronicle of Midwestern Rural Life, 1853–1865*, ed. J. Merton England (Bowling Green, Ky.: Bowling Green State University Popular Press, 1996), 224; "Where Is the Once Proud Southern Rights Party?," *Augusta Daily Chronicle and Sentinel*, April 15, 1857; "The Meeting in Tammany Hall," *New York Herald*, October 22, 1856.

109. John C. Chase, "How I Became a Socialist," *Comrade* 2 (November 1902): 109.

110. W. B. Miller, "A Letter from a Neighbor," *Outlook*, March 8, 1916, 536.

111. "A Sturdy Pioneer Passes to Reward," *Keith County (Neb.) News*, October 1, 1931.

112. McCarthy, "When I First Voted a Democratic Ticket."

113. J. McCarthy, "Speech Made by J. J. McCarthy at Kearney, Nebraska."

114. B. G. Mathews, interviewed by Bessie Jollensten, November 5, 1938, American

Life Histories Interviews; Mary McCarthy, interviewed by Bessie Jollensten, October 19, 1938, American Life Histories Interviews; "Sturdy Pioneer Passes to Reward."

115. "Sturdy Pioneer Passes to Reward." For a thorough if morbid study of the evolving place of obituaries in society, see Janice Hume, *Obituaries in American Culture* (Oxford: University Press of Mississippi, 2000).

116. Mary McCarthy interview.

117. "Sturdy Pioneer Passes to Reward."

118. "Independent Twenty-Onesters."

Chapter 4

1. See the following in the *Baltimore Sun*: "Proceedings of the Courts," January 21, 1861; "Outrages at the Polls," November 3, 1859; "Funeral of Adam Barklee Kyle, Jr.," November 5, 1859; "The Homicide of Adam Barklie Kyle, Jr.," November 8, 1859; "The Trial of James Logan," January 19, 1861; "Trial and Acquittal of James Logan for the Murder of A. Barkley Kyle," January 22, 1861; "The Habeas Corpus in the Case of Joseph H. Edwards," January 31, 1861.

2. "The Murder of Mr. A. B. Kyle Jr.," *Baltimore Sun*, November 8, 1859; Frank Towers, *The Urban South and the Coming of the Civil War* (Charlottesville: University of Virginia Press, 2004), 149.

3. Towers, *Urban South*, 150.

4. Ibid., 149–51; Jacob Frey, *Reminiscences of Baltimore* (Baltimore: Maryland Book Concern, 1893), 83–100; Tracy Matthew Melton, *Hanging Henry Gambrill: The Violent Career of Baltimore's Plug Uglies, 1854–1860* (Baltimore: Johns Hopkins University Press, 2005).

5. "Murder of Mr. A. B. Kyle Jr."

6. Quoted in Towers, *Urban South*, 151.

7. "Outrages at the Polls."

8. Ibid.; "Proceedings of the Courts."

9. "Outrages at the Polls"; "Proceedings of the Courts"; *House of Delegates of the State of Maryland, Baltimore City Contested Election, Papers in the Contested Election Case from Baltimore City, Feb. 13, 1860* (Annapolis: B. H. Richardson, Printers, 1860).

10. "Murder of Mr. A. B. Kyle Jr."; "Proceedings of the Courts."

11. "Outrages at the Polls."

12. Richard Franklin Bensel, *The American Ballot Box in the Mid-Nineteenth Century* (Cambridge: Cambridge University Press, 2004), 179; "Outrages at the Polls."

13. Towers, *Urban South*, 151; Frey, *Reminiscences of Baltimore*, 85–100.

14. It is always possible that James Logan did not kill Adam Kyle, and the prosecution certainly failed to prove that he did. This may have been because a number of witnesses changed their testimony in the fourteen months between the shooting and the trial. At least two claimed they were threatened by members of the Tigers. My account of the November 2 shoot-out gives preference to the testimony that Regina Dochtermann and several other seemingly unbiased witnesses gave to the grand jury and newspapers in the days after the murder. These early accounts regularly identify

James Logan as Kyle's shooter. "Outrages at the Polls"; "Funeral of Adam Barklee Kyle Jr."; "Homicide of Adam Barklie Kyle, Jr."; "Trial of James Logan"; "Proceedings of the Courts"; "Trial and Acquittal of James Logan for the Murder of A. Barkley Kyle"; "Habeas Corpus in the Case of Joseph H. Edwards."

15. "Murder of Mr. A. B. Kyle Jr."

16. Henry Liddell, *The Evolution of a Democrat: A Darwinian Tale* (New York: Paquet, 1888).

17. Edmund Keyser Diary, December 22, 1867, Historical Society of Pennsylvania, Philadelphia; "Gratifying Indication of Progress," *Washington Post*, September 12, 1882; James Michael Curley, *I'd Do It Again* (New York: Arno Press, 1976), 17–33; William L. Riordan, *Plunkitt of Tammany Hall: A Series of Very Plain Talks on Very Practical Politics* (New York: E. P. Dutton, 1963), 8–14.

18. Samuel Tilden, "To perfect the organization of the democracy of this state," circular to New York State Democrats, March 31, 1868, Printed Ephemera Collection, Library of Congress.

19. Though patronage played a central role in party structures, there were always far more campaigners than there were jobs available, so most workers went unrewarded. Walter Licht, *Getting Work: Philadelphia, 1840–1950* (Cambridge, Mass.: Harvard University Press, 1992), 34.

20. Charles Dickens, *American Notes* (London: Everyman Press, 1997), 246.

21. Edmund Keyser Diary, December 22, 1867; Michael F. Campbell Diary, November 8, 1881, Sterling Library, Yale Special Collections, New Haven, Conn.; Franklin Buck, September 22, 1852, in *A Yankee Trader in the Gold Rush: The Letters of Franklin A. Buck*, comp. Katherine A. White (Boston: Houghton Mifflin, 1930); "Electioneering," *New Haven Register*, October 15, 1884; Rolf Johnson, November 6, 1876, *Happy as a Big Sunflower: Adventures in the West, 1876–1880*, ed. Richard E. Jensen (Lincoln: University of Nebraska Press, 2000), 33.

22. Michael F. Campbell Diary, November 8, 1881.

23. Marianne Marbury Slaughter, writing as "Letter from Pleasant Riderhood," *New Orleans Times Picayune*, August 25, 1878, 3.

24. In his satire of the political system, *Solid for Mulholly*, writer Rufus Shapley asked, "Why continue to talk of the free-school on the hillside as the hope of the Republic, when every day, under your very eyes, you see the indubitable proof that the despised grog-shop is the true birthplace of statesmanship, and the maligned gin-mill the very cradle in which shall be rocked into manhood the coming American politician?" Rufus Edmonds Shapley, *Solid for Mulhooly* (New York: G. W. Carleton, 1881), 21.

25. Curley, *I'd Do It Again*, 18; Joseph J. Mersman, October 18, 1848, *The Whiskey Merchant's Diary*, ed. Linda A. Fisher (Athens: Ohio University Press, 2007), 137; Riordan, *Plunkitt of Tammany Hall*, 77; Digest of Election Cases, Cases of Contested Election in the House of Representatives, from 1865 to 1871 Inclusive, 38th Cong., 2nd Sess., Misc. Doc. No 152 (1870), 697.

26. George Foster, *New York in Slices: By an Experienced Carver* (New York: W. H. Graham, 1849), 81.

27. J. Frank Kernan, *Reminiscences of the Old Fire Laddies and Volunteer Fire Departments of New York and Brooklyn* (New York: M. Crane, 1885), 47–50.

28. Ibid., 47–50; G. Foster, *New York in Slices*, 22–29; Tyler Anbinder, *Five Points* (New York: Free Press, 2001).

29. Kernan, *Reminiscences of the Old Fire Laddies*, 47–50. On the other hand, some women ran stores and saloons frequented by the opposing party, much to their irritation. Emily Hawley Gillespie, November 1861, *A Secret to Be Buried: The Diary and Life of Emily Hawley Gillespie* (Iowa City: University of Iowa Press, 1989), 295.

30. G. Foster, *New York in Slices*, 81.

31. John M. Roberts, *Buckeye Schoolmaster: A Chronicle of a Midwestern Rural Life, 1853–1865*, ed. J. Merton England (Bowling Green, Ky.: Bowling Green State University Popular Press, 1996), 184; Paul E. Johnson, *A Shopkeeper's Millennium* (New York: Hill and Wang, 1978).

32. David Schenck Papers, Southern Historical Collection, University of North Carolina, Chapel Hill, N.C.; J. Roberts, *Buckeye Schoolmaster*; "A Triumph of Young America," *Milwaukee Daily Sentinel*, May 14, 1867.

33. John I. Young, interviewed by Henry Muir, Montgomery County, Ohio, Works Progress Administration, Ex-Slave Narratives, Ohio Historical Society, "The African-American Experience in Ohio, 1850–1920," http://dbs.ohiohistory.org/africanam/page.cfm?ID=13937&Current=001&View=Text (last accessed December 21, 2013).

34. Ibid.

35. "Many Candidates," *Philadelphia Inquirer*, December 31, 1893.

36. Lyman Abbott, *Reminiscences* (Boston: Houghton Mifflin, 1914), 110. For other examples of active young hustlers, see Edmund Keyser Diary, December 22, 1867; September 15, 1868–November 3, 1868; Mersman, October 18, 1848, *Whiskey Merchant's Diary*, 137; Riordan, *Plunkitt of Tammany Hall*, 8–14; R. Johnson, November 6, 1876, *Happy as a Big Sunflower*, 33; and James Witham, *Fifty Years on the Firing Line: My Part in the Farmer's Movement* (Chicago: Privately published, 1924), 18–22.

37. Frank Leach, *Recollections of a Newspaperman; A Record of Life and Events in California* (San Francisco: S. Levinson Co., 1917), 17–21; Abbott, *Reminiscences*, 110. The best information on ballot tricks can be found in Mark Wahlgren Summers, *Party Games: Getting, Keeping, and Using Power in Gilded Age Politics* (Chapel Hill: University of North Carolina Press, 2004), 94–130; and Patricia Crain, "Potent Papers: Secret Lives of the Nineteenth-Century Ballot," *Common-Place* 9 (October 2008), http://www.common-place.org/vol-09/no-01/crain (last accessed September 2, 2015).

38. Leach, *Recollections of a Newspaperman*, 17–21. Another popular trick, related by Frank Leach, was the "tapeworm ballot," printed just half an inch wide, so that voters who wished to split their vote would have no room to write in the names of other candidates.

39. William Mills Ivin, *Machine Politics and Money in Elections in New York City* (New York: Harper and Brothers, 1887), 52. William Mills Ivin stressed how controlling printing presses allowed New York City bosses to dominate the political process. More recently, Michael McGerr and Richard Bensel addressed this issue, arguing that,

on the one hand, the system of printing ballots allowed for easy entry of new tickets and third parties, but on the other, this system enabled parties to dominate the political process. Michael E. McGerr, *The Decline of Popular Politics: The American North, 1865–1928* (Oxford: Oxford University Press, 1986), 214; Bensel, *American Ballot Box*, 15.

40. Leach, *Recollections of a Newspaperman*, 17.

41. Daniel J. Ryan, "Clubs in Politics," *North American Review* 146, no. 375 (February 1888): 177.

42. Leach, *Recollections of a Newspaperman*, 18.

43. Abbott, *Reminiscences*, 110.

44. Ibid., 110.

45. "Increase of Political Excitement," *New York Herald*, October 1, 1844. Another article on the rise of "political fighting clubs" in 1844 hoped that "the election will scatter these gangs of rowdies" who would return, after November, to "the old business of plunder, boxing, and crime." "Political Rowdyism," *New York Herald*, October 17, 1844.

46. G. Foster, *New York in Slices*, 44.

47. Owen Kildare, *My Mamie Rose* (New York: Baker and Taylor, 1903), 78.

48. October 5 through 13, 1868, Edmund Keyser Diary; "First Demonstration of the Clay Party in This City," *New York Herald*, September 28, 1841; "The Alleged Election Frauds," *Milwaukee Daily Journal*, April 22, 1886; "The Model Young Man," *Hinds County (Miss.) Gazette*, March 25, 1857; "Our Best Young Men Talk It Over," *Central City (Col.) Daily Register-Call*, November 25, 1881; "Young Men's Convention," *New-York Spectator*, October 6, 1836.

49. Paul Prowler, "Glimpses of Gotham," *National Police Gazette*, October 4, 1879.

50. R. Johnson, *Happy as a Big Sunflower*, 33; Erastus Flavel Beadle, *Ham, Eggs, and Corn Cake: A Nebraska Territory Diary*, ed. Ronald Naugle (Lincoln: University of Nebraska Press, 2001), 101; Bayard Taylor, *El Dorado; or, Adventures in the Path of Empire*, vol. 2 (London: Henry G. Bohn, 1850), 189; C. S. Bundy, *Early Days in the Chippewa Valley* (Menomonie, Wis.: Flint Douglas, 1916), 6; Horace Bell, *Reminiscences of a Ranger: Early Times in Southern California* (Los Angeles: Yarnell, Caystile and Mathes, Printers, 1881), 73; Enos Christman, *One Man's Gold: The Letters and Journal of a Forty-Niner*, ed. Florence Morrow Christman (New York: Whittlesey House, 1930), 117; Sim Moak, *The Last of the Mill Creeks* (Chico, Calif.: Privately published,1923); David R. Leeper, *The Argonauts of 'Forty-Nine: Some Recollections of the Plains and of the Diggings* (South Bend, Ind.: J. B. Stoll, 1894), appendix 4.

51. William E. Gienapp, "Politics Seem to Enter into Everything: Political Culture in the North, 1840–1860," in *Essays on American Antebellum Politics, 1840–1860*, ed. Stephen E. Maizlish (College Station: Texas A&M University Press, 1982), 27; Bensel, *American Ballot Box*, xii–xiii, 83–96.

52. "Volunteers after the Wide Awakes," *New York Herald*, November 6, 1860.

53. Cases of Contested Elections in Congress, 1834 to 1865, 38th Cong., 2nd Sess., Miscellaneous Document No. 57 (1862), 620; Bensel, *American Ballot Box*, xii–xiii, 83–96.

54. Albion Winegar Tourgée, *Letters to a King* (Cincinnati: Cranston and Stowe, 1888), 166.

55. Andreas Ueland, *Recollections of an Immigrant* (New York: Minton, Balch, 1929), 51.

56. "Letter," *Chronicle: Student Magazine of University of Michigan* 7 (September 1880–June 1881): 243. For a thorough view of the worst examples of vote buying, see Summers, *Party Games*, 91–107.

57. "Young Reformers Club," *American Reformer*, November 8, 1884, 364.

58. *An American Almanac and Treasury of Facts, Statistical, Financial, and Political, for the Year 1886*, ed. Ainsworth R. Spofford (New York: American News, 1886), 241.

59. Susan Bradford Eppes, *Through Some Eventful Years* (Macon, Ga.: J. W. Burke, 1926), 378.

60. William Saunders Brown Diary, October 30, 1844, University of Virginia Special Collections, Charlottesville.

61. Witham, *Fifty Years on the Firing Line*, 13. For more examples of young people introduced to politics by an older sibling or friend, see Charles Plummer Diary, September 27, 1840, Historical Society of Pennsylvania, Philadelphia; Michael F. Campbell Diary, August 23, 1880; Benjamin Brown Foster, *Downeast Diary*, ed. Charles H. Foster (Orono: University of Maine at Orono Press, 1975), 75; and Oscar Lawrence Jackson, *The Colonel's Diary: Journals Kept before and during the Civil War*, ed. David P. Jackson (Sharon, Pa.: Privately published, 1922), 17–36.

62. For a comparative survey of political club rosters, published in newspapers and club papers from 1832 to 1912, see *Proceedings of a National Republican Convention of Young Men*, Providence, R.I. November 2, 1832, Printed Ephemera Collection, Library of Congress; "Young Men's Ratification Meeting," *Boston Daily Advertiser*, August 25, 1857; "Democratic Douglas Arthur Association, Minute Book," 1858, Clubs and Association Records, Historical Society of Pennsylvania, Philadelphia; "Lincoln Wide Awakes," *Daily Cleveland Herald*, May 26, 1860; "Wide-Awakes," *Daily Cleveland Herald*, May 29, 1860; "Their First Vote," *Milwaukee Sentinel*, July 29, 1888; "Young Men of Hope, a Republican League to Fight for a New Philadelphia," *Philadelphia Inquirer*, November 23, 1890; and Young Republican Club, "Young Republican Club of the Twenty-Second Ward, Minute Book," Philadelphia, 1892–1912, Historical Society of Pennsylvania.

63. Jeremiah A. Wilcox Diary, April 3, 1860, Connecticut Historical Society, Hartford.

64. Michael Campbell, the "poor boy" of the James English Phalanx, reported bumping into club members whom he had lost touch with years later, rediscovering his political interest in the process. Michael F. Campbell Diary, November 8, 1881.

65. Mary Densel, "The Grand Procession," *Harper's Young People*, November 9, 1880.

66. Charles G. Leland, *Pipps among the Wide Awakes* (New York: Wevill and Chapin, 1860), 6, 14; "The Rival Bonfires," *Youth's Companion*, October 16, 1884, 57, 387; Matthew White, "The Roverings and the Parade," *Harper's Young People*, November 16, 1880.

67. William Dean Howells to Dune Dean, September 9, 1857, *Selected Letters of William Dean Howells*, ed. George Arms (Boston: Twayne, 1979), 1:10.

68. William Dean Howells, *Years of My Youth* (New York: Harper and Brothers, 1916), 110–203.

69. Susan Goodman and Carl Dawson, *William Dean Howells: A Writers Life* (Berkeley: University of California Press, 2005), 48–50; W. D. Howells, *Years of My Youth*, 166–75.

70. William Dean Howells, *The Lives and Speeches of Abraham Lincoln and Hannibal Hamlin* (Columbus, Ohio: Follett, Foster, 1860), xi.

71. Ibid., 21, 50–51.

72. Ibid., 50–51.

73. W. D. Howells, *Years of My Youth*, 138.

74. Goodman and Dawson, *William Dean Howells*, 68.

75. Howard Chudacoff, *The Age of the Bachelor* (Princeton: Princeton University Press, 1999), 70–71. See my conclusion for more on peer culture.

76. Blanche Butler Ames to Sarah Hildreth Butler, January 7, 1861, *Chronicles from the Nineteenth Century: Family Letters of Blanche Butler and Adelbert Ames*, comp. Blanche Butler Ames, vol. 1 (Clinton, Mass.: Privately published, 1957), 63. For strong examples of this sense of peer rivalry, see William Wheeler, December 23, 1860, *Letters of William Wheeler of the Class of 1855, Y.C.* (Cambridge: Privately published, 1875); B. Foster, *Downeast Diary*, 10–12; William Saunders Brown Diary, November 5, 1844; and Moses Puterbaugh to Uriah Oblinger, June 26, 1868, and Mattie V. Thomas to Uriah W. Oblinger, Uriah W. Oblinger Family Collection, Nebraska State Historical Society, Lincoln, digitally collected at the Library of Congress, http://memory.loc.gov/ammem/award98/nbhihtml/pshome.html.

77. B. Foster, *Downeast Diary*, 75.

78. Jackson, *Colonel's Diary*, 28.

79. David Ross Locke, *Nasby: Divers Views, Opinions and Prophecies of Petroleum V. Nasby* (Cincinnati: R. W. Carroll, 1867), 25; "A Political Lecture by a Pious Wife," *New York Herald*, September 22, 1860; Ella Gertrude Clanton Thomas, November 1852, in *The Secret Eye: The Journal of Ella Gertrude Clanton Thomas, 1848–1889*, ed. Virginia Ingraham Burr (Chapel Hill: University of North Carolina Press, 1990), 117.

80. Rebecca Edwards, *Angels in the Machinery: Gender in American Party Politics from the Civil War to the Progressive Era* (New York: Oxford University Press, 1997), 3–9; Charlotte Howard Conant, October 19, 1880, and September 19, 1888, *A Girl of the Eighties at College and at Home*, ed. Martha Pike Conant (Boston: Houghton Mifflin, 1931), 261; Isabelle Maud Rittenhouse Mayne, January 1882, *Maud*, ed. Richard Lee Strout (New York: Macmillan, 1939), 48–52; Ellen K. Rothman, *Hands and Hearts: A History of Courtship in America* (New York: Basic Books, 1984), 190–95.

81. Uriah W. Oblinger to Mattie V. Thomas, August 18, 1864, Oblinger Family Collection.

82. Ibid., May 11, 1864.

83. Mattie V. Thomas to Uriah W. Oblinger, November 4, 1866, ibid.

84. Rothman, *Hands and Hearts*.

85. Uriah W. Oblinger to Mattie V. Thomas, August 26, 1866, Oblinger Family Collection.

86. Ibid., May 3, 1868, September 14, 1866.

87. Ibid., October 25, 1866.

88. Mattie V. Thomas to Uriah W. Oblinger, August 13, 1868, ibid.

89. Mark Wahlgren Summers, *A Dangerous Stir: Fear, Paranoia, and the Making of Reconstruction* (New York: Oxford University Press, 2009).

90. Mattie V. Thomas to Uriah W. Oblinger, June 7, 1868, Oblinger Family Collection.

91. Ibid., November 4, 1866.

92. Ibid., June 7, 1868.

93. Uriah W. Oblinger to Mattie V. Thomas, June 28, 1868, ibid.

94. Mattie V. Thomas to Uriah W. Oblinger, August 13, 1868, ibid.

95. Ibid., September 1, 1868.

96. Ibid., September 3, 1868. Mattie was not alone in pressuring her man to vote for the Republicans. Nan Ewing wrote her soldier husband, Mack, during the Civil War, pushing him to vote for Lincoln in 1864 and warning that he had better not "turn butter nut." ("Butternut," like "Copper," worked as a reference to Democrats, originally referring to Ohio River settlers of southern heritage.) Jonathan W. White, "'For My Part I Don't Care Who Is Elected President': The Union Army and the Election of 1864," in *This Distracted and Anarchical People: New Answers for Old Questions about the Civil War–Era North*, ed. Andrew Slap and Michael Thomas Smith (New York: Fordham University Press, 2013), 104–7.

97. Mattie V. Thomas to Uriah W. Oblinger, June 8, 1865, Oblinger Family Collection.

98. L. W. Monson to Uriah W. Oblinger, March 10, 1869, ibid.

99. William Fletcher King, *Reminiscences* (New York: Abingdon Press, 1915), 64; E. Anthony Rotundo, *American Manhood: Transformations in Masculinity from the Revolution to the Modern Era* (New York: Basic Books, 1993), 21, 56; E. L. Godkin, "The Political Campaign of 1872," *North American Review* 115 (October 1872): 401–22; *Young Men! Vote for Edgar Tehune for Congress* (Chicago, 1886), broadside in Printed Ephemera Collection, Library of Congress.

100. *Proceedings of a National Republican Convention of Young Men*, November 2, 1832; "Great Whig Meeting in New York, Nominations for Governor," September 8, 1833, Library of Congress; "Young Men's Ratification Meeting"; Young Man's Republican Union, *Report From Young Men's Republican Union, Head Quarters Stuyvesant Institute*, November 5, 1860, Printed Ephemera Collection, Library of Congress; "New England Maine," *Boston Daily Advertiser*, March 6, 1878; "A Political Sangerfest," *Milwaukee Daily Sentinel*, August 27, 1880.

101. Abraham Lincoln to William H. Herndon, July 10, 1848, *Abraham Lincoln: The Collected Works*, 9 vols., ed. Roy P. Basler (New Brunswick: Rutgers University Press, 1953), 1:498.

Chapter 5

1. Robert Kelley, "The Thought and Character of Samuel J. Tilden: The Democrat as Inheritor," *Historian* 26 (Spring 1964): 176–205; John Bigelow, *The Life of Samuel J. Tilden* (New York: Harper and Brothers, 1895).

2. Alexander Clarence Flick, *Samuel Jones Tilden: A Study in Political Sagacity* (New York: Dodd, Mead, 1939), 6; Bigelow, *Life of Samuel J. Tilden*, 47; Kelley, "Thought and Character of Samuel J. Tilden," 189.

3. Kelley, "Thought and Character of Samuel J. Tilden," 176–85.

4. Roy Morris Jr., *The Fraud of the Century: Rutherford B. Hayes, Samuel J. Tilden, and the Stolen Election of 1876* (New York: Simon and Schuster, 2003), 105.

5. Horatio Seymour to Samuel Tilden, January 13, 1867, *Letters and Literary Memorials of Samuel J. Tilden*, ed. John Bigelow, 2 vols. (New York: Harper and Brothers, 1908), 1:214; Samuel Tilden, "To perfect the organization of the democracy of this state," circular to New York State Democrats, March 31, 1868, Printed Ephemera Collection, Library of Congress.

6. Tilden, "To perfect the organization of the democracy of this state."

7. "A Neighbor's Complaint," *New Haven Evening Register*, April 28, 1892.

8. Claims of being the preferred party of young Americans proliferated in the press of each major and minor party. For National Republican and Whig assertions, see *Young Men of Boston! Broadside for Charles Wells as Boston Mayor*, 1832, Printed Ephemera Collection, Library of Congress; *Nominating Rally for Delegates to National Convention of Young Men, National Republican Party* (Baltimore: Sand and Neilson, 1831); "The True Spirit," *Daily Cleveland Herald*, October 9, 1843; and "Young Whigs," *Mississippian and State Gazette*, May 28, 1852.

For Republican claims, see "The Duty of the Republican Party," *Boston Daily Atlas*, November 26, 1856; "The Party for Young Men," *Boston Daily Advertiser*, July 30, 1880; "Migma," *Continent: An Illustrated Weekly Magazine*, June 27, 1883; and Daniel J. Ryan, "Clubs in Politics," *North American Review* 146, no. 375 (February 1888): 172–77.

For Democrats, see "Wm. A. Neil, Esq.," *Daily Ohio Statesman*, October 2, 1850; "10 out of 12 of the Young Voters," *Macon Weekly Telegraph*, October 17, 1876; and *News and Courier*, July 28, 1884.

For third party claims, see "Young Men of Massachusetts," *Emancipator and Weekly Chronicle*, September 3, 1840; *Emancipator and Weekly Chronicle*, December 18, 1844; "Young America," *Semi-Weekly Raleigh Register*, August 16, 1856; and "The New York Greenbackers," *Milwaukee Daily Journal*, August 30, 1884.

9. Tilden, "To perfect the organization of the democracy of this state"; Horatio Seymour to Samuel Tilden, July 20, 1868, *Letters and Literary Memorials of Samuel J. Tilden*, 1:242.

10. Kelley, "Thought and Character of Samuel J. Tilden," 176–205.

11. Samuel J. Tilden, "The Political Duties of Young Men—Address to the Young Men's Democratic Club," Fall 1874, *The Writings and Speeches of Samuel J. Tilden*, ed. John Bigelow, vol. 2 (New York: Harper and Bros., 1885), 16.

12. The unresponsive nature of nineteenth-century party structures is best ex-

plained by Roy F. Nichols in *The Disruption of American Democracy* (New York: Macmillan, 1948), 20.

13. John Parsons, *A Tour through Indiana in 1840: The Diary of John Parsons of Petersburg, Virginia*, ed. Kate Milner Rabb (New York: R. M. McBride, 1920), 1–3.

14. Ibid., 16.

15. David Waldstreicher, *In the Midst of Perpetual Fetes: The Making of American Nationalism, 1776–1820* (Chapel Hill: University of North Carolina Press, 1997).

16. J. Parsons, *Tour through Indiana in 1840*, 4–5; Robert Gray Gunderson, *The Log Cabin Campaign* (Lexington: University Press of Kentucky, 1957), 1.

17. J. Parsons, *Tour through Indiana in 1840*, 26–28; Frank H. Heck, "Robert Perkins Letcher," *Kentucky's Governors*, ed. Lowell H. Harrison (Lexington: University Press of Kentucky, 2004), 57.

18. J. Parsons, *Tour through Indiana in 1840*, 80–87, 246.

19. Daniel Dupre, "Barbeques and Pledges," *Journal of Southern History* 60, no. 3 (August 1994): 479–512; Waldstreicher, *In the Midst of Perpetual Fetes*; Carolyn Eastman, *A Nation of Speechifiers: Making an American Public after the Revolution* (Chicago: University of Chicago Press, 2009); Joseph Kett, *Rites of Passage: Adolescence in America, 1790 to the Present* (New York: Basic Books, 1977), 12–64.

20. Glenn Wallach charts this need to justify young people's involvement in politics in the 1830s particularly well, quoting the young Democrats of New York's claims that the economic crisis of 1837 provided "sufficient apology" for their activism. Glenn Wallach, *Obedient Sons: The Discourse of Youth and Generations in American Culture, 1630–1860* (Amherst: University of Massachusetts Press, 1997), 74. Also see National Republican Young Men's Meeting, March 22, 1832, Washington, D.C., Library of Congress; *Proceedings of a National Republican Convention of Young Men*, November 2, 1832, Providence, R.I., Printed Ephemera Collection, Library of Congress; "Great Whig Meeting in New York, Nominations for Governor," September 8, 1833, Library of Congress; and "History," *American Monthly Review*, December 1833.

21. "Publico," letter to the editor, *Colored American*, July 14, 1838; "A Phoenixonian," letter to the editor, ibid., August 18, 1838.

22. Wallach, *Obedient Sons*, 82–83; Nic Wood, "'A Sacrifice on the Altar of Slavery': Doughface Politics and Black Disenfranchisement in Pennsylvania, 1837–1838," *Journal of the Early Republic* 31 (Spring 2011): 75–106; "Publico"; "A Phoenixonian."

23. Joel Silbey, *The American Political Nation, 1838–1893* (Stanford: Stanford University Press, 1994), 23, 45.

24. Wallach, *Obedient Sons*, 78.

25. See, on the role of food prices in the rise of the Whig Party in the late 1830s, Michael Holt, "The Election of 1840, Voter Mobilization, and the Emergence of the Second Party System," in *A Master's Due: Essays in Honor of David Herbert Donald*, ed. John McCardell (Baton Rouge: Louisiana State University Press, 1985), 16–58, and Alasdair Roberts, *America's First Great Depression: Economic Crisis and Political Disorder after the Panic of 1837* (Ithaca: Cornell University Press, 2012).

26. Quoted in Silbey, *American Political Nation*, 36–37; Robert Gray Gunderson, *The Log Cabin Campaign* (Lexington: University Press of Kentucky, 1957), 149.

27. Gunderson, *Log Cabin Campaign*, 52; *Proceedings of State Convention of Whig Young Men of Connecticut* (Hartford, Conn.: Courant Office Printing, 1840), 4; Wallach, *Obedient Sons*, 194.

28. Gunderson, *Log Cabin Campaign*, 1; Reid, *Horace Greeley* (New York: Charles Scribner's Sons, 1879), 8.

29. Gunderson, *Log Cabin Campaign*, 285.

30. An examination of Whig campaign banners from 1840 reveals nearly identical appeals from all over the country. See "Tippecanoe Clubs of Georgia," "Norfolk County Harrison & Reform," "Lynn New England Convention," "Ohio We Know Him," and many others in the Political Campaign Collections, Smithsonian Institution, National Museum of American History, Washington, D.C., and Silbey, *American Political Nation*, 27.

31. "Harrison, Democracy, Reform and Better Times: Gathering of the Young Men," *Pennsylvania Inquirer and Daily Courier*, March 12, 13, 14, 16, 17, 18, 1840; "Another Great Meeting in Philadelphia, The Young Men in Motion," ibid., March 19, 1840.

32. Silbey, *American Political Nation*, 36. For more on women in the 1840 campaign, see Ronald J. Zboray and Mary Saracino Zboray, *Voices without Votes: Women and Politics in Antebellum New England* (Durham: University of New Hampshire Press, 2010), 79–98; Elizabeth Varon, "Tippecanoe and the Ladies, Too: White Women and Party Politics in Antebellum Virginia," *Journal of American History* 82 (September 1995): 494–521; Jayne Crumpler DeFiore, "Come, and Bring the Ladies: Tennessee Women and the Politics of Opportunity during the Presidential Campaigns of 1840 and 1844," *Tennessee Historical Quarterly* 51, no. 4 (December 1992): 197–212; and "The Ladies," *Westfield Courier and Chautauqua County Whig*, August 21, 1840.

33. The Democrats' frustration serves as a reminder that no one party ever monopolized the youth vote. Many young Democrats participated for the first time in 1840—the party won nearly 50 percent more votes than it had the last time around—and some Whig campaigners paid no attention to young people. Though the rising Whigs made the more concerted bid for youth, their efforts were neither exclusive nor exhaustive. Parmenas Taylor Turnley, *Reminiscences of Parmenas Taylor Turnley: From the Cradle to Three-Score and Ten* (Chicago: Donohue and Henneberry, 1892), 22; "Female Politicians," *United States Democratic Review* 30 (April 1852): 355. Also see "Hurra for the Young Democracy," *Weekly Ohio Statesman*, May 29, 1844; "To the Young Men of Orleans Co.," *Vermont Patriot*, July 13, 1840; and "Our Glorious Hickory Club," *Ohio Statesman*, November 29, 1843.

34. Robert Walker Johannsen, *The Frontier, the Union, and Stephen A. Douglas* (Urbana: University of Illinois Press, 1989), 80; Yonatan Eyal, *The Young America Movement and the Transformation of the Democratic Party, 1828–1861* (Cambridge: Cambridge University Press, 2007), 3.

35. Eyal, *Young America Movement*, 3. David Hackett Fischer cleverly explores the implication of the titles "young" and "old" in nineteenth-century America. David Hackett Fischer, *Growing Old in America* (New York: Oxford University Press, 1977), 131–33.

36. Eyal, *Young America Movement*, 7–8. For a strong study of O'Sullivan and the lit-

erary aspects of the Young America movement, see Edward L. Widmer, *Young America: The Flowering of Democracy in New York City* (New York: Oxford University Press, 2000).

37. "Wm. A. Neil, Esq.," *Daily Ohio Statesman*, October 2, 1850.

38. *An Appeal to the Young Democrats of Frederick, Virginia*, broadside, University of Virginia Special Collections, Charlottesville.

39. F. A. Wagler, "Govr. Polk's March and Quick Step" (Baltimore: Geo. Willis Jr., 1844); A. Tennessean, "Hickory Waltz and Gallopade" (New York: John F. Nunns, 1844); Lewis Clark, "Polk Quadrilles" (Baltimore: Samuel Carusi, 1844); John F. Goneke, "James K. Polk's Grand March and Quick Step" (Philadelphia: G. Willis, 1844), all from the collection Music for the Nation: American Sheet Music, ca. 1820–1860, Library of Congress, last modified June 11, 2013, http://www.loc.gov/collection/american-sheet-music-1820-to-1860/about-this-collection/.

40. *An Appeal to the Young Democrats of Frederick, Virginia*.

41. David Hackett Fischer explores the emergence of the term "Old Fogy" in the antebellum era in *Growing Old in America*, 91.

42. Eyal, *The Young America Movement*, 147.

43. Ibid., 147–49; Mark Lause, *Young America: Land, Labor, and the Republican Community* (Urbana: University of Illinois Press, 2005).

44. William Gienapp, *Origins of the Republican Party, 1852–1856* (New York: Oxford University Press, 1987).

45. For the most enjoyable book on Frémont and Benton, read Sally Denton's *Passion and Principle: John and Jessie Frémont* (New York: Bloomsbury, 2007). See Lyman Abbott's *Reminiscences* (Boston: Houghton Mifflin, 1914), 107–11, for a stirring portrait of the cult of personality Jessie Benton Frémont in 1856.

46. Whether young people preferred younger candidates is open to debate. Campaigners certainly believed they did and were sure to stress the youth of any politician under fifty. Sometimes this got out of hand, with "bald and toothless" old candidates asserting their youth in print. On the other hand, some of the most popular candidates among young voters, men like William Henry Harrison and Andrew Jackson, were well over sixty-five. Ultimately, young people had little say in the nominating process, so a candidate's age was often an afterthought, mentioned when convenient. "Gratifying Indication of Progress," *Washington Post*, September 12, 1882; *Young Men! Vote for Edgar Tehune for Congress* (Chicago, 1886), broadside in Printed Ephemera Collection, Library of Congress; "A Ticket for Young Republicans," *Philadelphia Inquirer*, August 10, 1890.

47. Gienapp, *Origins of the Republican Party*, 325. What experience Frémont did have, Greeley noted, was as a Democrat, proving that the Republicans were not merely a "Whig trick." *New York Tribune*, June 7, 1856.

48. Francis Preston Blair, Martin Van Buren, and Horace Greeley among them. Gienapp, *Origins of the Republican Party*, 324; Denton, *Passion and Principle*, 234.

49. Gienapp, *Origins of the Republican Party*, 324.

50. "The Flag-Bearer of the Republicans," *New York Times*, June 19, 1856.

51. Jonathan Earle, *Jacksonian Antislavery and the Politics of Free Soil: 1824–1854* (Chapel Hill: University of North Carolina Press, 2004), 135–38.

52. "Duty of the Republican Party."

53. Gienapp, *Origins of the Republican Party*, 413–47.

54. Quoted in ibid., 415.

55. Silbey, *American Political Nation*, 36–37.

56. Thurlow Weed, "The Revolution of the Parties," *Albany Evening Register*, July 6, 1860.

57. Henry T. Sperry, *The Republican Wide-Awakes of Hartford, Organized March 3, 1860* (Hartford, 1860), pamphlet, Connecticut Imprints, Connecticut Historical Society, Hartford; Julius G. Rathbun, "'The Wide Awakes': The Great Political Organization of 1860," *Connecticut Quarterly* 1 (October 1895): 335.

58. George Templeton Strong, *Diary: Young Man in New York, 1835–1849*, ed. Allan Nevins and Milton Halsey Thomas (New York: Macmillan, 1952), 43.

59. Elizur Wright, "An Eye-Opener for the Wide Awakes" (Boston, 1860), Historical Society of Pennsylvania, Philadelphia; Carl Schurz, *The Reminiscences of Carl Schurz* (New York: McClure, 1907), 2:193; Mary A. Logan, *Reminiscences of a Soldier's Wife* (New York: Charles Scribner's Sons, 1916), 65.

60. Jon Grinspan, "'Young Men for War': The Wide Awakes and Lincoln's 1860 Presidential Campaign," *Journal of American History* 96 (September 2009): 360; Rathbun, "'Wide Awakes,'" 335.

61. Schurz, *Reminiscences*, 2:194–95.

62. "Mr. Seward and Party En Route," *New York Herald*, September 4, 1860; "Senator Seward Down East," ibid., August 15, 1860; "Political Affairs," ibid., September 3, 1860.

63. The push and pull between the Wide Awakes and the national leadership resembled the development of the phrases "virgin vote" and "start right." Though established leaders did not introduce the Wide Awake clubs or the term "virgin vote," they quickly adapted these trends to their own interests. Often, adult politicians during the age of popular politics proved better at managing existing youth movements than they were at introducing their own organizations.

64. Weed, "Revolution of the Parties."

65. Fanny Seward, September 1, 3, 8, October 1, 1860, in "Stumping for Lincoln in 1860: Excerpts from the Diary of Fanny Seward," ed. Patricia C. Johnson, *University of Rochester Library Bulletin*, 16, no. 1 (Autumn 1960).

66. "Mr. Seward to the Wide Awakes," *Milwaukee Daily Sentinel*, September 10, 1860. For a dramatic account of this trip and a fifteen-year-old girl's view of the Wide Awakes, see Seward's daughter's diary entries from the trip: Seward, "Stumping for Lincoln in 1860: Excerpts from the Diary of Fanny Seward."

67. Charles Sumner, "The Victory and the Present Duties," *The Works of Charles Sumner* (Boston: Lee and Shephard, 1875–83), 5:351.

68. Strong, *Diary*, 57.

69. "Mass Meeting at Woodsville," *Trenton State Gazette*, September 15, 1860; John P. McIver, *Historical Statistics of the United States, Millennial Edition*, ed. Susan B. Carter and Scott Sigmund Gartner (Cambridge: Cambridge University Press 2006), series Eb62–113.

70. "The Struggle in Pennsylvania," *New York Herald*, October 8, 1860.

71. Walter Dean Burnham, *Presidential Ballots: 1836–1892* (Baltimore: Johns Hopkins University Press, 1955), 260; Phillip Shaw Paludan, *The Presidency of Abraham Lincoln* (Lawrence: University Press of Kansas, 1994), 274–93; Oscar O. Winther, "The Soldier Vote in the Election of 1864," *New York History* 25 (October 1944): 440–58.

More recently, Jonathan W. White has skillfully challenged the idea that among many northerners, service in the Union army automatically meant a long-term commitment to the Republicans. Jonathan W. White, "'For My Part I Don't Care Who Is Elected President': The Union Army and the Election of 1864," in *This Distracted and Anarchical People: New Answers for Old Questions about the Civil War–Era North*, ed. Andrew Slap and Michael Thomas Smith (New York: Fordham University Press, 2013).

72. For a study of William Dean Howells's GOP-leaning tenure at the *Atlantic Monthly*, see Louis J. Budd, "Howells, the *Atlantic Monthly*, and Republicanism," *American Literature* 24 (May 1952): 140. For an example of Will Howells's close relationship with Ulysses S. Grant, see Susan Goodman and Carl Dawson, *William Dean Howells: A Writer's Life* (Berkeley: University of California Press, 2005), 196. For Rutherford B. Hayes, see William Dean Howells to Rutherford B. Hayes, July 20, 1876, and September 7, 1876, in *Selected Letters of William Dean Howells*, ed. George Arms (Boston: Twayne, 1979), 2:131–32, 137, and Goodman and Dawson, *William Dean Howells*, 61, 192. For James A. Garfield, see Goodman and Dawson, *William Dean Howells*, 2–6.

73. William Dean Howells, August 1852, "1852 Diary and Spanish Exercises," Houghton Library, Harvard Special Collections, Cambridge, Mass.; William Dean Howells, *Years of My Youth* (New York: Harper and Brothers, 1916), 138.

74. William Dean Howells, *Sketch of the Life and Character of Rutherford B. Hayes* (Cambridge: H. Houghton, 1876); William Dean Howells to Webb C. Hayes, August 23, 1876, in *Selected Letters of William Dean Howells*, 2:135–36.

75. William Dean Howells to Thomas S. Perry, August 15, 1884, in *Selected Letters of William Dean Howells*, 3:108.

76. Ibid.

77. William Dean Howells, *A Boy's Town: Described for "Harper's Young People"* (New York: Harper and Brothers, 1890), 228.

78. William Dean Howells to William Cooper Howells, November 9, 1884, *Selected Letters of William Dean Howells*, 3:113.

79. Ibid., November 12, 1876, 2:141; William Dean Howells to James Russell Lowell, August 8, 1876, ibid., 2:131–32.

80. James L. Vallandigham, *A Life of Clement L. Vallandigham* (Baltimore: Turnbull Brothers, 1872), 338.

81. Horatio Seymour to Samuel Tilden, July 20, 1868, *Letters and Literary Memorials of Samuel J. Tilden*, 1:242; Rebecca Edwards, *Angels in the Machinery: Gender in American Party Politics from the Civil War to the Progressive Era* (New York: Oxford University Press, 1997), 27; Edward Lee Gambill, *Conservative Ordeal: Northern Democrats and Reconstruction, 1865–1868* (Ames: Iowa State University Press, 1981); Mark Wahlgren Summers, *A Dangerous Stir: Fear, Paranoia, and the Making of Reconstruction* (Chapel Hill: University of North Carolina Press, 2009).

82. Abraham Lincoln to William H. Herndon, June 22, 1848, *Abraham Lincoln: The*

Collected Works, 9 vols., ed. Roy P. Basler (New Brunswick: Rutgers University Press, 1953), 1:491.

83. Horatio Seymour to Samuel Tilden, July 20, 1868, Letters and Literary Memorials of Samuel J. Tilden, 1:242.

84. This cycle of excited youths and burned-out older activists was a constant refrain in politicians' search for new, energetic campaigners. "The Continuation of a Political Reconnaissance of the Key Stone State," New York Herald, September 28, 1848; Marianne Marbury Slaughter, "Letter from Pleasant Riderhood," New Orleans Times Picayune, August 25, 1878; Washington Post, September 12, 1882; "The Grand Army Anniversary," Philadelphia Inquirer, August 5, 1891.

85. "A Great Day for Joliet," Chicago Tribune, October 12, 1860.

86. "The Young Man in Politics," Daily Inter Ocean, January 12, 1892.

87. "Private Dalzell," Wheeling Register, September 8, 1887; "A Dinner Given for Carl Schurz," Hartford Daily Courant, April 28, 1875; "Other Republican Rallies," Boston Daily Advertiser, October 11, 1879; A Young Voter, "Young Men and the War Issues," Century 33 (March 1887): 312; "Narrow Partisanship," New York Times, January 8, 1888. Even historians, those most prone to linger on the conflict, began to introduce a "reunion school" of Civil War interpretation, shaving down the rough edges and old grudges, in the 1880s. Thomas Pressly, Americans Interpret Their Civil War (New York: Free Press, 1965).

88. "Peets Store," Houston Union, January 16, 1869. For other examples of young southerners' desire to move on after the conflict, see Sarah Ann Ross Pringle interview; Marcus Sterling Hopkins Diary, November 3, 1868, University of Virginia Special Collections, Charlottesville; Edward Ayers, The Promise of the New South: Life after Reconstruction (Oxford: Oxford University Press, 1992), 34–55; and Summers, Dangerous Stir.

89. "Young Men and the Union," Bangor Daily Whig and Courier, March 30, 1880.

90. "A Word to Our Young Men," Rocky Mountain News (Denver, Colo.), September 17, 1880. Denver Democrats went on to accuse Republicans of being "fossils who have bonanzas," echoing the young Texans who felt constrained by rich "old suckers." Relying on a mixture of class and age resentments, the Democrats offered a future to younger, poorer voters who had not made their identity, or their fortunes, in the 1860s. "Peets Store"; also see Edwards, Angels in the Machinery, 60, for a strong discussion of this trend, and William Allen White, The Autobiography of William Allen White (New York: Macmillan, 1947), 101.

91. This suggests that all the waving of the bloody shirt done by Republican politicians was not an initial response to the Civil War but a delayed effort to remind a younger generation, a decade or more after Appomattox, of events they had not experienced. "Party for Young Men"; "The Mothers Vote This Year," Salt Lake Tribune, June 26, 1884; "To Honest Young Men," Wisconsin State Journal, August 1, 1884.

92. "Letter," Boston Transcript, October 16, 1879. The New York Tribune also published a notable editorial titled "Why the Nation Forgets," accusing new voters of ungratefully scoffing at veterans. The Tribune sarcastically blamed school textbooks for being "delightfully nonpartisan" when they should have been heaping scorn on

the Democrats for slavery, secession, and war. "Why the Nation Forgets," *New York Tribune*, May 27, 1888.

93. Mark Lawrence Kornbluh, *Why America Stopped Voting: The Decline of Participatory Democracy and the Emergence of Modern American Politics* (New York: New York University Press, 2000), 13–16.

94. Harry Germaine, "A Campaign Club's Equipment," *Daily Inter Ocean*, May 31, 1896; "The Making of Campaign Banners," *Harper's Weekly*, September 10, 1892; "In a Campaign Banner Factory," *Rocky Mountain News*, August 23, 1896.

95. There were 2,270 American newspapers in 1840, 4,459 papers in 1860, and 13,489 papers by 1890. As far as citizens per newspaper, in 1840 America had 7,519 citizens per paper, in 1860 the ratio was 7,051 citizens per paper, and it was 4,666 citizens per paper by 1890. After this historic low, the ratio went back up as newspapers began to consolidate in the twentieth century. Krissy Clark and Geoff McGhee, "Did the West Make Newspapers, or Did Newspapers Make the West?," *Stanford University, Rural West Initiative*, last modified February 22, 2013, http://www.stanford.edu/group/ruralwest/cgi-bin/drupal/content/rural-newspapers-history.

96. "Grant in Chicago," *Milwaukee Daily Sentinel*, October 23, 1879.

97. "The Young Vote," *New York Times*, October 13, 1897.

98. "Mothers Vote This Year"; "Dinner Given for Carl Schurz"; *New Mississippian*, November 18, 1884.

99. Michael R. Haines and Richard H. Steckel, *A Population History of North America* (New York: Cambridge University Press, 2000), 702–4. Though the other momentous realization of 1890—that America no longer had a single line of frontier—has received frequent discussion, the significance of the change in American age and demographics still needs exploration.

100. This phrase appears in over five hundred political articles from 1840 to 1890. For a brief sampling of its uses, see Abraham Lincoln, "Letter to William H. Herndon," July 10, 1848, *Abraham Lincoln*, 1:497; Jacob Frey, *Reminiscences of Baltimore* (Baltimore: Maryland Book Concern, 1893), 69; "Duty of the Republican Party"; and Tilden, "To perfect the organization of the democracy of this state."

101. "It Is Gratifying," *Washington Post*, September 19, 1882.

102. *"Don't pitch your tent among the dead." An appeal to young men, 1879*, Blaine and Logan campaign pamphlet, 1884, Library of Congress; "Garfield to Young Voters. Do Not Pitch Your Tent in the Camp of the Dead. Come into the Camp of Glory and Life," *Daily Inter Ocean*, November 5, 1888.

103. "Our Young Voters," *Trenton State Gazette*, October 30, 1884.

104. For strong work on the rise of independence as a politic virtue, see John G. Sproat, *The Best Men: Liberal Reformers in the Gilded Age* (Chicago: University of Chicago Press, 1982), 118–19, and Mark Wahlgren Summers, *The Press Gang* (Chapel Hill: University of North Carolina Press, 1994), 65–67.

105. "Over the Field, Pertinent Advice to Young Colorado Electors," *Rocky Mountain News*, October 5, 1880.

106. "Claims of Independence: The Young Voters," *Cleveland Gazette*, September 27, 1884; "The Year of the Full Vote," *Daily Inter Ocean*, November 6, 1888; "Etc.,"

Overland Monthly and Out West Magazine, September 1884, 327; "The Young Man's First Vote," *Rocky Mountain News*, November 1, 1890.

107. The popular bit by humorist and preacher Robert Jones Burdette advised young voters that if they supported "any candidate but the one I vote for," the country would be "ruined," and accused the opposition of throwing banana peels on the sidewalk and planning to force married men to live with their mothers-in-law. Robert Jones Burdette, "Burdette's Advice to Young Voters," *Burlington Hawkeye*, August 1884, "Advice to Young Voters," *Wheeling Sunday Register*, August 17, 1884; "Burdette's Advice to Young Voters," *Wisconsin State Register*, September 13, 1884; "Burdette's Advice to Young Voters," *San Francisco Daily Evening Bulletin*, September 19, 1884.

108. "A Fresh Suggestion," *Daily Inter Ocean*, March 30, 1876; Albion Winegar Tourgée, *Letters to a King* (Cincinnati: Cranston and Stowe, 1888), 43; D. Ryan, "Clubs in Politics"; "Young Voter," *Trenton State Gazette*, September 10, 1878.

109. "Young Men in Politics," *Trenton State Gazette*, July 3, 1884; Edward A. Ross, "Raising the Standard of Suffrage," *La Follette's Weekly Magazine*, April 1, 1911, 7.

110. "Among Our Exchanges," *American Nonconformist*, November 9, 1893.

111. "Young Reformers Club," *American Reformer*, November 8, 1884, 364; "Mothers Vote This Year"; "Claims of Independence: The Young Voters," 2; "Violent Little Partisans," *Newark Evening News*, October 10, 1884; Tourgée, *Letters to a King*.

112. Michael McGerr, *A Fierce Discontent: The Rise and Fall of the Progressive Movement in America, 1870–1920* (New York: Free Press, 2003), 80; Robert H. Wiebe, *The Search for Order, 1877–1920* (New York: Hill and Wang, 1967), 111–96.

113. Wiebe, *Search for Order*, 167–70.

114. Alexander Keyssar, *The Right to Vote: The Contested History of Democracy in the United States* (New York: Basic Books, 2009), 94–139; Michael E. McGerr, *The Decline of Popular Politics: The American North, 1865–1928* (Oxford: Oxford University Press, 1986), 43–65.

Conclusion

1. "'Plunky,' the Picturesque" *New York World*, June 8, 1901; "George W. Plunkitt Dies at 82 Years," *New York Times*, November 20, 1924; William L. Riordan, *Plunkitt of Tammany Hall: A Series of Very Plain Talks on Very Practical Politics* (New York: McClure, Phillips, 1905).

2. "'Plunky,' the Picturesque"; "George W. Plunkitt Dies at 82 Years"; "Senator Plunkitt's 'Office,'" *New York Times*, January 29, 1902.

3. Riordan, *Plunkitt of Tammany Hall*, 8.

4. "George W. Plunkitt Dies at 82 Years"; Riordan, *Plunkitt of Tammany Hall*, 8–10.

5. Riordan, *Plunkitt of Tammany Hall*, xxiii.

6. "'Plunky,' the Picturesque."

7. Riordan, *Plunkitt of Tammany Hall*.

8. Ibid., 7.

9. "To Sweep Plunkitt Out," *New York Tribune*, January 24, 1902; Riordan, *Plunkitt of Tammany Hall*, 25–35, 49.

10. Riordan, *Plunkitt of Tammany Hall*, 25.

11. Ibid., 14.

12. "'Plunky,' the Picturesque."

13. Riordan, *Plunkitt of Tammany Hall*, 11.

14. Ibid., 11–16.

15. John P. McIver, *Historical Statistics of the United States, Millennial Edition*, ed. Susan B. Carter and Scott Sigmund Gartner (Cambridge: Cambridge University Press, 2006), series Eb62–113.

16. Paul Kleppner calculated new voter turnout in the "metropole" (the center of population in the Northeast and Midwest) as 87.5 percent in 1888 and just 34.5 percent in 1924. Paul Kleppner, *Who Voted? The Dynamics of Electoral Turnout, 1870–1980* (New York: Praeger, 1982), 68–69.

17. Jane Addams, *The Spirit of Youth and the City Streets* (New York: Macmillan, 1909), 146.

18. "Young Reformers Club," *American Reformer*, November 8, 1884, 364.

19. Riordan, *Plunkitt of Tammany Hall*, 55.

20. The greatest source on the subject of elite reformers' renewed interest in politics in the 1880s and 1890s is Michael E. McGerr, *The Decline of Popular Politics: The American North, 1865–1928* (Oxford: Oxford University Press, 1986), 42–107. This chapter owes a great debt to McGerr's work on the subject.

21. Howard Chudacoff, *How Old Are You? Age Consciousness in American Culture* (Princeton: Princeton University Press, 1989); Joseph Kett, *Rites of Passage: Adolescence in America, 1790 to the Present* (New York: Basic Books, 1977); Addams, *Spirit of Youth and the City Streets*; Howard Chudacoff, *The Age of the Bachelor* (Princeton: Princeton University Press, 1999); Steven Mintz, *Huck's Raft: A History of American Childhood* (Boston: Belknap Press of Harvard University Press, 2006); Jon Savage, *Teenage: The Prehistory of Youth Culture, 1875–1945* (New York: Penguin, 2008); David Nasaw, *Children of the City: At Work and at Play* (New York: Oxford University Press, 1986).

22. Robert H. Wiebe's *Search for Order, 1877–1920* (New York: Hill and Wang, 1967) makes the best case for this impulse, though he views it as an attempt to establish a new order to replace the lost "island communities" of pre-industrial America. Writing about this lost "order" implies a period of stability in American life that has never really existed. It is more accurate to view this movement as the newest in a succession of reconfigurations of elements that have been rearranged across American history.

23. "To Sweep Plunkitt Out"; "Plunkitt Tries Diplomacy," *New York Tribune*, January 25, 1902; "Senator Plunkitt's 'Office'"; "Plunkitt Dares the Town," *New York Sun*, March 15, 1902; "George W. Plunkitt Dies at 82 Years."

24. "To Sweep Plunkitt Out"; "Plunkitt Tries Diplomacy"; "Senator Plunkitt's 'Office'"; "Plunkitt Dares the Town"; "George W. Plunkitt Dies at 82 Years."

25. "To Sweep Plunkitt Out."

26. "Night after Night; November," *Philadelphia Inquirer*, September 8, 1880; "State Legislature Remarks," *Raleigh Register, and North-Carolina Gazette*, February 24, 1843; "Riot," *Liberator*, December 20, 1850; "Political Painters," *St. Louis Globe-Democrat*, January 12, 1876; "The Ball Opens," *St. Louis Globe-Democrat*, June 20, 1876; "To Anti-gang

Democrats," *Daily Inter Ocean*, March 26, 1893; "Latent Forces and How to Develop Them," *Independent*, February 14, 1895.

27. McGerr, *Decline of Popular Politics*, 42–69; Alexander Keyssar, *The Right to Vote: The Contested History of Democracy in the United States* (New York: Basic Books, 2009), 94–139; John G. Sproat, *The Best Men: Liberal Reformers in the Gilded Age* (Chicago: University of Chicago Press, 1982).

28. Daniel Dupre, "Barbeques and Pledges," *Journal of Southern History* 60 (August 1994): 479–512; Morton Keller, *America's Three Regimes* (New York: Oxford University Press, 2007), 7–67; Glenn C. Altschuler and Stuart M. Blumin, *Rude Republic: Americans and Their Politics in the Nineteenth Century* (Princeton: Princeton University Press, 2000), 9, 125–51.

29. William A. Alcott, *Familiar Letters to Young Men on Various Subjects: Designed as a Companion to the Young Man's Guide* (Buffalo: Geo. H. Derby, 1850), 96; Elizabeth Emma Sullivan Stuart to William Chapman Baker, March 2, 1855, *Stuart Letters of Robert and Elizabeth Sullivan Stuart and Their Children, 1819–1864* (New York: Privately published, 1961), 2:479; Andrew Dickson White, *Autobiography of Andrew Dickson White* (New York: Century, 1904), 1:46.

30. Charles Astor Bristed, *The Upper Ten Thousand* (New York: Stringer and Townsend, 1852), 285; Junius Henri Browne, *The Great Metropolis: A Mirror of New York* (Hartford, Conn.: American Publishing, 1869), 73; Wilder Dwight, *Life and Letters of Wilder Dwight* (Boston: Ticknor, 1891), 349; *Daily Inter Ocean*, March 26, 1893.

31. Henry Seidel Canby, *The Age of Confidence: Life in the Nineties* (New York: Farrar and Rinehart, 1934), 249.

32. For a few of the upper-middle-class youths who tended to look down on popular politics, see George Templeton Strong, *Diary: Young Man in New York, 1835–1849*, ed. Allan Nevins and Milton Halsey Thomas (New York: Macmillan, 1952), 94, 137; John Parsons, *A Tour through Indiana in 1840: The Diary of John Parsons of Petersburg, Virginia*, ed. Kate Milner Rabb (New York: R. M. McBride, 1920), 5–15; Rutherford B. Hayes, *Diary and Letters of Rutherford Birchard Hayes,* ed. Charles Richard Williams (Columbus: Ohio State Archaeological and Historical Society, 1922), 69, 126; Almira Heard to John Theodore Heard, November 2, 1860, Letters of J. Theodore Heard, University of Virginia Special Collections, Charlottesville; "Young Men in Council: The Conference of Young Republicans," *Boston Daily Advertiser*, August 27, 1878; and E. L. Godkin, "The Political Campaign of 1872," *North American Review* 115 (October 1872): 410.

33. George Boutwell, "Young Men in Politics," *North American Review* 129, no. 277 (December 1879): 537–44; Dwight, *Life and Letters of Wilder Dwight*, 349; Alcott, *Familiar Letters to Young Men*, 96; T. H. Hoskins, "Editor," *Vermont Watchman*, June 25, 1884. Advice writers frequently warned "respectable" young people to stay away from public democracy. See James Isaac Vance, *The Young Man Foursquare* (New York: F. H. Revell, 1894), 57–60; Constance Cary Harrison, "Boys, Evenings, and Amusements," in *Before He Is Twenty: Five Perplexing Phases of Boyhood Considered: Essays from "Ladies' Home Journal,"* ed. Edward Bok (New York: F. H. Revell, 1894), 80–96; L. K. Wash-

burn, "A Lecture to Young Men," *Boston Investigator*, October 3, 1888; and "The Morals of the Campaign," *Congregationalist*, August 28, 1884.

34. Whitelaw Reid, "The Oration before the Societies," Amherst College, Amherst, Mass., *Circulars of Information of the Bureau of Education for the Year 1873* (Washington, D.C.: Government Printing Office, 1874), 34; Mark Wahlgren Summers, *The Press Gang* (Chapel Hill: University of North Carolina Press, 1994), 68.

35. Canby, *Age of Confidence*, 250–51.

36. "Young Men in Council"; John Lockwood Dodge, "College Republicans," *North American Review* 154 (June 1892): 753–55; "Young Men Dissatisfied," *Baltimore Sun*, November 25, 1881; "Young Men in Politics," *Trenton State Gazette*, July 3, 1884; "Young Men Should Be Independent," *Kansas City Evening Star*, August 1, 1884; "The Young Voters Party," *Philadelphia Inquirer*, August 7, 1888; "Religion in Politics," *Weekly Register-Call*, September 5, 1890.

37. Boutwell, "Young Men in Politics," 537–39.

38. Albion Winegar Tourgée, *Letters to a King* (Cincinnati: Cranston and Stowe, 1888), 58.

39. Ibid., 49, 70.

40. Ibid., 70.

41. Edwin Lawrence Godkin, *The Problems of Modern Democracy* (New York: Charles Scribner's Sons, 1896), 202; also see Keyssar, *Right to Vote*, 126.

42. James Russell Lowell, *Lowell's Works, Literary and Political Addresses* (Boston: Houghton Mifflin, 1886), 6:201; McGerr, *Decline of Popular Politics*, 42–85; Keyssar, *Right to Vote*, 94–139.

43. Robert Kelley, "The Thought and Character of Samuel J. Tilden: The Democrat as Inheritor," *Historian* 26 (Spring 1964): 176–205; John Bigelow, *The Life of Samuel J. Tilden* (New York: Harper and Brothers, 1895).

44. "Tilden," *Kansas City Evening Star*, October 25, 1884; McGerr, *Decline of Popular Politics*, 71.

45. McGerr, *Decline of Popular Politics*, 83; "Letters to the People," *Daily Inter Ocean*, July 14, 1888; Dodge, "College Republicans"; Rebecca Edwards, *Angels in the Machinery: Gender in American Party Politics from the Civil War to the Progressive Era* (New York: Oxford University Press, 1997), 66–68; Daniel J. Ryan, "Clubs in Politics," *North American Review* 146, no. 375 (February 1888): 172–77.

46. McGerr, *Decline of Popular Politics*, 70–75.

47. Dodge, "College Republicans."

48. Chauncey F. Black to Daniel Lamont, August 18, 1888, quoted in McGerr, *Decline of Popular Politics*, 83.

49. James Poster, William Walter Phelps, Henry Cabot Lodge, et al., "Permanent Republican Clubs," *North American Review* 146 (March 1888): 241–65; "Republican Clubs," *Laramie Daily Boomerang*, March 5, 1890.

50. McGerr, *Decline of Popular Politics*, 79; D. Ryan, "Clubs in Politics," 172–77; Poster, Phelps, Lodge, et al., "Permanent Republican Clubs," 241–65; John F. Hogan, ed., *The History of the National Republican League of the United States* (Detroit: National

Republican League of the United States, 1898), 316; Executive Committee of the Republican League of Oregon, *The Republican League Register* (Portland: Republican Register, 1894); James S. Clarkson, "The Politician and the Pharisee," *North American Review* 152, no. 414 (May 1891): 613–23.

51. D. Ryan, "Clubs in Politics," 173. For examples of the Republican League's focus on recruiting young members over the following years, see "Thurston in Tennessee: The Nebraska Orator Talks Politics to the Republican League," *Omaha World Herald*, March 5, 1890; "Young Men in Politics," *Daily Inter Ocean*, March 26, 1890; "Young Men of Hope, a Republican League to Fight for a New Philadelphia," *Philadelphia Inquirer*, November 23, 1890; "Private from Clarkson, Kentucky," *New York Times*, August 9, 1892; "Students for Sound Money," *Sioux City Journal*, August 2, 1896; and "Legislative Acts or Legal Proceedings," *Duluth News-Tribune*, August 28, 1896.

52. Hogan, *History of the National Republican League of the United States*, 316.

53. National Democratic Committee, "National Association of Democratic Clubs," in *The Campaign Text Book for the Democratic Party of the United States* (New York: Brentano's, 1888), 436.

54. D. Ryan, "Clubs in Politics," 175, 177; Poster, Phelps, Lodge, et al., "Permanent Republican Clubs," 241–65.

55. Mark Lawrence Kornbluh, *Why America Stopped Voting: The Decline of Participatory Democracy and the Emergence of Modern American Politics* (New York: New York University Press, 2000), 123.

56. Tourgée, *Letters to a King*, 71.

57. Canby, *Age of Confidence*, 52, 9.

58. Savage, *Teenage*; Chudacoff, *How Old Are You?*; Kett, *Rites of Passage*.

59. Mintz, *Huck's Raft*, 134–98; David Nasaw, *Schooled to Order: A Social History of Public Schooling in the United States* (New York: Oxford University Press, 1979), 87–156.

60. Chudacoff, *How Old Are You?*, 6, 49; Kett, *Rites of Passage*, 111–211.

61. David Hackett Fischer, "The Revolution in Age Relations" and "The Cult of Youth in America," *Growing Old in America* (New York: Oxford University Press, 1977); Richard L. Rapson, ed., *The Cult of Youth in Middle-Class America* (Lexington, Mass.: Heath, 1971).

62. Historians discussing *Adolescence* often forget that Hall's work synthesized and codified decades of reformist sentiment and social research. Kent Baxter, *Modern Age: Turn-of-the-Century American Culture and the Invention of Adolescence* (Tuscaloosa: University of Alabama Press, 2008), 24.

63. Reprinted in Frances Hodgson Burnett, "When He Decides," in Bok, *Before He Is Twenty*, 31.

64. Chudacoff, *How Old Are You?*, 50–51.

65. Bok, *Before He Is Twenty*; Vance, *Young Man Foursquare*.

66. Mintz, *Huck's Raft*, 136.

67. James Schmidt, *Industrial Violence and the Legal Origins of Child Labor* (Cambridge: Cambridge University Press, 2010).

68. Chuducaoff, *How Old Are You?*, 94–96; McIver, *Historical Statistics of the United States*.

69. Mintz, *Huck's Raft*, 174–75, 187; Kett, *Rites of Passage*, 130.

70. Chudacoff, *How Old Are You?*, 68; William Allen White, *The Autobiography of William Allen White* (New York: Macmillan, 1947), 38; Darrel Drury and Justin Baer, *The American Public School Teacher: Past, Present, and Future* (Cambridge, Mass.: Harvard Education Press, 2011); Paul H. Mattingly, *The Classless Profession: American Schoolmen in the Nineteenth Century* (New York: New York University Press, 1975).

71. Nasaw, *Children of the City*, 42–44.

72. Harpo Marx, *Harpo Speaks!*, ed. Rowland Barber (New York: : Bernard Geis Associates, 1961) 36.

73. Nasaw, *Children of the City*, 42–51; Chudacoff, *How Old Are You?*, 92, 103.

74. Henry James, *The American Scene* (New York: Harper and Brothers, 1907), 127; Nasaw, *Children of the City*, 16.

75. Addams, *Spirit of Youth and the City Streets*, 5–8.

76. Ibid., 13.

77. Ibid.

78. G. Stanley Hall, "The High School versus the Fitting School," *Pedagogical Seminary: A Quarterly*, ed. G. Stanley Hall (Worchester, Mass.: Louis N. Wilson, 1902), 9:66.

79. Addams, *Spirit of Youth and the City Streets*, 27; David Nasaw, *Going Out: The Rise and Fall of Public Amusements* (Cambridge, Mass.: Harvard University Press, 1993).

80. Kathy Peiss, *Cheap Amusements: Working Women and Leisure in Turn-of-the-Century New York* (Philadelphia: Temple University Press, 1986).

81. E. Anthony Rotundo, *American Manhood: Transformations in Masculinity from the Revolution to the Modern Era* (New York: Basic Books, 1993), 239–41.

82. Marx, *Harpo Speaks!*, 39.

83. Chudacoff, *How Old Are You?*, 6; For typical examples of the "loafer"-hating young men who often expressed hostility toward their peers, see David Schenck Papers, Southern Historical Collection, University of North Carolina, Chapel Hill; Strong, *Diary*; Benjamin Brown Foster, *Downeast Diary*, ed. Charles H. Foster (Orono: University of Maine at Orono Press, 1975), 10–12; Blanche Butler Ames to Sarah Hildreth Butler, January 7, 1861, *Chronicles from the Nineteenth Century: Family Letters of Blanche Butler and Adelbert Ames*, comp. Blanche Butler Ames, vol. 1 (Clinton, Mass.: Privately published, 1957), 63; William Wheeler, December 23, 1860, *Letters of William Wheeler of the Class of 1855, Y.C.* (Cambridge: Privately published, 1875); William Saunders Brown Diary, November 5, 1844, University of Virginia Special Collections, Charlottesville; and Moses Puterbaugh to Uriah Oblinger, June 26, 1868, and Mattie V. Thomas to Uriah W. Oblinger, Uriah W. Oblinger Family Collection, Nebraska State Historical Society, Lincoln, digitally collected at the Library of Congress, http://memory.loc.gov/ammem/award98/nbhihtml/pshome.html.

84. Glenn Wallach, *Obedient Sons: The Discourse of Youth and Generations in American Culture, 1630–1860* (Amherst: University of Massachusetts Press, 1997); and George Forgie, *Patricide in the House Divided: A Psychological Interpretation of Lincoln and His Age* (New York: W. W. Norton, 1981).

85. Jon Grinspan, "'Young Men for War': The Wide Awakes and Lincoln's 1860 Presidential Campaign," *Journal of American History* 96 (September 2009): 357–78.

86. Savage, *Teenage*, 160–90.

87. Randolph S. Bourne, "The Two Generations," *Atlantic Monthly*, May 1911, 592.

88. Addams, *Spirit of Youth and the City Streets*, 3; Savage, *Teenage*, 180–84.

89. These changes can be charted using Google Books' Ngram Viewer, which tracks the appearance of words in published works in Google Books' broad collection. Though such charts offer a wonderful glimpse of linguistic changes, it is important to remember that Google's collections are not exhaustive, that the Ngram Viewer has been criticized for lack of transparency, and that such charts neglect the specific implications of these words within the original text. For use of "grown-up," see https://books.google.com/ngrams/graph?content=grown-up&year_start=1800&year_end=2000&corpus=15&smoothing=3&share=&direct_url=t1%3B%2Cgrown%20-%20up%3B%2Cco. For "fellows," see https://books.google.com/ngrams/graph?content=fellows&year_start=1800&year_end=2000&corpus=15&smoothing=3&share=&direct_url=t1%3B%2Cfellows%3B%2Cco. And for "young" and "old," see https://books.google.com/ngrams/graph?content=young%2C+old&year_start=1800&year_end=2000&corpus=15&smoothing=3&share=&direct_url=t1%3B%2Cyoung%3B%2Cco%3B.t1%3B%2Cold%3B%2Cco.

90. Bourne, "Two Generations," 592.

91. Canby, *Age of Confidence*, 82–86, 69.

92. Ibid.; D. Ryan, "Clubs in Politics," 175, 177; Poster, Phelps, Lodge, et al., "Permanent Republican Clubs," 241–65.

93. D. Ryan, "Clubs in Politics," 175, 177; Poster, Phelps, Lodge, et al., "Permanent Republican Clubs," 241–65.

94. For examples of club rosters from the beginning of the age of popular politics until the introduction of permanent clubs in 1887, see *Proceedings of a National Republican Convention of Young Men*, Providence, R.I., November 2, 1832, Printed Ephemera Collection, Library of Congress; "Great Whig Meeting in New York, Nominations for Governor," September 8, 1833, Printed Ephemera Collection, Library of Congress; "Young Men's Ratification Meeting," *Boston Daily Advertiser*, August 25, 1857; Young Man's Republican Union, *Report from Young Men's Republican Union, Head Quarters Stuyvesant Institute*, November 5, 1860, Printed Ephemera Collection, Library of Congress; "New England Maine," *Boston Daily Advertiser*, March 6, 1878; and "A Political Sangerfest," *Milwaukee Daily Sentinel*, August 27, 1880.

For rosters following the shift to permanent political clubs, see "Their First Vote," *Milwaukee Sentinel*, July 29, 1888; "Young Men of Hope, a Republican League to Fight for a New Philadelphia"; Young Republican Club, "Young Republican Club of the Twenty-Second Ward, Minute Book," Philadelphia, 1892–1912, Historical Society of Pennsylvania, Philadelphia; National Democratic Committee, "National Association of Democratic Clubs," 436; Executive Committee of the Republican League of Oregon, *Republican League Register*; "Political Organizations, National, State, Local Members," *Brooklyn Daily Eagle Almanac, 1901* 16 (January 1901): 311; Young Republican Club, "Young Republicans of Philadelphia, Minutes 1903–1919," Historical Society of Pennsylvania, Philadelphia.

95. McGerr, *Decline of Popular Politics*, 75–88.

96. "Private from Clarkson, Kentucky"; "Young Men of Hope, a Republican League to Fight for a New Philadelphia"; Young Republican Club, "Young Republican Club of the Twenty-Second Ward, Minute Book"; "Political Organizations, National, State, Local Members," 311.

97. D. Ryan, "Clubs in Politics," 175.

98. Young Republican Club, "Young Republican Club of the Twenty-Second Ward, Minute Book"; Young Republicans of Philadelphia; Robert William Fogel and Stanley L. Engerman, *Reinterpretation of American Economic History* (New York: Harper and Row, 1971), 40.

99. Young Republican Club, "Young Republican Club of the Twenty-Second Ward, Minute Book."

100. Some more nimble political organizations, like Tammany Hall, turned such clubs into permanent community bases where the needy could come for relief or to find jobs, replacing saloon-based political headquarters. Yet even these long-lived organizations, like the Delaware Club or the Narragansett Club, enforced the growing notion that politics should be removed from everyday life. Terry Golway, *Machine Made: Tammany Hall and the Creation of Modern American Politics* (New York: W. W. Norton, 2014), 153–55.

101. "A New Republican Club House the Young Voters of Chester," *Philadelphia Inquirer*, October 7, 1889; "Young Men of Hope, a Republican League to Fight for a New Philadelphia"; National Young Men's Taft Club, broadside, University of Virginia Special Collections, Charlottesville; D. Ryan, "Clubs in Politics," 172–77; Hogan, *History of the National Republican League of the United States*; McGerr, *Decline of Practical Politics*, 82–83.

102. Engravings, *Harper's Weekly*, August 29, 1896; September 5, 1896; October 24, 1896; October 31, 1896.

103. Harvey A. Levenstein, *Revolution at the Table: The Transformation of the American Diet* (Berkeley: University of California Press, 1988), 10–22.

104. "The Young Man in Politics," *Daily Inter Ocean*, January 12, 1892; "Banquet Held for the Republican City Committee," *Boston Daily Advertiser*, January 20, 1888; "Feasting Republicans Banquet of the Union Club," *Rocky Mountain News* (Denver, Colo.), April 1, 1888; "In Hotel Rotundas Cleveland Will Be Beaten in New York," *Daily Inter Ocean*, September 9, 1892; "Richmond's Democratic Banquet," *Raleigh News and Observer*, January 26, 1893; "Banquet by Democrats: The Jefferson Club's Spread at the Pabst Hotel," *Milwaukee Sentinel*, March 5, 1893.

105. Nasaw, *Children of the City*, 52; Addams, *Spirit of Youth and the City Streets*, 9; Roy Rosenzweig, *Eight Hours for What We Will: Workers and Leisure in an Industrial City, 1870–1920* (Cambridge: Cambridge University Press, 1985); Nasaw, *Going Out*; Marx, *Harpo Speaks!*, 30–32.

106. Savage, *Teenage*, 134–35, 184–85.

107. McGerr, *Decline of Popular Politics*, 145–53; Peiss, *Cheap Amusements*.

108. "Letters to the People"; McGerr, *Decline of Popular Politics*, 69–107; "Republican Clubs," *Daily Boomerang*; "Protection to Home Industries," *Daily Inter Ocean*, September 22, 1888; "Young Voters and the Money Question," *Omaha World Herald*,

August, 1, 1896; "Legislative Acts or Legal Proceedings"; D. Ryan, "Clubs in Politics," 175; "Private from Clarkson, Kentucky"; "Republican Clubs," *Atchison Daily Globe*, March 5, 1890; "Religion in Politics."

109. One Democratic proponent of direct mailing bragged that a voter who received campaign literature would feel "as if he were personally known to the sender, and he unconsciously feels that his importance as a voter is recognized." A canvasser in a saloon, however, could offer that same sense, as well as a few beers and cigars along the way. The main drawback was that the canvasser cost more and was not likely to be a member of the "better class." William Andrews to Daniel S. Lamont, February 3, 1888, in McGerr, *Decline of Politics*, 85. For concerns over the cost of canvassers, see Horatio Seymour to Samuel Tilden, July 20, 1868, *Letters and Literary Memorials of Samuel J. Tilden*, ed. John Bigelow, vol. 1 (New York: Harper and Brothers, 1908); McGerr, *Decline of Popular Politics*, 69–85; and "Night after Night; November."

110. "Legislative Acts or Legal Proceedings"; "Letters to the People"; "Republican Clubs," *Daily Boomerang*; "Protection to Home Industries"; "The Registry of Voters and Population," *San Francisco Daily Evening Bulletin*, November 3, 1888; "Students for Sound Money."

111. Kornbluh, *Why America Stopped Voting*, 123–26. The new ballots also made voting harder for illiterate, non-English-speaking, and poorly informed voters. Selecting names on a complicated government document required better English skills than simply handing in a ballot. Kornbluh, *Why America Stopped Voting*, 124–25; Patricia Crain, "Potent Papers: Secret Lives of the Nineteenth-Century Ballot," *Common-Place* 9 (October 2008), http://www.common-place.org/vol-09/no-01/crain (last accessed September 2, 2015); Lyman Abbott, *Reminiscences* (Boston: Houghton Mifflin, 1914), 112; Charles A. Murdock, *A Backward Glance at Eighty* (San Francisco: P. Elder, 1921), 122–23; "Complicated and Expensive," *Bangor Daily Whig and Courier*, December 1, 1890.

112. "A Chicago Boy's First Vote," *Daily Inter Ocean*, May 17, 1896; "A Suggestion as to the Ceremony Marking the First Vote of Young Men, Thomas P. Ballard," *Daily Inter Ocean*, May 16, 1892; "Among Publishers and Agents," *School Board Journal* 11 (June 1896): 16.

113. Thomas Ballard and the Union League were not alone in wishing that the value of a virgin vote be more explicit. Edward W. Bok, Dutch immigrant and editor of the *Ladies' Home Journal*, wrote in his autobiography about his struggle to determine the meaning of his first vote in his adopted country in 1884. American political socialization was so casual and social that he could find no clear, official explanation of the meaning of voting. Bok was one of the reformers who went on to champion age separation and to encourage "respectable" young men to avoid public politics. Edward W. Bok, *The Americanization of Edward Bok* (New York: Scribner and Sons, 1920), 441–46; Bok, "The Boy in the Office," in Bok, *Before He Is Twenty*, 55.

114. "Among Publishers and Agents"; "Notes," *Nation*, June 25, 1885, 522; "Personal," *Indiana School Journal* 35 (1890): 223.

115. Addams, *Spirit of Youth and the City Streets*, 140,

116. Tourgée, *Letters to a King*, 71.

117. Addams, *Spirit of Youth and the City Streets*, 140, 152, 145, 52.

118. McIver, *Historical Statistics of the United States*, series Eb62–113.

119. "The Young Man in Politics," *Daily Inter Ocean*, January 18, 1892; "Young Men in Politics," *Daily Inter-Ocean*, March 26, 1890; "A New Crop of Republicans," *Grand Forks Herald*, September 28, 1896. For a thoughtful analysis of nineteenth-century partisan newspaper style, see one of William Dean Howells's many memoirs: *Years of My Youth* (New York: Harpers and Brothers, 1916), 140–59.

120. "Young Men in Politics," *Daily Inter Ocean*, March 26, 1890; "The Young Man in Politics," *Daily Inter Ocean*, January 18, 1892; "Young Men's Victory," *New York Times*, June 5, 1884; George B. McClellan Jr., *The Gentleman and the Tiger: The Autobiography of George B. McClellan, Jr.* (New York: J. B. Lippincott, 1956); Albert J. Beveridge, *The Young Man and the World* (New York: D. Appleton, 1905).

121. "Gratifying Indication of Progress," *Washington Post*, September 12, 1892.

122. McGerr, *Decline of Popular Politics*, 145–46.

123. William Dean Howells to *New York Tribune*, November 12, 1887, *Selected Letters of William Dean Howells*, ed. George Arms (Boston: Twayne, 1979), 3:204.

124. William Dean Howells to Aurelia Howells, November 7, 1896, ibid., 4:133; William Dean Howells to William Cooper Howells, November 6, 1892, ibid., 29.

125. Susan Goodman and Carl Dawson, *William Dean Howells: A Writers Life* (Berkeley: University of California Press, 2005), 248.

126. This is the case in Google Books' Ngram Viewer; see http://books.google.com/ngrams/graph?content=virgin+vote%2C+maiden+vote&year_start=1800&year_end=2000&corpus=15&smoothing=3&share=.

127. Abbott, *Reminiscences*, 112; Murdock, *Backward Glance at Eighty*, 122–23; Frank Leach, *Recollections of a Newspaperman: A Record of Life and Events in California* (San Francisco: S. Levinson, 1917), 13–14; Andreas Ueland, *Recollections of an Immigrant* (New York: Minton, Balch, 1929), 51–53; Jared Benedict Graham, *Handset Reminiscences: Recollections of an Old-Time Printer and Journalist* (Salt Lake City: Century, 1915), 105–7.

128. For examples of American Life History interviews with Americans who recalled the age of popular politics and their first vote and spoke mostly about "elections," see John J. McCarthy, "When I First Voted a Democratic Ticket," collected by Bessie Jollensten, October 19, 1938; Sarah Ann Ross Pringle, interviewed by Effie Cowan, McLennan County, Tex. (undated); W. A. Boyter, interviewed by Ethel Deal, Newton, N.C., September 4, 1939; Mrs. Charley Huyck (first name unknown), interviewed by Harold J. Moss, January 24, 1939; and Emil R. Kaiser, interviewed by Francis Donovan, Thomaston, Conn., December 15, 1938.

For examples of Americans born after the 1870s who did not mention their first vote and spoke primarily about who was "elected," see Frank Perciful, interviewed by Annie McAulay, Robert Lee, Tex., September 1, 1938; James Dowling, interviewed by Edward Welch, Pittsfield, Mass., December 22, 1938; DeWitt Hines, interviewed by Adyleen G. Merrick, Columbia, N.C., February 2, 1939; St. Elmo W. Acosta, interviewed by Rose Shepherd, Jacksonville, Fla., July 17, 1938; and Cora Lovell, interviewed by Rosalie Smith, Peru, Mass., January 4, 1939, American Life Histories Interviews.

129. Emil R. Kaiser interview.

130. Don Powers and Susie Powers, interviewed by John William Prosser, Columbia, S.C., February 6, 1939, American Life Histories Interviews; McGerr, *Decline of Popular Politics*, 150.

131. Emil R. Kaiser interview. As the *New York Times* put it in a 1924 piece on the decline of rural communities, "We are all children of the movie and the radio," *New York Times*, July 17, 1924; McGerr, *Decline of Popular Politics*, 151.

132. "We're Going Backwards," *San Jose Evening News*, December 21, 1917.

133. Ibid.; McGerr, *Decline of Popular Politics*, 147.

134. The fact that Yvonne was in the first generation of young women raised knowing that they could legally vote mattered less than her culture's growing political ambivalence, demonstrating the power of political culture in the face of constitutional change. Yvonne Blue, January 16, 1926, in "The Diary of Yvonne Blue," *Private Pages: Diaries of American Women, 1830s–1970s*, ed. Penelope Franklin (New York: Ballantine, 1986), 69–70.

135. Sally McCarty Pleasants, *Old Virginia Days and Ways: Reminiscences of Mrs. Sally McCarty Pleasants* (Menasha, Wis.: George Banta, 1916), 12.

136. B. Foster, *Downeast Diary*, 140.

137. Oscar Lawrence Jackson, *The Colonel's Diary: Journals Kept before and during the Civil War*, ed. David P. Jackson (Sharon, Pa: Privately published, 1922), 27.

138. "Chicago Boy's First Vote."

139. Riordan, *Plunkitt of Tammany Hall*, 14.

140. Ibid., 22.

Afterword

1. Perhaps we would no longer devote the majority of federal benefits to the 13 percent of the population over age 65. David Leonhardt, "The Generation Gap Is Back," *New York Times*, June 22, 2012.

2. "2014 Youth Turnout and Youth Registration Rates Lowers Ever Recorded," Center for Information and Research on Civic Learning and Engagement, http://www.civicyouth.org/2014-youth-turnout-and-youth-registration-rates-lowest-ever-recorded-changes-essential-in-2016 (last accessed September 9, 2015).

3. In the United Kingdom and across the European Union, youth voting often falls below 40 percent of eligible young people. In Canada in 2011, just 38.8 percent of eighteen- to twenty-four-year-olds turned out, up from the abysmal 22 percent of eighteen- to twenty-year-old Canadians who voted in 2000. Murray Print, "Citizenship Education and Youth Participation in Democracy," *British Journal of Educational Studies* 55, no. 3 (September 2007): 329; Andre Barnes and Erin Virgint, "Youth Voter Turnout in Canada," *Library of Parliament Research Publications*, last modified January 12, 2014, http://www.parl.gc.ca/Content/LOP/ResearchPublications/2010–19-e

.htm#a6; "Estimation of Voter Turnout by Age Groups at the 2008 General Election," *Elections Canada: Working Paper Series*, last modified January 12, 2014, http://www .elections.ca/res/rec/part/estim/estimation40_e.pdf.

4. "All Together Now: Collaboration and Innovation for Youth Engagement," *Report of the Commission on Youth Voting and Civic Knowledge*, Center for Information & Research on Civic Learning and Engagement (CIRCLE), 2013, 5.

5. Ibid., 8.

6. Paul Allen Peck and M. Kent Jennings, "Family Traditions, Political Periods, and the Development of Partisan Orientations," *Journal of Politics* 53, no. 3 (August 1991): 742–63; John Gross, "The Influence of Parents in the Voting Behavior of Young People," *Public Opinion and Survey Research*, December 13, 2007; "All Together Now: Collaboration and Innovation for Youth Engagement," 5–6, 30–1, 31.

7. "All Together Now: Collaboration and Innovation for Youth Engagement," 15.

8. Daniel Hart, Thomas M. Donnelly, James Youniss, and Robety Atkins, "High School Community Service as a Predictor of Adult Voting and Volunteering," *American Educational Research Journal* 44, no. 1 (March 2007): 197–219; Julianna Dandell and Eric Plutzer, "Divorce and Voter Turnout in the US," *Political Behavior* 27, no. 2 (June 2005): 133–62.

9. "Youth and Gender Voting Fact Sheet," *Center for Information and Research on Civic Learning and Engagement*, 2013, 8–9.

10. "All Together Now: Collaboration and Innovation for Youth Engagement," 13–14, 30–31.

11. Juliana Sandell Pacheco, "Political Socialization in Context: The Effect of Political Competition on Youth Voter Turnout," *Political Behavior* 30, no. 4 (December 2008): 415–36.

12. "All Together Now: Collaboration and Innovation for Youth Engagement," 11.

13. Ibid., 18; David E. Campbell, "Sticking Together: Classroom Diversity and Civic Engagement," *American Politics Research* 35, no. 1 (2007): 51–78.

14. "All Together Now: Collaboration and Innovation for Youth Engagement," 16; "Young Women Drive Youth Turnout," *Center for Information and Research on Civil Learning Fact Sheet*, last modified January 12, 2014, http://www.civicyouth.org/ young-women-drive-youth-turnout.

15. "What Affects Youth Voting," CIRCLE Quick Facts: Youth Voting, http://www .civicyouth.org/quick-facts/youth-voting (accessed January 14, 2014); "Young Voter Mobilization Tactics," compiled by CIRCLE with George Washington University's Graduate School of Political Management, http://www.civicyouth.org/PopUps/ Young_Voters_Guide.pdf.

16. Elizabeth A. Bunion and David W. Nickerson, "The Cost of Convenience: An Experiment Showing E-mail Outreach Decreases Voter Registration," *Political Research Quarterly* 64, no. 4 (December 2011): 858–69; "What Affects Youth Voting."

17. Michelle Theret, "Predicting Civic Engagement in Young Adults: The Effects of Celebrity-Endorsed Public Service Announcements," *Xavier Journal of Politics* 1, no. 1 (2010): 49–66.

18. "Young Reformers Club," *American Reformer*, November 8, 1884, 364.

Bibliography

Primary Materials

Archival Sources

Cambridge, Mass.
    Houghton Library, Harvard Special Collections
        William Dean Howells, "1852 Diary and Spanish Exercises"
Chapel Hill, N.C.
    University of North Carolina, Southern Historical Collection
        David Schenck Papers
Charlottesville, Va.
    University of Virginia Special Collections
        An Appeal to the Young Democrats of Frederick, Virginia. 1851. Broadside.
        Susan M. Eaton Ashworth Diaries
        Richard Henry Baker Papers
        William Matthews Blackford Diaries
        William Saunders Brown Diary
        Francis E. Butler Papers
        Diary of an unknown resident of Madison County
        John Muscoe Garnett Diary
        Bettie Ann Graham Diary
        Susan B. Gray Diary
        Mary Susan Gregory Papers
        J. Theodore Heard Letters
        Jacob Heffelfinger Diaries
        John Hunton Diaries
        Mary Johnston Papers
        Robert Larimer Diaries and Papers
        Louisa A. Minor Diary
        National Young Men's Taft Club broadside
        Stephen Parrish Papers
        John W. Peyton Diary
        Levi Pitman Papers

Thomas W. Springer Diary

Marcus Sterling Hopkins Diary

Lewis Preston Summers Papers

John Toole Papers

Robert Whitehead Papers

Hartford, Conn.

Connecticut Historical Society

Jane Chaney Papers

Gilman Family Papers

Tracey Peck Letters

Sperry, Henry T. *The Republican Wide-Awakes of Hartford, Organized March 3, 1860.* Hartford, 1860. Pamphlet.

————. *To the Republican Wide Awake Ladies of Hartford.* Hartford, 1860. Pamphlet.

Jeremiah A. Wilcox Diary

Lincoln, Neb.

Nebraska State Historical Society

Uriah W. Oblinger Family Collection

Madison, Wis.

William B. Cairns Special Collections, University of Wisconsin

Carrie Ball Diary

Melissa Bishop Diary

Lizzie Ferris Papers

Lulu Ethel Kenison Diaries

Helen Nelson Maynard Diary

Frances R. Paige Diary

K. Mathilde Paulsen Diary

S. Elisa Sleight Diary

Wisconsin Historical Society

Ellen Stanford Smith Diary

New Haven, Conn.

Beinecke Rare Book Library, Yale University

Henry Austin Papers

Sterling Library, Yale Special Collections

Michael F. Campbell Diaries

Philadelphia, Pa.

Historical Society of Pennsylvania

William Bigler Papers

John H. Campbell Papers

Edmund Keyser Diary

Charles Godfrey Leland Papers

List of Registered Voters of the Town of New Haven, Connecticut. New Haven: Thomas J. Stafford Printer, 1858.

Samuel R. Marshall Papers

Joseph Hampton Moore Papers

Newtown Township Poll Books, Camden, N.J., November 4, 1856, March 11,
November 3, 1857, March 3, 1858, November 6, 1860

Charles Plummer Diary

"Poll Book," assembled by George M. Robeson, Gloucester, N.J., 1864

"Register of Lawful Voters of Township of Mannington, Salem County,"
Mannington, N.J., October 16, 1866

Republican Campaign Committee of Philadelphia, "Poll Book, Division 11,
Ward 8," 1896

Sierra County (Calif.) Clerk, "Great register of Sierra County, California,
Voters," 1877, 1878,1879, 1886, 1888, 1890, Balch Institute Library and
Archives

Robert Lincoln Sinclair Papers

Young Republican Club of the Twenty-Second Ward, "Young Republicans of
Philadelphia, Minutes 1892–1912"

Library Company of Philadelphia

Brooklyn Young Republican Club. *Young Republican Campaign Song Book.*
Compiled by Henry Camp. Brooklyn, N.Y.: Harrison & Morton Press,
1888.

Democratic Party of Montgomery County, Pennsylvania. "Young Men's
Meeting, Porter & Democracy!" Montgomery County, Pa., 1838.

Democratic Party of Philadelphia County. "To the Democrats of the
wards and townships, residing in the city and county of Philadelphia."
Philadelphia, Pa., 1844.

National Republican Young Men of the Fifth Congressional District. *Meeting
of Young Men.* Baltimore: Printed by Sands & Neilson, 1832.

Young White Men's League of Jackson. "A Blast from the Youth: The Young
Men of Jackson Utter their Ultimatum." Jackson, Miss., 1890.

Tallahassee, Fla.

Florida State University Strozier Library

Diary of an unknown traveler in Florida

Washington D.C.

Library of Congress, Printed Ephemera Collection

*Great Democratic and Anti-Tariff Meeting of the Young men of Portland, Office of
the Eastern Argus.* Portland, Maine, September 3, 1828.

Proceedings of a National Republican Convention of Young Men. Providence, R.I.,
November 2, 1832.

Tilden, Samuel. *To perfect the organization of the democracy of this state.* Circular
to New York State Democrats, March 31, 1868.

To the people of Waldo. Great Whig meeting in New York. Waldo, N.Y.,
September 8, 1833.

*Young Men! Vote for Edgar Tehune for Congress—To the Young Men of the First
Congressional District.* Chicago, Ill., 1886.

Young Men of Boston! Broadside for Charles Wells as Boston Mayor. Boston, 1832.

Young Men's Fillmore and Donelson Association. *An Address to the Young Men of Massachusetts*. Boston, 1856.

Young Men's Republican Club. *Facts For Workingmen! As Told By Hon. James G. Blaine*. Brooklyn, N.Y., 1884.

Young Men's Republican Union. *Report From Young Men's Republican Union, Head Quarters Stuyvesant Institute*. New York, N.Y, November 5, 1860.

National Museum of American History, Smithsonian Institution, Collections of the Division of Political History

Bidlack, Benjamin. *In Defense of the Young Hickory*. Washington, D.C.: Globe Offices, 1844.

Boston Harrison Club. *The Log Cabin and Straight-out Harrison Songbook*. Boston, 1840.

Bristol, Pennsylvania, Poll Book. Bristol Township, Pa., 1888.

G. F. Foster, Sons & Co. *Catalog of Campaign Goods*. Chicago, Ill., 1896.

Harding, Bythe. *The Honest American Voter's Little Catechism for 1880*. New York, N.Y., 1880.

Lincoln Campaign Songster. Philadelphia: Mason & Co., 1864.

A Red-Hot Campaign for 1880! Great Sale: Fine Art Campaign Pictures! New York, N.Y., 1880.

Seymour, Horatio. *Address of Hon. Horatio Seymour Before the Young Men's Democratic Club*. New York, N.Y., 1880. Collections of the Division of Political History.

The Unexcelled Campaign Fireworks Company. *Illustrated Campaign Handbook*. New York, N.Y., 1888.

Wallace, William A. *Democratic State Committee Meeting*. Philadelphia, Pa., 1867.

Young Men's Shifler's Association. Young Men's Shifler's Association Invitation to Meeting. Philadelphia, Pa., 1844.

American Life Histories Interviews,
Federal Writers' Project, Library of Congress

Acosta, St. Elmo W. Interviewed by Rose Shepherd. Jacksonville, Fla. July 17, 1938.

Boyter, W. A. Interviewed by Ethel Deal. Newton, N.C. September 4, 1939.

Dowling, James. Interviewed by Edward Welch. Pittsfield, Mass. December 22, 1938.

Hines, DeWitt. Interviewed by Adyleen G. Merrick. Columbus, N.C. February 2, 1939.

Huyck, Mrs. Charley. Interviewed by Harold J. Moss. Lincoln, Neb. January 24, 1939.

Kaiser, Emil R. Interviewed by Francis Donovan, Thomaston, Conn. December 15, 1938.

Lovell, Cora. Interviewed by Rosalie Smith. Peru, Mass. January 4, 1939.

Mathews, B. G. Interviewed by Bessie Jollensten. Ogallala, Neb. November 5, 1938.

McCarthy, John J. "A Speech Made by J. J. McCarthy at Kearney, Nebraska." Collected by Bessie Jollensten. Ogallala, Neb. October 19, 1938.

———. "When I First Voted a Democratic Ticket." Collected by Bessie Jollensten. Ogallala, Neb. October 19, 1938.

McCarthy, Mary. Interviewed by Bessie Jollensten. Ogallala, Neb. October 19, 1938.

Perciful, Frank. Interviewed by Annie McAulay. Maverick County, Tex. September 1, 1938.

Powers, Don, and Susie Powers. Interviewed by John William Prosser. Columbia, S.C. February 6, 1939.

Pringle, Sarah Ann Ross. Interviewed by Effie Cowan. Marlin, Tex. (undated).

Slave Narratives

Bryant, Robert. *Born in Slavery: Slave Narratives from the Federal Writers' Project, 1936–1938. Missouri Narratives*, 10:61.

Cancer, Polly Turner. Transcribed by Ann Allen Geoghegan. *Mississippi Narratives Prepared by the Federal Writers' Project of the Works Progress Administration for the State of Mississippi*, http://msgw.org/slaves/cancer-pollyt-xslave.htm. Last accessed April 28, 2015.

Davis, Louis. Transcribed by Ann Allen Geoghegan. *Mississippi Narratives Prepared by the Federal Writers' Project of the Works Progress Administration for the State of Mississippi*, http://msgw.org/slaves/davis-xslave.htm. Last accessed April 28, 2015.

Gray, Callie. Transcribed by Ann Allen Geoghegan. *Mississippi Narratives Prepared by the Federal Writers' Project of the Works Progress Administration for the State of Mississippi*, http://msgw.org/slaves/gray-xslave.htm. Last accessed April 28, 2015.

Hill, Louis. Farmington, Mo. *Born in Slavery: Slave Narratives from the Federal Writers' Project, 1936–1938. Missouri Narratives*, 10:186.

Holsell, Rhody. *Born in Slavery: Slave Narratives from the Federal Writers' Project, 1936–1938. Missouri Narratives*, 10:191.

Jones, Aaron. Transcribed by Ann Allen Geoghegan. *Mississippi Narratives Prepared by the Federal Writers' Project of the Works Progress Administration for the State of Mississippi*, http://msgw.org/slaves/jones-aaron-xslave.htm. Last accessed April 28, 2015.

Nealy, Wylie. Interviewed by Irene Robertson, Biscoe, Ark. *Born in Slavery: Slave Narratives from the Federal Writers' Project, 1936–1938. Arkansas Narratives*, 2:188.

Pope, John. Interviewed by Irene Robertson, Biscoe, Ark. *Born in Slavery: Slave Narratives from the Federal Writers' Project, 1936–1938. Arkansas Narratives*, 2 (pt. 5): 359.

Ramsay, George Washington. Transcribed by Ann Allen Geoghegan. *Mississippi Narratives Prepared by the Federal Writers' Project of the Works Progress Administration for the State of Mississippi*, http://msgw.org/slaves/ramsey-xslave.htm. Last accessed April 28, 2015.

Wamble, Reverend. Interviewed by Archie Koritz, Valparaiso, Ind. *Born in Slavery: Slave Narratives from the Federal Writers' Project, 1936–1938. Indiana Narratives*, 5:198.

Young, John I. Interviewed by Henry Muir, Montgomery County, Ohio. Works

Progress Administration, Ex-Slave Narratives. Ohio Historical Society, "The African-American Experience in Ohio, 1850–1920."

Published Diaries

Allibone, Susan. *A Life Hid with Christ in God*. Philadelphia: J. B. Lippincott, 1856.

Andrews, Eliza Frances. *The War-Time Journal of a Georgia Girl, 1864–1865*. Edited by Spencer B. King Jr. New York: Appleton-Century-Crofts, 1908.

Andrews, Sidney. *The South since the War, as Shown by Fourteen Weeks of Travel and Observation in Georgia and the Carolinas*. Boston: Ticknor, 1866.

Beadle, Erastus Flavel. *Ham, Eggs, and Corn Cake: A Nebraska Territory Diary*. Edited by Ronald Naugle. Lincoln: University of Nebraska Press, 2001.

Beardsley, David. "Birthday Commentaries on His Life." In *Visions of the Western Reserve*, edited by Robert A. Wheeler, 183–92, 319–40. Columbus: Ohio State University Press, 2000.

Beck, Edward. "Diary." In *"A Funnie Place, No Fences": Teenagers' Views of Kansas, 1867–1900*, edited by C. Robert Haywood and Sandra Jarvis. Lawrence: University of Kansas, Division of Continuing Education, 1992.

Bierce, Chloe Bridgman Conant. *Journal and Biological Notice of Chloe B. Conant Bierce*. Cincinnati: Elm Street Printing, 1869.

Bircher, William. *A Drummer-Boy's Diary*. St. Paul: St. Paul Book and Stationery Co., 1889.

Blackwell, Alice Stone. *Growing Up in Boston's Gilded Age*. New Haven: Yale University Press, 1990.

Blue, Yvonne. "Diary." In *Private Pages: Diaries of American Women, 1830s–1970s*, edited by Penelope Franklin, 60–70. New York: Ballantine, 1986.

Bradford Eppes, Susan. *Through Some Eventful Years*. Macon, Ga.: J. W. Burke, 1926.

Brown, Spencer Kellogg. *Spencer Kellogg Brown, His Life in Kansas and His Death as a Spy, 1843–1863, as Disclosed in His Diary*. Edited by George Gardner Smith. New York: D. Appleton, 1903.

Burns, Amanda McDowell. *Fiddles in the Cumberland*. Edited by Amanda McDowell and Lela McDowell Blankenship. New York: Richard R. Smith, 1943.

Channing, Elizabeth Parsons. *Autobiography and Diary of Elizabeth Parsons Channing: Gleanings of a Thoughtful Life*. Boston: American Unitarian Association, 1907.

Chesnutt, Charles Waddell. *The Journals of Charles W. Chesnutt*. Edited by Richard Brodhead. Durham: Duke University Press, 1993.

Claytor, William Quesenbury. *Diary of William Claytor, 1849–1896*. Alexandria, Va.: Alexander Street Press, 2002.

Cooper, Annie Burnham. *Private Pages: Diaries of American Women, 1830s–1970s*. Edited by Penelope Franklin. New York: Ballantine Books, 1986.

Dawson, Sarah Ida Fowler Morgan. *A Confederate Girl's Diary*. Boston: Houghton Mifflin, 1913.

Doten, Alfred. *The Journals of Alfred Doten, 1849–1903*. Reno: University of Nevada Press, 1973.

Dougherty, Michael. *Prison Diary of Michael Dougherty*. Bristol, Pa.: C. A. Dougherty, Printer, 1908.

Downing, Alexander G. *Downing's Civil War Diary*. Edited by Olynthus B. Clark. Des Moines: Iowa State Department of History and Archives, 1916.

Eastman, Elaine Goodale. *Journal of a Farmer's Daughter*. New York: G. P. Putnam's Sons, 1881.

Farnsworth, Martha. *Plains Woman: The Diary of Martha Farnsworth, 1882–1922*. Edited by Marlene Springer and Haskell Springer. Bloomington: Indiana University Press, 1986.

Foster, Benjamin Brown. *Downeast Diary*. Edited by Charles H. Foster. Orono: University of Maine at Orono Press, 1975.

Gillespie, Emily Hawley. *A Secret to Be Buried: The Diary and Life of Emily Hawley Gillespie*. Iowa City: University of Iowa Press, 1989.

Grimké, Charlotte L. Forten. *The Journals of Charlotte Forten Grimké*. Edited by Brenda Stevenson. Oxford: Oxford University Press, 1988.

Havens, Catherine Elizabeth. *The Diary of a Little Girl in Old New York*. New York: Henry Collins Brown, 1919.

Hayes, Rutherford B. *Diary and Letters of Rutherford Birchard Hayes*. Edited by Charles Richard Williams. Columbus: Ohio State Archaeological and Historical Society, 1922.

Herrington, Margaret Virginia. "A Very Nice Girl's School Diary." In *"A Funnie Place, No Fences": Teenagers' Views of Kansas, 1867–1900*, edited by C. Robert Haywood and Sandra Jarvis. Lawrence: University of Kansas, Division of Continuing Education, 1992.

Jackson, Oscar Lawrence. *The Colonel's Diary: Journals Kept before and during the Civil War*. Edited by David P. Jackson. Sharon, Pa.: Privately published, 1922.

Johnson, Rolf. *Happy as a Big Sunflower: Adventures in the West, 1876–1880*. Edited by Richard E. Jensen. Lincoln: University of Nebraska Press, 2000.

Jones, Jenkin Lloyd. *An Artilleryman's Diary*. Madison: Wisconsin History Commission, 1914.

Kemble, Frances Anne. *Journal of Frances Anne Butler*. Vol. 1. Philadelphia: Carey, Lea and Blanchard, 1835.

Lynch, Charles H. *The Civil War Diary, 1862–1865, of Charles H. Lynch*. Hartford, Conn.: Case, Lockwood and Brainard, 1915.

Mayne, Isabella Maud Rittenhouse. *Maud*. Edited by Richard Lee Strout. New York: Macmillan, 1939.

Mersman, Joseph J. *The Whiskey Merchant's Diary*. Edited by Linda A Fisher. Athens: Ohio University Press, 2007.

Northrop, John Worrell. *Chronicles from the Diary of a War Prisoner in Andersonville: and Other Military Prisons of the South in 1864*. Wichita: J. W. Northrop, 1904.

Ober, Merril. "A Journal of Village Life in Vermont in 1848." Edited by Wilson O. Clough. *New England Quarterly* 1, no. 2 (January 1928): 32–40.

Ridgely, Anna. "A Girl in the Sixties." Edited by Octavia Roberts Corneau. *Journal of the Illinois State Historical Society* 2 (October 1929): 1–48.

Roberts, John M. *Buckeye Schoolmaster: A Chronicle of Midwestern Rural Life, 1853–1865*. Edited by J. Merton England. Bowling Green, Ky.: Bowling Green State University Popular Press, 1996.

Seward, Francis. "Stumping for Lincoln in 1860: Excerpts from the Diary of Fanny Seward." Edited by Patricia C. Johnson. *University of Rochester Library Bulletin* 16, no. 1 (Autumn 1960): 1–15.

Spottswood, Wilson Lee. *Brief Annals*. Harrisonburg, Va.: Publishing Department M. E. Book Room, 1888.

Stanton, Elizabeth Cady. *Elizabeth Cady Stanton, as Revealed in Her Letters, Diary and Reminiscences*. Vol. 2. Edited by Harriot Stanton Blatch and Theodore Stanton. New York: Harper and Brothers, 1922.

Strong, George Templeton. *Diary: Young Man in New York, 1835–1849*. Edited by Allan Nevins and Milton Halsey Thomas. New York: Macmillan, 1952.

Taylor, Marion. *Private Pages: Diaries of American Women, 1830s–1970s*. Edited by Penelope Franklin. New York: Ballantine, 1986.

Thomas, Ella Gertrude Clanton. *The Secret Eye: The Journal of Ella Gertrude Clanton Thomas, 1848–1889*. Edited by Virginia Ingraham Burr. Chapel Hill: University of North Carolina Press, 1990.

Tyler, Mason Whiting. *Recollections of the Civil War: With Many Original Diary Entries and Letters Written from the Seat of War, and with Annotated References*. Edited by William S. Tyler. New York: G. P. Putnam's Sons, 1912.

Ward, Lester. *Young Ward's Diary*. Edited by Bernhard J. Stern. New York: G. P. Putnam's Sons, 1935.

Wells, Ida Barnett. *The Memphis Diary of Ida B. Wells: An Intimate Portrait of the Activist as a Young Woman*. Edited by Miriam Decosta-Willis. Boston: Beacon Press, 1995.

Youmans Van Ness, Anne L. *Diary of Annie L. Youmans Van Ness, 1864–1881*. Alexandria, Va.: Alexander Street Press, 2004.

Published Memoirs / Reminiscences / Autobiographies

Abbott, Lyman. *Reminiscences*. Boston: Houghton Mifflin, 1914.

Adams, Charles Francis, Jr. *Charles Francis Adams, 1835–1915: An Autobiography*. Boston: Houghton Mifflin, 1916.

Albee, John. *Confessions of Boyhood*. Boston: Gorham Press, 1910.

Anderson, Rasmus Bjorn. *Life Story of Rasmus Bjorn Anderson*. Madison, Wis.: Privately published, 1915.

Barbour, Sylvester. *Reminiscences*. Hartford, Conn.: Case, Lockwood and Brainard, 1908.

Bell, Horace. *Reminiscences of a Ranger: Early Times in Southern California*. Los Angeles: Yarnell, Caystile and Mathes, Printers, 1881.

Billings, John David. *Hardtack and Coffee: The Unwritten Story of Army Life*. Lincoln: University of Nebraska Press, 1993.

Bok, Edward W. *The Americanization of Edward Bok*. New York: Scribner and Sons, 1920.

Bruce, Henry Clay. *The New Man: Twenty-Nine Years a Slave, Twenty-Nine Years a Free Man, Recollections of Henry Clay Bruce.* York, Pa.: P. Anstadt and Sons, 1895.

Buck, Franklin A. *A Yankee Trader in the Gold Rush: The Letters of Franklin A. Buck.* Compiled by Katherine A. White. Boston: Houghton Mifflin, 1930.

Bundy, C. S. *Early Days in the Chippewa Valley.* Menomonie, Wis.: Flint Douglas, 1916.

Canby, Henry Seidel. *The Age of Confidence: Life in the Nineties.* New York: Farrar and Rinehart, 1934.

Claiborne, John Herbert. *Seventy-Five Years in Old Virginia.* New York: Neale, 1904.

Cobb, Ned. *All God's Dangers: The Life of Nate Shaw.* Compiled by Theodore Rosengarten. Chicago: University of Chicago Press, 1974.

Culp, Frederick M. *Gibson County, Past and Present.* Paducah, Ky.: Turner, 1961.

Curley, James Michael. *I'd Do It Again.* New York: Arno Press, 1976.

Ellis, W. T. *Memories: My Seventy-Two Years in the Romantic County of Yuba, California.* Eugene: University of Oregon Press, 1939.

Frey, Jacob. *Reminiscences of Baltimore.* Baltimore: Maryland Book Concern, 1893.

Graham, Jared Benedict. *Handset Reminiscences: Recollections of an Old-Time Printer and Journalist.* Salt Lake City: Century, 1915.

Graves, Jackson A. *My Seventy Years in California.* Los Angeles: Times Mirror Press, 1927.

Hampton, Charles G. "Twelve Months in Rebel Prisons." In *War Papers Read before the Michigan Commandery of the Loyal Legion of the United States.* Vol. 2. Detroit: James H. Stone, 1898.

Haugen, Nils. *Pioneer and Political Reminiscences.* Evansville, Wis.: Antes Press, 1930.

Haven, Alice Bradley. *Cousin Alice: A Memoir of Alice B. Haven.* Edited by Cornelia Richards. New York: D. Appleton, 1868.

Howard, Robert M. *Reminiscences.* Columbus, Ga.: Gilbert, 1912.

Howells, William Cooper. *Recollections of Life in Ohio, from 1813 to 1840.* Cincinnati: Robert Clarke, 1895.

Howells, William Dean. *A Boy's Town: Described for "Harper's Young People."* New York: Harper and Brothers, 1890.

——. *Imaginary Interviews.* New York: Harper and Brothers, 1910.

——. *Years of My Youth.* New York: Harper and Brothers, 1916.

Johnston, William G. *Life and Reminiscences from Birth to Manhood.* New York: Knickerbocker Press, 1901.

Kernan, J. Frank. *Reminiscences of the Old Fire Laddies and Volunteer Fire Departments of New York and Brooklyn.* New York: M. Crane, 1885.

Kildare, Owen. *My Mamie Rose: The Story of My Regeneration.* New York: Baker and Taylor, 1903.

King, William Fletcher. *Reminiscences.* New York: Abingdon Press, 1915.

Leach, Frank. *Recollections of a Newspaperman: A Record of Life and Events in California.* San Francisco: S. Levinson, 1917.

Leeper, David R. *The Argonauts of 'Forty-Nine: Some Recollections of the Plains and of the Diggings.* South Bend, Ind.: J. B. Stoll, 1894.

Logan, Mary A. *Reminiscences of a Soldier's Wife*. New York: Charles Scribner's Sons, 1916.

Lynch, John Roy. *The Reminiscences of an Active Life: The Autobiography of John Roy Lynch*. Edited by John Hope Franklin. Chicago: University of Chicago Press, 1970.

Marx, Harpo. *Harpo Speaks!* Edited by Rowland Barber. New York: Bernard Geis Associates, 1961).

McClellan, George B., Jr. *The Gentleman and the Tiger: The Autobiography of George B. McClellan, Jr.* New York: J. B. Lippincott, 1956.

Moak, Sim. *The Last of the Mill Creeks*. Chico, Calif.: Privately published, 1923.

Murdock, Charles A. *A Backward Glance at Eighty*. San Francisco: P. Elder, 1921.

Olmstead, Frederick Law. *Journeys and Explorations in the Cotton Kingdom*. London: S. Low, 1862.

Parsons, Albert R. *Life of Albert Parsons: With a Brief History of the Labor Movement in America*. Edited by Lucy Parsons. Chicago: Privately published, 1903.

Parsons, John. *A Tour through Indiana in 1840: The Diary of John Parsons of Petersburg, Virginia*. Edited by Kate Milner Rabb. New York: R. M. McBride, 1920.

Parvin, Theodore Sutton. *The Life and Labors of Theodore Sutton Parvin*. Edited by Joseph E. Morcombe. Clifton, Iowa: Allen, 1906.

Pleasants, Sally McCarty. *Old Virginia Days and Ways: Reminiscences of Mrs. Sally McCarty Pleasants*. Menasha, Wis.: George Banta, 1916.

Pomeroy, Marcus. *Reminiscences and Recollections of "Brick" Pomeroy*. New York: Advance Thought Company, 1890.

Schurz, Carl. *The Reminiscences of Carl Schurz*. New York: McClure, 1907.

Selby, Julian A. *Memorabilia and Anecdotal Reminiscences of Columbia, South Carolina*. Columbia: R. L. Bryan, 1905.

Shields, Art. *My Shaping-Up Years: The Early Years of Labor's Great Reporter*. New York: International, 1983.

Steele, Eliza R. *Summer Journey in the West*. New York: John S. Taylor, 1841.

Stephenson, Isaac. *Recollections of a Long Life, 1829–1915*. Chicago: Privately published, 1915.

Stillwell, Leander. *The Story of a Common Soldier of Army Life in the Civil War, 1861–1865*. Kansas City, Mo.: Frank Hudson, 1920.

Taylor, Bayard. *El Dorado; or, Adventures in the Path of Empire*. Vol. 2. London: Henry G. Bohn, 1850.

Thompson, B. F. "The Wide Awakes of 1860." *Magazine of History with Notes and Queries* 10 (November 1909): 293–96.

Turnley, Parmenas Taylor. *Reminiscences of Parmenas Taylor Turnley: From the Cradle to Three-Score and Ten*. Chicago: Donohue and Henneberry, 1892.

Ueland, Andreas. *Recollections of an Immigrant*. New York: Minton, Balch, 1929.

Wallace, Lew. *An Autobiography*. Vol. 1. New York: Harper and Brothers, 1906.

White, Andrew Dickson. *Autobiography of Andrew Dickson White*. Vol. 1. New York: Century, 1904.

White, William Allen. *The Autobiography of William Allen White*. New York: Macmillan, 1947.

Willard, Frances E. *Glimpses of Fifty Years: The Autobiography of an American Woman*. Chicago: Women's Temperance Publication Association, H. J. Smith and Co., 1889.

Witham, James. *Fifty Years on the Firing Line: My Part in the Farmers' Movement*. Chicago: Privately published, 1924.

Published Letters

Ames, Blanche Butler, comp. *Chronicles from the Nineteenth Century: Family Letters of Blanche Butler and Adelbert Ames*. Vol. 1. Clinton, Mass.: Privately published, 1957.

Barton, H. Arnold, ed. *Letters from the Promised Land: Swedes in America, 1840–1915*. Minneapolis: University of Minnesota Press, 1975.

Botta, Anne Charlotte Lynch. *Memoirs of Anne C. L. Botta Written by Her Friends*. Edited by Vincenzo Botta. New York: J. Selwin Tait, 1893.

Child, Lydia Maria. *Letters of Lydia Maria Child*. Edited by Wendell Phillips. Boston: Houghton Mifflin, 1882.

Christman, Enos. *One Man's Gold: The Letters and Journal of a Forty-Niner*. Edited by Florence Morrow Christman. New York: Whittlesey House, 1930.

Conant, Charlotte Howard. *A Girl of the Eighties at College and at Home*. Edited by Martha Pike Conant. Boston: Houghton Mifflin, 1931.

Dickinson, Emily Elizabeth. *The Letters of Emily Dickinson*. Vol 1. Edited by Mabel Todd Loomis. Boston: Roberts Bros., 1894.

Dwight, Wilder. *Life and Letters of Wilder Dwight*. Boston: Ticknor, 1891.

Emerson, Ellen Tucker. *The Letters of Ellen Tucker Emerson*. Edited by Edith W. Gregg. Kent, Ohio: Kent State University Press, 1982.

FitzGerald, Emily McCorkle. *An Army Doctor's Wife on the Frontier: Letters from Alaska and the Far West, 1874–1878*. Pittsburgh: University of Pittsburgh Press, 1962.

Hale, Susan. *Letters of Susan Hale*. Edited by Caroline P. Atkinson. Boston: Marshall Jones, 1918.

Hancock, Cornelia Oatis. *Letters of a Civil War Nurse: Cornelia Hancock, 1863–1865*. Edited by Henrietta Stratton Jaquette. Lincoln: University of Nebraska Press, 1871.

Howells, William Dean. *Selected Letters of William Dean Howells*. 6 vols. Edited by George Arms. Boston: Twayne, 1979.

Judson, Emily Chubbuck. *The Life and Letters of Mrs. Emily C. Judson*. New York: Sheldon, 1860.

Life and Letters of Judge Thomas J. Anderson and Wife. Edited by James House Anderson and Nancy Anderson. Cincinnati: Press of F. J. Heer, 1904.

Lincoln, Abraham. *Abraham Lincoln: The Collected Works*. 9 vols. Edited by Roy P. Basler. New Brunswick: Rutgers University Press, 1953.

Segale, Sister Blandina. *At the End of the Santa Fe Trail*. Columbus, Ohio: Columbian Press, 1932.

Stuart, Elizabeth Emma Sullivan. *Stuart Letters of Robert and Elizabeth Sullivan Stuart and Their Children, 1819–1864*. New York: Privately published, 1961.

Sumner, Charles. *The Works of Charles Sumner*. 7 vols. Boston: Lee and Shephard, 1875–83.

Thompson, Harriet Jane Parsons. *Civil War Wife: The Letters of Harriet Jane Thompson*. Edited by Glenda Riley. Iowa City: State Historical Society of Iowa, 1978.

Tilden, Samuel J. *Letters and Literary Memorials of Samuel J. Tilden*. Edited by John Bigelow. 2 vols. New York: Harper and Brothers, 1908.

———. *The Writings and Speeches of Samuel J. Tilden*. Edited by John Bigelow. Vol. 2. New York: Harper and Bros., 1885.

Townsend, Elizabeth G. *Life of Abby Hopper Gibbons: Told Chiefly through Her Correspondence*. Vol. 2. Edited by Sarah Hopper Emerson. New York: G. P. Putnam's Sons, 1896.

The Welsh in America: Letters from the Immigrants. Edited by Alan Conway. Minneapolis: University of Minnesota Press, 1961.

Wheeler, William. *Letters of William Wheeler of the Class of 1855, Y.C.* Cambridge: Privately published, 1875.

Newspapers and Periodicals

Albany Evening Register
American Federationist
American Heritage
American Monthly Review
American Nonconformist
American Reformer
Arizona Journal-Miner
Atchison Daily Globe
Atlantic Monthly
Augusta Daily Chronicle and Sentinel
Baltimore Patriot
Baltimore Sun
Bangor Daily Whig and Courier
Bismarck Daily Tribune
Boston Daily Advertiser
Boston Daily Atlas
Boston Investigator
Boston Transcript
Brooklyn Daily Eagle
Burlington (Del.) Hawkeye
Century
Central City (Col.) Daily Register-Call
Charleston Courier
Chicago Press and Tribune

Chicago Tribune
Chillicothe Scioto Gazette
Chronicle: Student Magazine of University of Michigan
Cleveland Gazette
Colored American
Comrade
Congregationalist
Continent: An Illustrated Weekly Magazine
Daily Cleveland Herald
Daily Inter Ocean (Chicago)
Daily Ohio Statesman
Des Moines Daily State Register
Duluth News-Tribune
Emancipator and Weekly Chronicle
Emporia (Kans.) Daily Gazette
Forum
Galveston Daily News
Grand Forks Herald
Harper's Weekly
Harper's Young People
Harrisburg Weekly Patriot and Union
Hartford Daily Courant

Hinds County (Miss.) Gazette
Houston Union
Indiana School Journal
Kansas City Evening Star
Keith County (Neb.) News
Knoxville Journal
La Follette's Weekly Magazine
Laramie (Wyo.) Daily Boomerang
Liberator
Los Angeles Daily Times
Lowell Citizen and News
Macon Weekly Telegraph
Memphis Enquirer
Milwaukee Daily Journal
Milwaukee Daily Sentinel
Mississippian and State Gazette
Portland (Ore.) Morning Oregonian
Nation
National Police Gazette
Newark (Ohio) Evening News
New Haven Evening Register
New Mississippian
New Orleans Times Picayune
Charleston News and Courie
New York Evening Post
New York Herald
New York Independent
New-York Spectator
New York Sun
New York Times
New York Tribune
New York World
North American and United States
    Gazette
North American Review
Ogallala (Neb.) Reflector

Ohio State Journal
Omaha World Herald
Outlook
Overland Monthly and Out West Magazine
Pennsylvania Inquirer and Daily Courier
Philadelphia Inquirer
Pittsfield (Mass.) Sun
Pomeroy's Democrat
Windsor (Ontario, Canada) Provincial
    Freeman
Puck
Raleigh News and Observer
Republican Magazine
Richmond News and Observer
Richmond Planet
Rocky Mountain News (Denver, Colo.)
San Francisco Daily Evening Bulletin
St. Louis Globe-Democrat
Salt Lake Tribune
San Jose Evening News
School Board Journal
Semi-Weekly Raleigh Register
Sioux City Journal
Tariff Review
Trenton State Gazette
Vermont Patriot
Vermont Watchman
Washington Bee
Washington Daily National Intelligencer
Washington Post
Westfield (N.Y.) Courier and Chautauqua
    County Whig
Wheeling (W.Va.) Register
Wisconsin State Journal
Wisconsin State Register
Youth's Companion

Books

Addams, Jane. *The Spirit of Youth and the City Streets.* New York: Macmillan, 1909.

Alcott, William A. *Familiar Letters to Young Men on Various Subjects: Designed as a Companion to "The Young Man's Guide."* Buffalo: Geo. H. Derby, 1850.

———. *The Young Man's Guide.* Boston: Lilly, Wait, Colman, and Holden, 1834.

Anonymous. *Maidenhead Stories, Told by a Set of Joyous Students.* New York: Erotica Biblion Society, 1897.

Austin, Reverend John Mather. *A Voice to Youth: Addressed to Young Men and Young Ladies*. Utica: Grosh and Hutchinson, 1839.

Beveridge, Albert J. *The Young Man and the World*. New York: D. Appleton, 1905.

Bigelow, John. *The Life of Samuel J. Tilden*. New York: Harper and Brothers, 1895.

Blaine, James G. *Life and Public Services of Hon. James G. Blaine*. Edited by James P. Boyd. Philadelphia: Publishers Union, 1893.

Bodine, Lester. *Off the Face of the Earth*. Omaha: Festner, 1894.

Bok, Edward, ed. *Before He Is Twenty: Five Perplexing Phases of Boyhood Considered: Essays from "Ladies' Home Journal."* New York: F. H. Revell, 1894.

Bristed, Charles Astor. *The Upper Ten Thousand*. New York: Stringer and Townsend, 1852.

Browne, Junius Henri. *The Great Metropolis: A Mirror of New York*. Hartford, Conn.: American Publishing, 1869.

Buckingham, James Silk. *America, Historical, Statistic, and Descriptive*. 2 vols. New York: Harper and Brothers, 1841.

Chevalier, Michael. *Society, Manners and Politics in the United States*. Boston: Weeks, Jordan, 1839.

Dickens, Charles. *American Notes*. London: Everyman Press, 1997.

———. *American Notes for General Circulation*. London: J. M. Dent, 1907.

Dineen, Joseph F. *Ward Eight*. New York: Harper and Brothers, 1936.

Executive Committee of the Republican League of Oregon. *The Republican League Register*. Portland: Republican Register, 1894.

Foster, George. *New York in Slices: By an Experienced Carver*. New York: W. H. Graham, 1849.

Godkin, Edwin Lawrence. *The Problems of Modern Democracy*. New York: Charles Scribner's Sons, 1896.

Hall, G. Stanley. *Youth: Its Education, Regimen, and Hygiene*. New York: D. Appleton, 1907.

Hogan, John F., ed. *The History of the National Republican League of the United States*. Detroit: National Republican League of the United States, 1898.

Ivin, William Mills. *Machine Politics and Money in Elections in New York City*. New York: Harper and Brothers, 1887.

Leland, Charles G. *Memoirs*. London: William Heinemann, 1894.

———. *Pipps among the Wide Awakes*. New York: Wevill and Chapin, 1860.

Liddell, Henry. *The Evolution of a Democrat: A Darwinian Tale*. New York: Paquet, 1888.

Locke, David Ross. *Nasby: Divers Views, Opinions and Prophecies of Petroleum v. Nasby*. Cincinnati: R. W. Carroll, 1867.

Lowell, James Russell. *Lowell's Works, Literary and Political Addresses*. Boston: Houghton Mifflin, 1886.

National Democratic Committee. "National Association of Democratic Clubs." In *The Campaign Text Book for the Democratic Party of the United States*, 436. New York: Brentano's, 1888.

Nordhoff, Charles. *Politics for Young Americans*. New York: Harper and Brothers, 1875.

Raymond, Walter Marion. *Rebels of the New South*. Chicago: Charles H. Kerr, 1905.

Reid, Whitelaw. *Horace Greeley*. New York: Charles Scribner's Sons, 1879.

Riordan, William L. *Plunkitt of Tammany Hall: A Series of Very Plain Talks on Very Practical Politics*. New York: McClure, Phillips, 1905. Reprint, New York: E. P. Dutton, 1963.

Shapley, Rufus Edmonds. *Solid for Mulhooly*. New York: G. W. Carleton, 1881.

Tourgée, Albion Winegar. *Letters to a King*. Cincinnati: Cranston and Stowe, 1888.

Vallandigham, James L. *A Life of Clement L. Vallandigham*. Baltimore: Turnbull Brothers, 1872.

Vance, James Isaac. *The Young Man Foursquare*. New York: F. H. Revell, 1894.

Von Raumer, Frederick. *America and the American People*. New York: J. and H. G. Langley, S. Astor House, 1841.

Woodbury, Augustus. *Plain Words for Young Men*. Concord: McFarland and Jenks, 1858.

Secondary Materials

Books

Altschuler, Glenn C., and Stuart M. Blumin. *Rude Republic: Americans and Their Politics in the Nineteenth Century*. Princeton: Princeton University Press, 2000.

Anbinder, Tyler. *Five Points*. New York: Free Press, 2001.

Bailey, Beth L. *From Front Porch to Back Seat: Courtship in Twentieth-Century America*. Baltimore: Johns Hopkins University Press, 1988.

Baxter, Kent. *Modern Age: Turn-of-the-Century American Culture and the Invention of Adolescence*. Tuscaloosa: University of Alabama Press, 2008.

Bederman, Gail. *Manliness and Civilization*. Chicago: University of Chicago Press, 1995.

Bensel, Richard Franklin. *The American Ballot Box in the Mid-Nineteenth Century*. Cambridge: Cambridge University Press, 2004.

Benson, Lee. *The Concept of Jacksonian Democracy: New York as a Text Case*. Princeton: Princeton University Press, 1961.

Bernstein, Iver. *The New York City Draft Riots: Their Significance in American Society and Politics in the Age of the Civil War*. New York: Oxford University Press, 1990.

Boyer, Paul, et al. *The Enduring Vision*. New York: Wadsworth, 2003.

Burnham, Walter Dean. *Presidential Ballots: 1836–1892*. Baltimore: Johns Hopkins University Press, 1955.

Carwardine, Richard J. *Evangelicals and Politics in Antebellum America*. New Haven: Yale University Press, 1993.

Chudacoff, Howard. *The Age of the Bachelor*. Princeton: Princeton University Press, 1999.

———. *How Old Are You? Age Consciousness in American Culture*. Princeton: Princeton University Press, 1989.

Cogan, Frances B. *All-American Girl: The Ideal of Real Womanhood in Mid-Nineteenth-Century America*. Athens: University of Georgia Press, 1989.

Cohen, Patricia Cline, Timothy J. Gilfoyle, and Helen Lefkowitz Horowitz. *The Flash Press: Sporting Male Weeklies in 1840s New York*. Chicago: University of Chicago Press, 2008.

Coontz, Stephanie. *Marriage, a History: From Obedience to Intimacy*. New York: Viking, 2005.

Cultice, Wendell W. *Youth's Battle for the Ballot*. New York: Praeger, 1992.

Curti, Merle. *The Making of an American Community: A Case Study in Democracy in a Frontier County*. Stanford: Stanford University Press, 1959.

Denton, Sally. *Passion and Principle: John and Jessie Frémont*. New York: Bloomsbury, 2007.

Drury, Darrel, and Justin Baer. *The American Public School Teacher: Past, Present, and Future*. Cambridge, Mass.: Harvard Education Press, 2011.

Earle, Jonathan. *Jacksonian Antislavery and the Politics of Free Soil, 1824–1854*. Chapel Hill: University of North Carolina Press, 2004.

Eastman, Carolyn. *A Nation of Speechifiers: Making an American Public after the Revolution*. Chicago: University of Chicago Press, 2009.

Edwards, Rebecca. *Angels in the Machinery: Gender in American Party Politics from the Civil War to the Progressive Era*. New York: Oxford University Press, 1997.

Eyal, Yonatan. *The Young America Movement and the Transformation of the Democratic Party, 1828–1861*. Cambridge: Cambridge University Press, 2007.

Feldberg, Michael. *The Philadelphia Riots of 1844*. Westport, Conn.: Greenwood Press, 1975.

Field, Corinne T. *The Struggle for Equal Adulthood: Gender, Race, Age, and the Fight for Citizenship in Antebellum America*. Chapel Hill: University of North Carolina Press, 2015.

Fischer, David Hackett. *Growing Old in America*. New York: Oxford University Press, 1977.

Fitzgerald, Michael W. *The Union League Movement in the Deep South: Politics and Agricultural Change During Reconstruction*. Baton Rogue: Louisiana State University Press, 1989.

Fogel, Robert William. *Without Consent of Contract: The Rise and Fall of American Slavery*. New York: W. W. Norton, 1989.

Fogel, Robert William, and Stanley L. Engerman. *Reinterpretation of American Economic History*. New York: Harper and Row, 1971.

Foner, Eric. *Free Labor, Free Soil, Free Men*. Oxford: Oxford University Press, 1970.

Forman-Brinell, Miriam, and Leslie Paris, eds. *The Girls' History and Culture Reader: The Nineteenth Century*. Urbana: University of Illinois Press, 2011.

Franklin, John Hope. *Reconstruction after the Civil War*. Chicago: University of Chicago Press, 1962.

Gambill, Edward Lee. *Conservative Ordeal: Northern Democrats and Reconstruction, 1865–1868*. Ames: Iowa State University Press, 1981.

Gibson, Campbell, and Kay Jung. *Historical Census Statistics on Population Totals by Race, 1790 to 1990*. Working Paper Series No. 56. Washington, D.C.: Population Division, U.S. Census Bureau, 2002.

Gienapp, William. *Origins of the Republican Party, 1852–1856.* New York: Oxford University Press, 1987.

Gilfoyle, Timothy. *City of Eros: New York City, Prostitution, and the Commercialization of Sex, 1790–1920.* New York: W. W. Norton, 1992.

Goodman, Susan, and Carl Dawson. *William Dean Howells: A Writer's Life.* Berkeley: University of California Press, 2005.

Greenberg, Amy S. *Cause for Alarm: The Volunteer Fire Department in the Nineteenth-Century City.* Princeton: Princeton University Press, 1998.

Gunderson, Robert Gray. *The Log Cabin Campaign.* Lexington: University Press of Kentucky, 1957.

Hahn, Steven. *A Nation under Our Feet.* Boston: Belknap Press, 2003.

Haines, Michael R., and Richard H. Steckel. *A Population History of North America.* New York: Cambridge University Press, 2000.

Halttunen, Karen. *Confidence Men and Painted Women: A Study of Middle-Class Culture in America, 1830–1870.* New Haven: Yale University Press, 1983.

Hessinger, Rodney. *Seduced, Abandoned, and Reborn: Visions of Youth in Middle-Class America, 1780–1850.* Philadelphia: University of Pennsylvania Press, 2005.

Holt, Michael F. *Forging a Majority: The Formation of the Republican Party in Pittsburgh, 1848–1860.* New Haven: Yale University Press, 1969.

Howe, Daniel Walker. *What Hath God Wrought.* Oxford: Oxford University Press, 2007.

Jabour, Anya. *Scarlett's Sisters: Young Women in the Old South.* Chapel Hill: University of North Carolina Press, 2007.

Johannsen, Robert Walker. *The Frontier, the Union, and Stephen A. Douglas.* Urbana: University of Illinois Press, 1989.

Johnson, Paul E. *A Shopkeeper's Millennium.* New York: Hill and Wang, 1978.

Josephson, Matthew. *The Politicos: 1865–1896.* New York: Harcourt, Brace, 1938.

Keller, Morton. *Affairs of State.* Cambridge, Mass.: Belknap Press of Harvard University Press, 1977.

———. *America's Three Regimes.* New York: Oxford University Press, 2007.

Kett, Joseph. *Rites of Passage: Adolescence in America, 1790 to the Present.* New York: Basic Books, 1977.

Keyssar, Alexander. *The Right to Vote: The Contested History of Democracy in the United States.* New York: Basic Books, 2009.

Kleppner, Paul. *Who Voted? The Dynamics of Electoral Turnout, 1870–1980.* New York: Praeger, 1982.

Kornbluh, Mark Lawrence. *Why America Stopped Voting: The Decline of Participatory Democracy and the Emergence of Modern American Politics.* New York: New York University Press, 2000.

Lause, Mark. *Young America: Land, Labor, and the Republican Community.* Urbana: University of Illinois Press, 2005.

Lebergott, Stanley. *The Americans: An Economic Record.* New York: Norton, 1984.

Licht, Walter. *Getting Work: Philadelphia, 1840–1950.* Cambridge, Mass.: Harvard University Press, 1992.

Lystra, Karen. *Searching the Heart: Women, Men, and Romantic Love in Nineteenth-Century America*. New York: Oxford University Press, 1992.

Macleod, David. *Building Character in the American Boy: The YMCA, the Boy Scouts, and Their Forerunners, 1870–1920*. Madison: University of Wisconsin Press, 1983.

Mattingly, Paul H. *The Classless Profession: American Schoolmen in the Nineteenth Century*. New York: New York University Press, 1975.

McGerr, Michael E. *The Decline of Popular Politics: The American North, 1865–1928*. Oxford: Oxford University Press, 1986.

———. *A Fierce Discontent: The Rise and Fall of the Progressive Movement in America, 1870–1920*. New York: Free Press, 2003.

McIver, John P. *Historical Statistics of the United States, Millennial Edition*. Edited by Susan B. Carter and Scott Sigmund Gartner. Cambridge: Cambridge University Press, 2006.

Melton, Tracy Matthew. *Hanging Henry Gambrill: The Violent Career of Baltimore's Plug Uglies, 1854–1860*. Baltimore: Johns Hopkins University Press, 2005.

Mintz, Steven. *Huck's Raft: A History of American Childhood*. Boston: Belknap Press of Harvard University Press, 2006.

Morris, Roy, Jr. *The Fraud of the Century: Rutherford B. Hayes, Samuel J. Tilden, and the Stolen Election of 1876*. New York: Simon and Schuster, 2003.

Nasaw, David. *Children of the City: At Work and at Play*. New York: Oxford University Press, 1986.

———. *Schooled to Order: A Social History of Public Schooling in the United States*. New York: Oxford University Press, 1979.

Neely, Mark E., Jr. *The Boundaries of American Political Culture in the Civil War Era*. Chapel Hill: University of North Carolina Press, 2005.

Nevins, Allan. *The War for Union*. Vol. 3, *The Organized War, 1863–1864*. New York: Charles Scribner's Sons, 1971.

Nichols, Roy F. *The Disruption of American Democracy*. New York: Macmillan, 1948.

Ohmann, Richard. *Selling Culture: Magazines, Markets, and Class at the Turn of the Century*. London: Verso, 1996.

Paludan, Phillip Shaw. *The Presidency of Abraham Lincoln*. Lawrence: University Press of Kansas, 1994.

Peiss, Kathy. *Cheap Amusements: Working Women and Leisure in Turn-of-the-Century New York*. Philadelphia: Temple University Press, 1986.

Pilkington, Colin. *The Politics Today Companion to the British Constitution*. Manchester: Manchester University Press, 1999.

Pressly, Thomas. *Americans Interpret Their Civil War*. New York: Free Press, 1965.

Rabinowitz, Howard N., ed. *Southern Black Leaders of the Reconstruction Era*, Champaign: University of Illinois Press, 1982.

Rapson, Richard L., ed. *The Cult of Youth in Middle-Class America*. Lexington, Mass.: Heath, 1971.

Reynolds, David. *Walt Whitman's America*. New York: Knopf, 1995.

Roberts, Alasdair. *America's First Great Depression: Economic Crisis and Political Disorder after the Panic of 1837*. Ithaca: Cornell University Press, 2012.

Rorabaugh, W. J. *The Alcoholic Republic: An American Tradition*. New York: Oxford University Press, 1979.

Rothman, Ellen K. *Hands and Hearts: A History of Courtship in America*. New York: Basic Books, 1984.

Rotundo, E. Anthony. *American Manhood: Transformations in Masculinity from the Revolution to the Modern Era*. New York: Basic Books, 1993.

Ryan, Mary. *Civic Wars*. Berkeley: University of California Press, 1998.

———. *Cradle of the Middle Class*. Cambridge: Cambridge University Press, 1981.

———. *Women in Public: Between Banners and Ballots, 1825–1880*. Baltimore: Johns Hopkins University Press, 1992.

Sap, Jan Willem. *The Netherlands Constitution, 1848–1998*. West Lafayette, Ind.: Purdue University Press, 2000.

Savage, Jon. *Teenage: The Prehistory of Youth Culture*. London: Penguin, 2008.

Schmidt, James. *Industrial Violence and the Legal Origins of Child Labor*. Cambridge: Cambridge University Press, 2010.

Sellers, Charles. *The Market Revolution*. Oxford: Oxford University Press, 1991.

Silbey, Joel. *The American Political Nation, 1838–1893*. Stanford: Stanford University Press, 1991.

Sproat, John. *The Best Men: The Liberal Reformers of the Gilded Age*. Chicago: University of Chicago Press, 1982.

Summers, Mark Wahlgren. *A Dangerous Stir: Fear, Paranoia, and the Making of Reconstruction*. New York: Oxford University Press, 2009.

———. *Party Games: Getting, Keeping, and Using Power in Gilded Age Politics*. Chapel Hill: University of North Carolina Press, 2004.

———. *The Plundering Generation: Corruption and the Crisis of the Union, 1849–1861*. New York: Oxford University Press, 1987.

Taylor, Alan. *William Cooper's Town*. New York: Alfred A. Knopf, 1995.

Tebeau, Mark. *Eating Smoke: Fire in Urban America, 1800–1950*. Baltimore: Johns Hopkins University Press, 2003.

Towers, Frank. *The Urban South and the Coming of the Civil War*. Charlottesville: University of Virginia Press, 2004.

Varon, Elizabeth R. *We Mean to Be Counted: White Women and Politics in Antebellum Virginia*. Chapel Hill: University of North Carolina Press, 1998.

Waldstreicher, David. *In the Midst of Perpetual Fetes: The Making of American Nationalism, 1776–1820*. Chapel Hill: University of North Carolina Press, 1997.

Wallach, Glenn. *Obedient Sons: The Discourse of Youth and Generations in American Culture, 1630–1860*. Amherst: University of Massachusetts Press, 1997.

West, Elliot. *Growing Up with the Country: Childhood on the Far Western Frontier*. Albuquerque: University of New Mexico Press, 1989.

Wiebe, Robert H. *The Search for Order, 1877–1920*. New York: Hill and Wang, 1967.

Zboray, Ronald J., and Mary Saracino Zboray. *Voices without Votes: Women and Politics in Antebellum New England*. Durham: University of New Hampshire Press, 2010.

Articles and Essays

Alexander, Thomas B. "The Dimensions of Voter Partisan Consistency in Presidential Elections from 1840 to 1860." In *Essays on American Antebellum Politics, 1840–1860*, edited by Stephen E. Maizlish, 70–122. College Station: Texas A&M University Press, 1982.

Australian Electoral Commission. "The Right to Vote in Australia." Last modified January 28, 2011, http://aec.gov.au/Elections/Australian_Electoral_History/righttovote.htm.

Bourne, Randolph S. "The Two Generations." *Atlantic Monthly*, May 1911.

Carson, Gerald. "Hair Today, Gone Tomorrow." *American Heritage* 17 (February 1966): 45.

Clark, Krissy, and Geoff McGhee. "Did the West Make Newspapers, or Did Newspapers Make the West?" *Stanford University, Rural West Initiative*. Last modified February 22, 2013, http://www.stanford.edu/group/ruralwest/cgi-bin/drupal/content/rural-newspapers-history.

Crain, Patricia. "Potent Papers: Secret Lives of the Nineteenth-Century Ballot." *Common-Place* 9 (October 2008), http://www.common-place.org/vol-09/no-01/crain. Last accessed September 2, 2015.

Davis, Susan G. "'Making the Night Hideous': Christmas Revelry and Public Disorder in Nineteenth-Century Philadelphia." *American Quarterly* 34, no. 2 (June 1982): 185–99.

DeFiore, Jayne Crumpler. "Come, and Bring the Ladies: Tennessee Women and the Politics of Opportunity during the Presidential Campaigns of 1840 and 1844." *Tennessee Historical Quarterly* 51, no. 4 (December 1992): 197–212.

Diemer, Andrew. "Reconstructing Philadelphia: African Americans and Politics in the Post–Civil War North." *Pennsylvania Magazine of History and Biography* 11, no. 1 (January 2009): 29–58.

Donald, David Herbert. "An Excess of Democracy." In *Lincoln Reconsidered: Essays on the Civil War Era*, 215–35. 3rd ed. New York: Vintage Books, 2001.

Dupre, Daniel. "Barbeques and Pledges." *Journal of Southern History* 60, no. 3 (August 1994): 479–512.

Durrill, Wayne K. "Political Legitimacy and Local Courts: 'Politicks at Such a Rage' in a Southern Community during Reconstruction." *Journal of Southern History* 70, no. 3 (2004): 577–617.

Field, Corinne T. "Are Women . . . All Minors? Women's Rights and the Politics of Aging in the Antebellum United States." *Journal of Women's History* 12 (Winter 2001): 113–37.

Gienapp, William E. "Politics Seem to Enter into Everything: Political Culture in the North, 1840–1860." In *Essays on American Antebellum Politics, 1840–1860*, edited by Stephen E. Maizlish, 14–61. College Station: Texas A&M University Press, 1982.

Grinspan, Jon. "'Young Men for War': The Wide Awakes and Lincoln's 1860 Presidential Campaign." *Journal of American History* 96 (September 2009): 357–78.

Holt, Michael F. "Change and Continuity in the Party Period: The Substance and Structure of American Politics, 1835–1885." In *Contesting Democracy: Substance and Structure in American Political History, 1775–2000*, edited by Byron E. Shafer and Anthony J. Badger, 93–115. Lawrence: University of Kansas Press, 2001.

Holt, Michael F. "The Election of 1840: Voter Mobilization, and the Emergence of the Second Party System." In *A Master's Due: Essays in Honor of David Herbert Donald*, edited by John McCardell, 16–58. Baton Rogue: Louisiana State University Press, 1985.

Kelley, Robert. "The Thought and Character of Samuel J. Tilden: The Democrat as Inheritor." *Historian* 26 (Spring 1964): 176–205.

Lowe, Richard. "The Freedmen's Bureau and Local Black Leadership." *Journal of American History* 80, no. 3 (December 1993): 989–98.

Mahnken, Robert R. "Ogallala—Nebraska's Cowboy Capital." *Nebraska History* 28 (April–June 1947): 85–109.

McCormick, Richard. "The Discovery That Business Corrupts Politics: A Reappraisal of the Origins of Progressivism." *American Historical Review* 86, no. 2 (April 1981): 247–74.

McPhee, Peter. "Electoral Democracy and Direct Democracy in France, 1789–1851." *European History Quarterly* 16 (1986): 77–96.

Phillips, John A., and Charles Wetherell. "The Great Reform Act of 1832 and the Political Modernization of England." *American Historical Review* 100 (April 1995): 413–14.

Rapson, Richard L. "The American Child as Seen by British Travelers, 1845–1935." *American Quarterly* 17 (Autumn 1965): 520–34.

Rathbun, Julius G. "'The Wide Awakes': The Great Political Organization of 1860." *Connecticut Quarterly* 1 (October 1895): 327–35.

Russ, William A., Jr. "Registration and Disfranchisement under Radical Reconstruction." *Mississippi Valley Historical Review* 21, no. 2 (September 1934): 163–80.

Smith-Rosenberg, Carroll. "Sex as Symbol in Victorian Purity: An Ethnohistorical Analysis of Jacksonian America." In *Turning Points: Historical and Sociological Essays on the Family*, edited by John Demos and Sarane Spence Boocock. Chicago: University of Chicago Press, 1978.

Ternstrom, Stephan, and Peter R. Knights. "Men in Motion: Some Data and Speculations about Urban Population Mobility in Nineteenth-Century America." *Journal of Interdisciplinary History* 1 (Autumn 1970): 7–35.

Varon, Elizabeth. "Tippecanoe and the Ladies, Too: White Women and Party Politics in Antebellum Virginia." *Journal of American History* 82 (September 1995): 494–521.

Winther, Oscar O. "The Soldier Vote in the Election of 1864." *New York History* 25 (October 1944): 440–58.

Acknowledgments

Writing a book is a pyramid scheme. You read hundreds of works, based on thousands more, to produce one. And you draw from just as many people. Decades of friends, family, and teachers contributed to these pages. Their names will not appear on the cover, but they deserve their own citations.

First and foremost, Gary W. Gallagher shaped this work, contributing his generous curiosity, his high expectations, and his finely tuned bullshit detector. Working with Gary taught me the virtues of rigor, restraint, and self-reliance; I'll never forget his advice to "be ruthless" in writing the book that *I* wanted to write. Though we spent much of our time discussing Petroleum Vesuvius Nasby and George Costanza, I'd like to think that some of his common sense and simple good taste wore off on this project.

I owe a host of teachers at the University of Virginia and elsewhere thanks as well. Corinne Field pushed me to think abstractly when I was inclined to be superficial and subtly made sure, without ever saying it, that I knew I wasn't the first person to write a book about young people. Cori guaranteed that this book reached as high as it could while building on a solid foundation. Michael F. Holt, Elizabeth Varon, and James Loeffler offered knowledge, much-needed feedback, odd jobs, and reassurance along the way. Stretching back through my years at Sarah Lawrence College and Friends' Central School, passionate educators like Grant Calder and Jack Briggs ensured that I followed this path.

I am also grateful to the staff at the Smithsonian's National Museum of American History. Larry Bird and Harry Rubenstein provided me with thrilling evidence, new perspectives, and undeserved good faith. Every day, enthusiastic and eclectic colleagues help me reshape my thinking and expand my sense of where history resides.

A number of other institutions provided funding, guidance, and nurturing intellectual climates. The Corcoran Department of History at the University of Virginia, the Jefferson Scholars Foundation, the Lynde and Harry Bradley Foundation, the Smithsonian Institution's National Museum of American History, the Massachusetts Historical Society, and the National Endowment for the Humanities all provided much-appreciated help. At each of these institutions, supportive researchers, librarians, administrators, and staff helped me move forward.

From our first conversation, Brandon Proia has shaped this book, balancing his unmatched enthusiasm with careful, objective editing. He is a joy to rant with but also a shrewd reviser, parsing each silly metaphor I threw his way. Every conversation we had renewed my excitement for the subject. Along with Brandon, I owe much thanks to the staff of the University of North Carolina Press.

Katherine Flynn first introduced me to Brandon and UNCP, and I owe her equal thanks. Katherine has been an agent and an advocate, bringing confidence and humor to our collaboration and ensuring that this manuscript found the right press and especially the right editor. At each stage, Katherine and everyone else at Kneerim, Williams & Bloom have made my long-term welfare their chief interest.

Friends, like Jenny Le Zotte, Oscar Ax, and Nic Wood, helped me figure out this project and talk about something (anything) else when I'd just had too much of nineteenth-century politics. Mike Caires played the greatest role; he has been a constant friend and support who saw the bigger meaning in my work and pushed me to think beyond my own narrow-mindedness. He encouraged me when I was flagging and reined me in when I was getting too arrogant. What a mensch.

Though it will probably incite merciless ridicule, I have to thank my family. Growing up a Grinspan has been a kind of training, teaching me how to read and write and debate and laugh, how to temper knowledge with irreverence, and how to have an opinion about everything.

Finally, Keiana Mayfield has shaped my work and my life in wonderful, surprising ways. We met during my first month of research—since then her energy, her honesty, her courage, and her complete inability to be anyone but herself has buoyed me through every step. She tolerated my compulsive work habits, my complaints about the historical accuracy of period movies, and my (terrible?) renditions of the "Battle Hymn of the Republic." This project is for her, as will be the next, and all of them after that.

Index

Illustrations are indicated by page numbers in italic.